"Why I Killed Strip[per]
Murder Diary."

The words jumped [out ...]
York Post. In a murder case run of shocking headlines, this "exclusive" was the topper. It alleged, in no uncertain terms, that not only had Paul Cortez killed Catherine Woods, but he'd also written down his confession in a "secret" diary.

The first line of the story by Laura Italiano was: "He had to save Catherine Woods from sin—by slashing her throat," and it went downhill from there, at least for Paul.

Anyone who knew Paul well understood his obsessive need to write down his innermost thoughts. His mother said he'd been doing it since he was a little boy. Paul's friend Jaki Levy was very familiar with the journals. Paul had often let him read them. "I've read his poetry before," Jaki said. "It's very, very easy to take a piece of poetry or whatever it is and interpret it in a million different ways. I believe someone went into his diary and looked at it and said, 'Oh, look at this journal entry. This is his confession right there.' You can take it out of context. It's very easy to do."

Jaki thought the whole thing was ridiculous. Detectives, however, didn't think the journals were ridiculous, not at all. They were especially keyed up about one phrase buried in a diary. It read: "She wipes clean the shaft that cuts her throat." Authorities thought that was just too close to the reality of how Catherine died.

DEATH OF A DREAM

PAUL LaROSA
AND ERIN MORIARTY

Pocket Star Books
New York   London   Toronto   Sydney

Pocket Star Books
A Division of Simon & Schuster, Inc.
1230 Avenue of the Americas
New York, NY 10020

First Pocket Star Books paperback edition April 2008

POCKET STAR and colophon are registered trademarks of
Simon & Schuster, Inc.

For information about special discounts for bulk purchases,
please contact Simon & Schuster Special Sales at
1-800-456-6798 or business@simonandschuster.com

Designed by Anna Dorfman; photo: Dave Crosier/Getty Images

Manufactured in the United States of America

10 9 8 7 6 5 4 3 2 1

ISBN-13: 978-1-4165-4661-0
ISBN-10:   1-4165-4661-8

From Paul . . . for my mother, Lucy

From Erin . . . for Nick

ACKNOWLEDGMENTS

This book would not have been possible without the assistance, goodwill, and reporting and producing skills of CBS News producer Patti Aronofsky. She played an integral role in securing interviews, reporting, producing, and helping to write the two broadcast hours aired by *48 Hours Mystery*. She was a tremendous help in making sure that this book was accurate and fair to all concerned.

As always, a word of thanks to executive producer Susan Zirinsky for representing the very essence of the broadcast and for being a strong supporter of the book series. Special thanks also to executive editor Al Briganti for his help and advice in shepherding this book along.

Thanks also to Elena DiFiore, Stephen McCain, and Jonathan Leach for their help in researching and reporting the hours aired by *48 Hours Mystery*.

Finally, Paul would like to thank his wife, Susan, and his children, Alexandra and Peter, for their love and support.

CONTENTS

PART I
THE MURDER

PART II
THE INVESTIGATION

PART III
THE TRIAL

Contents • xi

PART IV
AFTER THE VERDICT

PART I

THE MURDER

New York and, I suppose, Los Angeles are cities where people come to fulfill their dreams. People come here from other nearby cities. They come from rural America. They even come from foreign countries: all for the purposes of success, whether it be in the arts as actors, as musicians, as painters, as businessmen. They come to Manhattan because this is one of those places where you can find wealth and success and fame.

The evidence will show that Catherine Woods was one such dreamer.

Manhattan Assistant DA
Peter Casolaro

1

The Last Phone Call

Megan Wilkins will never forget the time of that last phone call. Cell phones are like that. They make it easy to go back and see exactly when you spoke to someone and for how long. On that night, November 27, 2005, Megan, a pretty blonde with long, straight hair, was in a coffee shop in Columbus, Ohio, when her best friend, Catherine Woods, called.

It was 5:41 p.m., and neither woman knew it, but twenty-one-year-old Catherine Woods had barely an hour left to live.

Catherine was one of Megan's friends from high school. They'd both graduated in January 2002, six months early. But while Megan and her classmates from Worthington Kilbourne High School were still making post-graduation plans, Catherine was already off and running, to New York City, determined to become a professional dancer, a dream her parents said she'd had since the age of three. She wanted to dance on the Broadway stage—or as close as she could get to it.

"She just wanted to be a star, the light on the stage," Megan said. "She wasn't the background person or the second person. She wanted to be the person that everybody went to see."

No doubt, Catherine looked like a star. She was five feet, seven inches tall and was obviously in tip-top shape. But it was not her body that made all the men stare—it was her gorgeous face. She was the epitome of the Girl Next Door, if only the girl next door was a stunning brunette. Catherine didn't really look as exotic as Angelina Jolie, her favorite actress, but she loved when people said she reminded them of Jolie. Katie Miller, another longtime friend from Columbus, had been in Ohio dance productions with Catherine and had noticed the effect Catherine had on those who watched her perform. All eyes were drawn to her, so much so that the other dancers onstage felt they were fading into the scenery. Katie, a pretty, clean-cut midwesterner, admitted to being envious but not in a mean-spirited way. "I wanted to say, 'Hey, I'm here, too,' " she joked.

Catherine's clear blue eyes were almond shaped, giving her that doe-eyed, sexy-but-innocent look that cannot be manufactured with all the makeup in the world. And her lips, Catherine's lips were something else: curvy and full and, as the expression goes, just waiting to be kissed. She had it all going on and she knew it.

"You're talking about somebody who was very comfortable in her own skin," Megan said. "She knew she was pretty. Every time she passed by a mirror—and she was always looking in a mirror—she'd be like, 'Oh, I'm so cute.' "

It was not unusual for Megan and Catherine to talk on the phone a lot, sometimes several times a day. That Sunday night, the last time Megan spoke to her, Catherine was on a high; "happy and cheery" was how Megan described her. It was the weekend after Thanksgiving and Catherine had chosen to spend the holiday in New York, with her roommate and on-again, off-again boyfriend David Haughn, who was then twenty-three years old. They'd been living together for nearly three years.

David, a tall aspiring hip-hop artist, was also from Columbus. On a first meeting, David can come off as a bit strange. He has a sweet-but-dumb nature, bringing to mind Lenny from the John Steinbeck classic *Of Mice and Men*. David is five-ten but appears bigger, and it was probably no accident that he had recently scored a job as a doorman at an upscale Manhattan apartment building. It's also one of the things Catherine liked about him: He looked like he could provide protection.

Catherine's introduction to New York was rough, and maybe subconsciously, she was looking for someone to take care of her. She had just turned eighteen years old, in July 2002, when she moved to the city. She didn't know a lot of people, and after winning acclaim for her dancing in Columbus, her life in the Big Apple was filled with rejection, as it is for any young performer. It was not surprising that for all her talent, she was getting cut at one audition after another. In New York, thousands of young, talented, beautiful dancers were chasing the very same dream as Catherine. "It was a wake-up call for sure," said Mary Rose Bushroe, one of Catherine's dance teachers from Columbus.

On a visit home back in the summer of 2002, Catherine, Megan, and some other friends were approached by David Haughn, who knew Megan's boyfriend, Zach. David was then selling home-produced rap CDs in the parking lot of a pool hall called Quarter Flash in East Columbus. He was immediately taken with Catherine. "She just seemed real nice. And I was like, 'Wow,' you know? I'd never seen this girl before. You know? She's beautiful," David said. "I knew she wasn't from around here but I definitely knew, like, she's beautiful and, you know, I didn't know her as a person then."

He got her phone number and the two bonded over their respective dreams, each seeing in the other a kindred creative spirit. It wasn't long before David began driving to New York on weekends to visit Catherine, and in September 2002, he blurted out that he wanted to move to the city full-time to be with her and try to make it in the world of rap music. Megan remembers when Catherine gave her the news: "She was like, 'I'm so happy.' And I remember the phone conversation. She was like, 'He's going to live with me. He's moving. He's giving up everything. I'm so excited!' "

So was David, who said, "I just kinda gave my boss

the two weeks' notice, rode that out, saved up a little bit of money, packed my stuff up in this car I had. Just crammed it, packed full. I really didn't know what was gonna happen. But I knew, you know, I knew she was there. That she was worth it."

On the surface, they seemed an unlikely couple. The energetic and outgoing Catherine was from a middle-class home in Worthington, a leafy suburb north of Columbus, while David, introspective and socially awkward, had spent a lot of his youth in foster homes after his mother was convicted of solicitation, child endangerment, and trafficking in cocaine. He and his younger sister were reunited years later by their father, who unfortunately died of natural causes not long after giving them a taste of what a stable family life could be like. For David, it was a cruel reality check, and he seemed to be searching for someone else to love when he and Catherine crossed paths in that parking lot. David readily admits that Catherine became his whole world. "I looked up to her, almost like a parent," he said.

But Catherine leaned on David, too. He became her best buddy and confidant in New York, someone who would not judge her, whom she could trust to do almost anything she needed. "I felt real comfortable around her," David said. "She felt real comfortable around me. I could speak to her about anything and really be myself. And I think that's what I liked about her the most, that she accepted me for who I was."

Catherine could have attracted better-looking guys

with more money, but that wasn't the point. She knew that she'd never find anyone more dedicated to her than David. He doted on her, running errands at a moment's notice. Whatever she wanted—a Starbucks cappuccino, an apple, a frozen dinner—she'd ask David and he'd go fetch, almost literally. He also would often drive her to work in the beat-up silver '87 Olds Cutlass that he somehow managed to keep in Manhattan, a city notoriously unfriendly to cars. Catherine's friends loved him like a big teddy bear. "We all love David," Catherine once said to Megan. "He's like a brother to me."

With David and Josie the Chihuahua, Catherine built a secure little family for herself in the big city—at least for a time. She was happy, and even though she wasn't getting any jobs on or off Broadway, she was at least honing her craft. She took advanced jazz and ballet classes at the Broadway Dance Center on West Fifty-seventh Street, taught dance classes to children, and blended into city life, working out at various gyms and drinking coffee nonstop. "It was her one drug," Megan said. Catherine's parents, Jon and Donna Woods, joked that they knew she'd become a real New Yorker when she began to wear all black and started yelling at cabdrivers.

As symbiotic as Catherine and David's relationship was, it wasn't perfect. After two years of living with him in typically cramped New York apartments, Catherine began complaining to friends that she was still paying most of the bills. She was teaching dance, working at a spa, and getting a one-thousand-dollar-a-month stipend from her parents, but until he got his doorman job, David wasn't contributing much at all. Sometime in the fall of 2005, David moved out at Catherine's urging, but he didn't have a lot of options. He stayed with a friend in Suffern, New York, about forty minutes north of the city, but there were days when he was practically living in his car. He was depressed, and Catherine knew it. She told friends she still loved him and felt responsible for him, and after two weeks, she welcomed him back into her one-bedroom apartment at 355 East Eighty-sixth Street, a safe Upper East Side neighborhood.

They agreed to be friends, not lovers. That arrangement seemed to work better for Catherine, and thanks to his new doorman job, David began contributing more money for rent and expenses. He also began earning extra money dog-walking for people who lived in the apartment building where he worked, and when those residents went out of town, David would keep their dogs in the apartment he shared with Catherine. In fact, that Thanksgiving weekend, he was taking care of a black Labrador.

After he moved back in, David spent his nights on the futon in the living room, while Catherine slept by herself in the bedroom. David knew she was dating other men but he ignored it, so long as he could be a part of her life.

"She never brought nobody home if she was datin' somebody," David said. "I think she respected me. She wouldn't of done that. I knew the way we were going about it wasn't a bad thing. We were best friends and that's pretty much it."

On the phone that November 27, Catherine told Megan how David had prepared her a Thanksgiving feast in their small kitchen. It was a good time, but Catherine definitely wanted to spend Christmas back home with her friends and family in Columbus, and was already making plans. She said things were better with David, and then she began talking about how she'd spent that day, a Sunday. She and friend and co-worker Christina Dupont had explored alternative religions. They went to a service at a small independent church called the Creative Light Church, on Lafayette Street in downtown New York, and then later went to a Spiritual Expo.

As Catherine talked, Megan was driving, having left the coffee shop where she'd been, to meet her sister at her sister's boyfriend's house. Megan pictured Catherine "sitting on the floor of her living room right in front of her huge mirror and doing her makeup and getting ready for work."

Megan knew the drill. She'd spent the previous summer living with Catherine and David. "It was tiny and cramped," Megan said of their apartment. "It was a little overbearing at times, but I bought an air mattress and slept on the floor." Maybe it was the close quarters or maybe it was just seeing how Catherine was living in New York, but the two friends seemed to grow closer than even during that visit. Megan even worked with Catherine in the job Catherine euphemistically referred to as "the restaurant" when speaking to her mother, Donna.

"Are you working tonight?" Megan asked that Sunday.

"Yeah, I'm going to work, but I wish I didn't have to," Catherine said. "Wouldn't it be great if you could just sit at home, watch TV, and get paid?"

"I wish," Megan said.

"Yeah, me, too."

The two friends talked a bit more, but back in Columbus, Megan had arrived at her destination. She told Catherine she had to sign off but promised to call her back.

The time was 6:03 p.m. The clock on Catherine's life was winding down. There were only minutes left.

While she'd been on that twenty-two-minute phone call with Megan, someone had been calling Catherine's cell phone, and Catherine had a pretty good idea of who it was. A friend named Paul Cortez had wanted to get together with her that day, but it had never happened. She took forty-five seconds to check her voice mail and then hung up. She didn't call Paul back, and that was the last time she'd ever use her cell phone.

David, who had been "messing around with my beat machine," says he was still in the apartment at that point. He'd told Catherine previously that he would drive her to work. "I'll go get the car while you're getting ready," he said.

"Okay, that's fine," she said before turning back to her mirror to apply the final touches of makeup. She was wearing a tan top and a pair of gray sweatpants. She would change into her uniform once she got to her job.

Her shift was to begin at 7:00 p.m.

2

Total Rage

The building where Catherine Woods lived with David Haughn at 355 East Eighty-sixth Street is an average New York City apartment building in many respects—a small, four-story building with no doorman and little glamour. Actually, their living space was pretty typical of the way a lot of New Yorkers live: a small apartment off an unadorned hallway. The building is located on Eighty-sixth Street between First and Second avenues, a big two-way thoroughfare with a lot of pedestrian and car traffic. A thousand or more people walk by the building on any given day. The surrounding stores—a supermarket, a locksmith, a corner diner—are, again, average for a New York City neighborhood.

But Catherine's building is a bit unusual because the entrance is not right off the sidewalk. Instead, the front door is set back a few dozen feet, in an alley. That is *not* a desirable feature, because tenants are slightly hidden from view when entering, making them more suscep-tible to muggings and other crimes. And in a place like New York, any alley attracts its share of homeless people. To keep out the riffraff and increase security, the building's management company erected a lockable wrought-iron gate at the entrance of the alley. A buzzer and intercom system on the gate allows visitors to buzz the building's residents to let them in. The problem, as any New Yorker knows, is that in a city where ordering in takeout is preferable to cooking, the stream of deliverymen in and out of a residential building is nearly nonstop. Many deliverymen don't speak English and will ring every buzzer to gain access. The result is that residents, tired of the constant buzzing, buzz anyone into the building without asking who it is.

Catherine's building did have a locked front door beyond the gate, but some residents later said it was often broken.

The building is in an enclave called Yorkville. Back in the nineteenth century and even into part of the twentieth century, Yorkville was a mostly German area, but there are few signs of that now. Rupert Towers, an apartment complex that was once the site of the old Rupert Brewery, is nearby, and so is Gracie Mansion, the elegant official residence of New York City's mayor, which sits on the East River. Most New York mayors are happy to call the mansion home, but not then-mayor Michael Bloomberg, a billionaire with his own elegant mansion just a few blocks away.

While there is petty crime in Yorkville, murders are unusual.

• • •

Eyewitnesses to a crime are notoriously unreliable, and as this case proved, so were some of the "earwitnesses." No one saw what happened to Catherine Woods, but at least four people *heard* her final moments. While there was some discrepancy about when they heard what they heard, one thing is certain: Not one of them called the police.

Catherine lived in apartment 2D, and the residents of apartment 2H, right next door, heard the screams first. They later reported the screams happening anywhere from 5:45 to 6:00 p.m. The problem was that at that time, Catherine was known to be speaking to Megan Wilkins. Cell phone records prove definitively that their twenty-two-minute call ended at 6:03 p.m. Nonetheless, Jessie Danzig and Amy VanDeussen of apartment 2H, whose wall abuts Catherine Woods's living room wall, reported that they were watching television when they began to hear what sounded like a child screaming. They hit the Mute button so they could hear better, and listened to what sounded like furniture being moved about. The last thing they heard were the sounds of dogs barking. That was unusual because the tenants of 2D were usually very quiet, and so was their tiny dog. The screams stopped after a few seconds, and Danzig and VanDeussen went back to watching television.

Andrew Gold, who lived directly above Catherine Woods, in apartment 3D, was having a phone conversation with his then-fiancée, Donna Propp, when he heard the screams. He'd been watching television when he took the call and was sitting facing the cable box, staring at the digital clock—it was 6:18 p.m. when the call started. He'd muted the sound on his television and was about five minutes into his conversation, he recalled, when he, too, heard a woman's scream, coming from downstairs. "I heard a scream and then I heard scuffling," he said. "It sounded like a scuffle, and I heard a dog barking and then I heard another scream and then I heard a thud and then nothing."

His girlfriend, on the other end of the phone, also heard the commotion. After hearing the first scream, Gold said to her, "Did you hear that?"

"Yes," she said. "What is it?"

"Shh, be quiet."

Then they both heard the barking, the scuffling, the second scream, and the thud. The second scream was "louder and longer" but lasted only about two seconds, Gold said. He and his fiancée listened for more sounds but heard nothing. They spoke for a few more minutes and then ended the conversation. Gold had an appointment a few blocks away, at 6:45, so he was very conscious of the time.

"Right after I got off the phone, I went outside [into the hallway] to see if there was anything going on because it was not normal to hear what I heard," he said. "I went out, looked around to my left and my right. I didn't see anyone sticking their head out. I actually went out and looked out the window on Eighty-sixth Street to see if there was any fire engine, something.

There was nothing. Then I went to the banister and looked up and down, down from the second floor to the fourth floor, and I yelled out, 'Is anyone out there?' and there was nothing. So I figured there was nothing going on."

He said he left the building by 6:40 but saw and heard nothing else.

Inside apartment 2D, a horrendous struggle had taken place. No one knows how the killer managed to get past the locked gate and front door, but police do know that the door to Catherine's apartment was unlocked. More than a year later, Manhattan Assistant District Attorney Peter Casolaro told a jury his account of what happened that night.

"The attack," he said, "was total rage. It was extreme violence. The moment [Catherine] opened the door she got pushed back into the bedroom. The bed is pushed in front of the door [by the killer] so she can't get out and she's attacked in the far side of the room. We know that she puts her arms up, because of the cuts all over her arms, her wrists, the stab wound through her, and then we know the attacker's still in front of her attacking, because he puts the knife right through her mouth.

"Surely that must have weakened her and stunned her so that her attacker could now get behind her and cut her throat for the first time. Now, how do we know that? We can look at this [a crime scene photograph] and we can see that all of the blood is on her shirt, a tremendous concentration of blood on the front of her shirt. If she were on the ground when her throat was cut, you wouldn't see this tremendous concentration of blood on her shirt. But if she's standing up, a lot of it, as it spurts out, is going to end up on the front of her.

"Then we know she probably fell to her knees. And how do we know that? Again, look at the enormous concentration of blood on the ground and you see the middle part of her body, there's hardly any blood at all.

"So she fell to her knees after she bled significantly and then we know almost certainly that the killer must have cut her throat again. And how do we know that? Because we see that she falls forward and she hits her hands on the bookcase. You can see her handprint right on the bookcase. She grabbed the bookcase as she fell down. So she's probably on her knees at this position to reach the bookcase at that level. And you'll see it in the other photograph that shows the whole bookcase. And then she falls on the ground and we know the killer stood on her back and held her down while she bled to death. We know that because the footprints are on her back.

"So this is not a robbery. This is not a burglary. This is not an accident. This is the product of extreme rage and total overkill. We also know that she put up a struggle but we know she didn't harm the person because look at her hands. The only thing on her hands is her own blood and the only thing under her fingernails is her own blood."

• • •

For all his exactitude concerning the crime scene, Casolaro neglected to mention a few heartbreaking details that are apparent in the crime scene photos. There on Catherine's bookcase shelf was her beat-up stuffed rabbit, Hop-Hop, a gift from her parents for her first Easter, when she was only nine months old. And Catherine was a reader; the bookcase was filled with the types of books any urban young woman might read: *Prozac Nation; Bitch; Valley of the Dolls; Girl, Interrupted; Crazy; In Her Shoes; Good Grief;* and *Angels & Demons.*

Her bloody handprint, as Casolaro suggests, is visible on the bookshelf, right beneath the book *Lucky,* by Alice Sebold, a memoir by the author of *The Lovely Bones,* a groundbreaking novel that tells the story of a young girl's murder, narrated by the young girl. *Lucky* is the true story of Sebold's survival after her own rape.

But there was no luck—or mercy—on that day in that apartment for Catherine Woods. Her jugular vein had been cut and she died a ghastly death, suffocating on her own blood. In crime scene photos, her beautiful eyes are open wide, looking incredulous at what is happening to her in those final moments. The killer left this spirited, vibrant young woman soaked in blood and lying facedown in a corner of her tiny bedroom. If he had looked down at her before he fled, he would have seen the tattoo that was visible on the small of her back: LOVE is all it said.

3

There Was Blood Everywhere

Brad Stewart lived in apartment 2J, on the same floor as Catherine. Though he says he heard nothing, he did notice something amiss when he went out to walk his two Huskies at, he says, 6:00 p.m. Again, the timing seemed a bit off, given the circumstances of everything that had happened in apartment 2D. It would be up to the police to piece it all together and make sense of it. But Brad never wavered from the time he says he noticed something was wrong. At 6:00 p.m., he says, he was on First Avenue, just down the block from his building, when he saw a dog off its leash, a black Lab that Brad immediately recognized as the dog belonging to David Haughn. The dog seemed frightened, but Brad caught up to it, brought it back to the building, and went out again to walk his dogs.

Meanwhile, David, who knew Catherine had to get to work by 7:00 p.m., was hustling back to pick her up. Catherine worked about forty blocks to the south, a ten-minute drive on a Sunday evening, when traffic, even in Manhattan, was light. David's car had been parked only about a block away, and as he turned left onto Eighty-sixth Street from Second Avenue, he dialed Catherine from his cell phone. "Usually I would call Catherine to let her know I was coming on the block and usually she would come down or let me know she was getting ready and she would be down in a second," he said.

This time, however, she didn't answer. Cell phone records would later show the time of that call to be 6:47 p.m.

David made a U-turn on Eighty-sixth Street so his car would be pointing west, the direction they'd have to drive. Unable to find a place to park, he pulled the car over to a space near a fire hydrant not far from the front entrance of 355 East Eighty-sixth Street. "I tried to call her again and there still wasn't an answer, so when I didn't get an answer, I didn't think anything of it," he said. "I just figured either she was still getting ready or something, so I go up to the buzzer."

He left the car running and buzzed the intercom on the front gate a few times, but Catherine didn't answer. "I just remember thinking, well, either she is coming down or just kind of confused," he said.

David went back to his car, shut it off, and returned to the front gate, where he ran into Brad Stewart, who was just then coming back from walking his dogs. "Hey, your dog got out," Brad told David.

"What do you mean?" David asked. "What dog?"

"Your black Lab. Your black Lab got out and was running down First Avenue."

Brad told David that he'd chased the dog down and had brought him back upstairs. At this point, the two men were walking side by side up the stairs. When they got to the second floor, David saw the black Lab had again escaped from the apartment and was now in the hallway. He thanked Brad and brought the Lab into the apartment with him. "I was still kind of confused how the dog got out," he said. "I walked into the apartment and the door was still unlocked. . . . I remember seeing my Chihuahua on the edge of the futon looking right at me. I let the Lab in and closed the door behind me. I passed the kitchen and see the bed pushed all the way up against the doorway."

The bed, which was on wheels, was normally pushed up against the far wall of the bedroom, but now it was blocking the doorway completely. "You couldn't get through, and there was blood everywhere," David said. "I remember seeing the walls, seeing the floor, and things were all over the place, and I see Catherine lying on the floor and I was just numb. I didn't know if it was an accident or what it was. I really didn't know. I was just in shock."

Catherine was lying on the floor on the far side of the bed. The room was awash in blood; it was spattered all over the walls and in heavy pools on the floor near Catherine. David had to have climbed over the bed to get to her. He had just walked into a horror movie, but there was no walking out. "'Baby, baby wake up,'" I said to her. "'Are you okay? Are you okay?'

"I was scared to touch her but at one point I had

grabbed the back of her shirt and tried to move her and lift her a little bit, and I couldn't get no movement out of her. My first instinct was to call 911. I had never seen so much blood in my life."

Just before 7:00 p.m., records show, David dialed 911. He was not overly excited; he was not crying. When the police and others later heard the tape, they couldn't agree. Some thought he sounded upset; some thought he was strangely unemotional. At times, he talks directly to Catherine, imploring her to be all right.

David: I just came home from . . . My girlfriend, I couldn't get her . . . there's blood all over the apartment. I don't know what happened. {to Catherine} Baby girl, Catherine. Catherine, baby girl. Oh, my goodness, I don't know what happened.

Operator: Is she there? I want to know if she's alive.

David: Okay, hold on. Okay, hold on. I don't even know if she's alive. There's blood everywhere. Oh, my goodness.

Operator: Okay, give me your location, where you're there.

David: 355 East Eighty-sixth Street.

Operator: And this is in the head, right?

David: And she's unconscious. We need to get her to wake up. I don't know if she's alive.

Operator: Okay. Hold on.

David: Catherine. Should I move her? Should I try to—

Operator: Don't—don't touch her. Don't touch her.

David: No. I did touch her, so—

Operator: Okay. Don't touch her. You're inside, right?

David: Yeah, but I just walked in. My car's parked out by a fire hydrant. I was picking her up for work.

Operator: Okay, you're in apartment what?

David: I'm in apartment 2D.

Operator: 2D as in David?

David: Yes, yes.

Operator: And that's on the second floor, right?

David: Yes, yes.

Operator: How old is she?

David: Twenty-one. She's twenty-one.

Operator: Okay. Don't hang up, please.

David: Okay, I'm not. Catherine! Oh no.

Operator: Did you do CPR?

David: I—I—I don't know how. I—I don't—

Operator: Okay, I'll tell you. EMS is on the phone.

David: You know what I just seen?

Operator: What—

David: Somebody was in here. Somebody did this, there's blood—there's—there's boot tracks on the bed. Oh my goodness, there's boot tracks on the bed.

Operator [talking to EMS operator]: Okay. Unconscious female. He just walked in, and his girlfriend is unconscious, blood all over the house.

Operator 2: Okay, so how old is she, sir?

David: She's twenty-one years old.

Operator 2: Okay, she's not breathing?

David: I—I can't get her to be conscious. I'm scared to move her. I—

Operator 2: I need to know, is she breathing? Sir, it's very important.

David: Okay, I will check. I will check right now.

Operator 2: All right, sir.

David: All right. This is crazy. It's crazy. Oh my goodness.

Operator 2: So what I said before, did you check the pulse on her neck?

David: She's facedown.

Operator 2: Can you put up—can you turn her on her back? Is that possible?

David: The bed was pushed up. I definitely can move the bed. Everything is kind of a mess. Catherine. Catherine, baby girl. Catherine, baby girl. I'm scared to look at her.

Operator 2: All—all right sir. 355 East Eighty-sixth Street. Hello?

David: 335 East Eighty-sixth Street, yes, apartment 2D. Catherine, baby girl. Baby girl.

Operator 2: Okay, so {unintelligible} 2D like David, right?

David: Yes, yes.

Operator 2: Second and First Avenue.

David: Yes.

Operator 2: All right, sir. We'll be there as soon as possible, okay?

David: Want me to stay on the phone?

Operator 2: No, you can hang up, sir.

David: Okay.

Operator 2: Okay, sir. Thank you.

Operator 3 [speaking to the other operator]: It looks like—it's a crime.

David says he was spooked and could not be in that apartment by himself for even another second. He walked into the hall and knocked on the door of Brad Stewart's apartment. Brad's girlfriend, Julia Jeon, answered. David was beside himself. "Something happened in my apartment," he told her. "There's blood everywhere. She's not breathing."

"Who, the dog?"

"No, my girlfriend. I think she's dead."

"Oh my God," Julia said. "Have you called the police?"

"Yeah, yeah."

They both walked down to David's apartment, and as soon as he opened the door, the black Lab bolted again. David could see how frightened the Lab was, "like it literally did not want to be in that apartment. It was trying to get down the stairs."

David showed Julia what happened in the apartment, and the moment she saw all the blood, she immediately turned and walked out. "I'll never forget the look on her face," David said.

Julia ran back to her apartment to get Brad. "Our neighbor is hurt," she said.

Everything was in chaos. Neighbors who heard the commotion were beginning to come out of their apartments. Dogs were barking. The black Lab had run downstairs already and Josie the Chihuahua, who had been lying next to Catherine, chased after the Lab. David went down to the mail room to bring the dogs back and heard static from police radios. Cops and the paramedics were at the front door. David let them in.

"I was only gone for about twenty minutes and she's all cut up," he told them. "I think she's dead."

Julia was back in the hallway watching David carefully. She noticed that he did not have any blood on him and that he seemed genuinely upset. "He looked dead, like he was in shock," she said.

4

Prime Suspect

Police Officer John Sheedy was one of those who met David at the door, along with Warren Lau, a paramedic who'd been on many emergency runs in his career. Sheedy and his partner had responded because they'd heard a call on the police radio for help in what the NYPD refers to as "an aided case," meaning simply that somebody needs help. They were only a few blocks away so they got there fast, in under five minutes. The time was now 7:07 p.m.

Sheedy, Lau, and their partners followed David up the stairs through the building's red-and-white hallways and into apartment 2D. The adrenaline was flowing. For a cop, entering a strange apartment is like stopping a car on a highway—it's never "routine" because anything can happen. You're never sure what you're walking into, especially when the guy meeting you is saying there might be a dead woman inside. Sheedy braced himself but also took the measure of this skinny, blond guy showing him the way: "White male, a little taller than myself, so I would say maybe five-ten, slim build, and he was maybe in a state of shock, disbelief. He was very flushed." If it was a homicide, this guy could be the murderer. Sheedy noticed that David was "calm," calmer than Sheedy felt inside.

The apartment was no more than four hundred square feet but, at least initially, there didn't seem to be anything amiss. But that's because Sheedy was looking into the living room. The bedroom was to the right, but he had not looked there, not yet.

"Where is she?" Sheedy asked David.

He pointed to the right, into the bedroom. "On the other side of the bed."

The EMTs took the lead. There were four paramedics in all: Lau, Kenny Guzman, Raphael Mohammed, and Claudia Salazar. They rushed past Sheedy, but at the bedroom doorway they stopped. The bed blocked the door. "When I saw the bloody walls," Lau said, "I looked to see where the patient would be and I couldn't see her. We were asking each other, me and my partner, 'Where's the patient?' So we looked around. We were getting ready to move the bed but we were afraid that the patient was under the bed, so we climbed over it."

Lau immediately noticed what David had told the 911 operator—there were reddish-brown footprints across the bedsheet.

The footprints concerned Lau; he knew those prints would be important to the murder investigation. What he didn't know was that the boots he was wearing— the Sketchers Cool Cat Bully II boot—were the very same style that had made those footprints. The only difference, it would turn out, was that Lau wore a size seven and the bloody boot prints were size ten and a half.

Once they spotted Catherine lying on the other side of the bed, they lifted the bed on its side so that it was vertical and pushed it up against the wall near the doorway, away from where Catherine was. This way, they had some room to work.

Sheedy watched from just a few feet away. "I saw a female laying on her right side," he said, "but twisted at the torso so that she was facedown, full of blood, and then blood on the walls, blood everywhere. The paramedics turned her over so they would be able to see her face, and at that point we just saw the huge laceration on her neck and there was no life left."

David stood next to Sheedy and watched the paramedics work. He seemed calmer with other people there and never turned away from the scene. The EMTs flipped Catherine over. Her body was still warm, indicating that the murder was very fresh. "We checked for breathing, if she had a heartbeat, pulse. Nothing," Lau said. "We checked for any other injuries and pretty much stopped as soon as we saw the cut."

The paramedics told Sheedy two things he already knew—this woman was dead and she had obviously been murdered.

Sheedy's police training kicked in. "We secured the crime scene, which means we brought everybody out.

Myself, the male that met us at the door, the EMTs, and the paramedics—they all had to stay right in that hallway."

Lau observed David. "He seemed somewhat scared and in shock," he said.

Sheedy closed the door of 2D behind them and called for his supervisors, letting them know that the Crime Scene Unit and detectives were needed. The first responders conferred in the hallway and looked at their watches. Catherine Woods, just twenty-one years old, was pronounced DOA at 7:10 p.m., barely an hour after she'd finished speaking to her high school friend Megan Wilkins.

All eyes were on David. No doubt, he was the prime suspect.

PART II

THE INVESTIGATION

Here this girl is, dead on the floor in her bedroom, and she has a family out there and they don't even know that she is dead.

NYPD detective Steven Goetz

5

Enemies?

Detective Steven Goetz was working the 4:00 p.m.–to–1:00 a.m. shift that Sunday. He'd been a cop for sixteen years and had the New York accent to prove it. Goetz has a way of speaking that just screams NYPD. Tall and good-looking, he doesn't let his guard down around civilians or the media, saving his compassion for the families of the victims. At the time of Catherine Woods's murder, he'd only recently been promoted to detective and was eager to take the lead on a big case, which is why he jumped when he heard about the murder on East Eighty-sixth Street.

Goetz and his partner, Detective Donna Torres, had just finished interviewing a witness in another case and were on their way back to "the one-nine," the Nineteenth Precinct station house, on East Sixty-seventh Street, when they heard the call.

"I can remember the night like it was yesterday," Goetz said. "Usually you don't get calls like this. Patrol had transmitted over the radio that they had a homicide on Eighty-sixth Street."

He turned to his partner. "Did I just hear what I think I heard?"

Goetz asked the dispatcher to repeat it, and it came through loud and clear: homicide on Eighty-sixth Street.

"Most of the times, you don't hear that on the Upper East Side," Goetz said. "Over the past decade, the amount of time that I have as a police officer, crime has definitely declined. Although there's millions of people who live in New York, especially Manhattan, you don't hear about these things every day. New York is a very safe place to live."

You couldn't miss the address on Eighty-sixth Street. Emergency lights from patrol cars and ambulances were lighting up the night. Goetz walked into the building and got a quick fill-in from Sheedy, who introduced David Haughn as the dead woman's roommate.

Goetz looked at David carefully. "Usually in a case like this, the first person you look to is the closest person to the victim, and that was David Haughn," he said. "He looked like he was in shock. He was obviously a suspect, but I can say that he was definitely in shock. He had the appearance that he couldn't believe what he just saw."

As Goetz says, David was wearing "baggy jeans that hung down past his sneakers." Goetz spotted blood on the bottom of David's jeans and told the patrol officers to keep an eye on David while he, Goetz, went into the apartment. New York cops exude a hard shell of "been there, done that," but Goetz admits he was taken aback by the amount of blood in Catherine Woods's tiny bedroom. "It was a brutal scene, just a violent struggle," he said. "The manner in which she was killed was just absolutely horrible. There was a violent struggle and there was a lot of anger involved. She definitely did try to fight for her life. Catherine was lying on the floor with large amounts of blood. With sixteen years as a police officer, never in my life have I seen anything so violent. There were footprints in blood, marks on the walls. We just obviously had to find out who did this. It's gotta be some type of rage, some type of jealousy.

"Because of the manner in which she was killed and the apparent struggle that she put up and the amount of anger that someone must have had to kill her, they had to know who she was. They had to know her personally."

There was a photograph of Catherine in the apartment, and Goetz could see for himself how beautiful she had been in life. What was she doing living with this weird skinny guy he'd just met in the hall, the guy who seemed all frayed edges? Goetz moved out into the hallway to question the kid.

An experienced cop, Goetz knew enough to let the suspect do all the talking, so he kept it simple: "What happened?"

"I left for about twenty minutes to get my car and when I came back, I found her like that. I was trying to call her but she didn't pick up. I mean, I don't know."

"Did she have any enemies?"

"No," David said, but a second later he did think of someone when Goetz asked the question a different way.

"You know anybody who may have done this?"

"She was having a problem with some guy. His name is Paul, Paul Vincent. He was kind of stalking her."

David told Goetz that Paul's CD was in a bag David had left in the living room. Goetz went to get it. The singer's phone number and photo were on the CD. In the photo this "Paul Vincent" had long hair, was good-looking, and appeared to be smirking.

It was another lead, but Goetz wasn't about to let this David guy off the hook so quickly. The detective needed to question David thoroughly, and that meant getting him away from all the neighbors and the excitement of the crime scene. "I'd like you to answer some questions, but not here. I need you to go down to the station house and I'll catch up with you, okay?"

"Okay," David said.

Two female police officers escorted David outside and into a waiting police car. He wasn't arrested and they didn't cuff him. On the way downtown, David pulled out his cell phone and called Catherine's parents, Jon and Donna Woods. David had met them many times and had even stayed with them when he and Catherine had returned to Columbus for various holidays. David tried calling them twice but they didn't answer, and he didn't leave a message.

Back at the crime scene, Detective Goetz was thinking along the same lines as David. Goetz knew the way the New York media operated, and this case was going to be a monster. It had everything: Upper East Side address, beautiful white female dancer from out of town with her head nearly cut off, a boyfriend who might or might not be the murderer, a potential killer on the loose. His thoughts turned to Catherine's family. This was going to be brutal on them, and he had to make sure they at least knew she was dead before the hyperaggressive New York reporters beat him to the punch.

Goetz called his superiors. Someone needed to get in touch with the Columbus Police Department. Goetz wanted them to hand-carry a message to Catherine's parents, asking them to call him in New York. Part of any homicide investigation was to find out more about the victim, to determine who would have wanted to kill her.

Goetz needed to find out more about Catherine Woods, a lot more.

6

Columbus

Sunday evenings at the Columbus, Ohio, police station located on the far north side of the city are often quiet, but the night of November 27, 2005, was unusually so. Cold weather, not to mention endless football games on television, kept people indoors during the Thanksgiving weekend. Out of bars and out of trouble. Patrolman Darren Egelhoff, a seven-year veteran of the force on duty that night, welcomed the break. He remembered a time when homicides in Columbus were a rarity; when the hours on his beat were spent breaking up domestic disputes and cleaning up after traffic accidents. No more. Columbus had grown, and so had its murder rate. That year, 105 people would be murdered in the city, averaging 2 every weekend. So when Egelhoff got a call from his dispatcher just before nine o'clock that evening, it wasn't the report of a murder that surprised him, but rather where it had occurred: five hundred miles away, in New York City.

Egelhoff was directed to call Thomas Ryan, a detective assigned to the Nineteenth Precinct of the NYPD.

Earlier that evening, Ryan told Egelhoff, a young woman had been stabbed to death inside her apartment on the East Side of Manhattan. Why Ryan was calling about a murder in another city soon became clear: the murder victim, only twenty-one years old, had grown up in Columbus, and someone had to notify her parents. Ryan knew it was only a matter of time before the New York tabloid press got a whiff of the murder, and he didn't want the parents to get the news from an insensitive reporter. Ryan had to be the one to tell them, and he wanted a Columbus police officer to be right there in the Woodses' home when he gently broke the news to them over the phone.

Few police officers volunteer for this kind of assignment. There is no joy in carrying news that will, in an instant, crush the hearts and lives of unsuspecting parents. But twenty-nine-year-old Darren Egelhoff had been training for months in crisis intervention and, by his own estimation, had been on "seven to ten similar missions." Although he was at the end of his shift, he offered to go, and by nine-thirty, he was on his way, along with his partner, Kim Boyer, and Officer Andre Leon.

Later, Officer Egelhoff would regret that he hadn't asked more questions about the family he would be visiting that night and that he hadn't spent more time wondering why the name Woods sounded so familiar. If he had, he would have realized that the Jon Woods he would comfort that night was not just a father but a man revered in Columbus.

The horrendous murder of Woods's oldest child would become front-page news by morning.

Jon Woods was and still is the director of the Ohio State University marching band. In most cities, a university band director would rarely attract much attention beyond the school's borders, but Columbus is not like most other cities, and the university is not just another "local school." Ohio State University, or OSU, sprawls across the heart of this city, both geographically and culturally. And *culture* in Columbus means one thing: sports. It is no exaggeration to say that residents are obsessed with their "Buckeyes," the name given to the Big Ten college's famed athletic teams. While it is not unusual to see souvenir stores lining college campuses, it's a bit different in Columbus. Here, shops throughout the city, even upscale ones, proudly display and sell the local uniform: bright scarlet-colored shirts and souvenirs emblazoned with a big gray *O*.

On fall Saturday afternoons, the fields and parking lots that surround the university become a swelling sea of red as more than one hundred thousand fans, the population of a small city, swarm "the Shoe," the horseshoe-shaped football stadium that sits alongside the Olentangy River. In this football-crazed environment, the name Jim Tressel, OSU's football coach, is far more recognizable than the mayor's.

And Jon Woods, the band director, is more widely known than the conductor of the Columbus Symphony Orchestra.

In person, Woods is a quiet, unassuming, bespectacled man in his late sixties, the personification of the lead character from Columbus-born writer James Thurber's short story "The Secret Life of Walter Mitty." Woods may look mild-mannered, but an amazing transformation takes place when he steps onto a football field, leading the university marching band in precise formations. Then, this Walter Mitty–type becomes a showman. Conducting from the sidelines, he seems to grow in stature as his musicians, who modestly call themselves "the best damn band in the land," work the Buckeye faithful into a frenzy. After more than two decades of honing the band into a national halftime attraction, Woods is something of a celebrity in town. Mike Harden, a longtime columnist for *The Columbus Dispatch*, the city's only major newspaper, chuckles when trying to explain Woods's popularity. "I'm not calling him and the band royalty, but certainly they are court musicians." As Harden describes it, football games and all that surrounds them form a ritual in Columbus—"a beloved ritual"—and Woods is "the magician who makes it all happen."

But on this terrible night in November, Egelhoff and his colleagues did not meet the man they had so often seen performing magic on a football field, but simply a father whose world was about to fall apart.

It was Catherine Woods's mother, Donna, who first came to the door. She had been doing laundry when the patrol car pulled up in front of the family's modest split-level home. It was now almost 10:00 p.m. and the sound of the doorbell had surprised her. It was too late for friends of her thirteen-year-old daughter, Tori, short for Victoria, to visit. And nineteen-year-old Stephen's pals, she knew, would never use the front door or ring the bell.

Donna was dressed as most homemakers would be late on a Sunday evening, casually and ready for bed. In her mid-fifties, she doesn't seem overly concerned with her appearance and often dresses in comfortable clothing, with little makeup. Her hair, dyed brown to cover the gray, is cut short in a simple, practical bob. If she had been the mother of a soldier in Iraq, the sight of three uniformed officers at the door would have filled Donna with dread. Instead, she felt only mild concern when Officer Egelhoff gave her a telephone number and asked her to call Detective Ryan in New York City. Donna considered for a moment that perhaps her oldest daughter, Catherine, had been hurt. "I thought maybe she had been mugged or attacked."

Not wanting to alarm her family, Donna asked the officers to remain outside with her on the porch while she called the number in New York. The line was busy. With a growing sense of apprehension, she called again. Still busy. Egelhoff and the other officers stood there awkwardly—shivering in the cold—as Donna called and called again. Egelhoff even pulled out his own cell phone and dialed, determined to get through. Again, still busy.

Finally, Egelhoff could take no more.

"Well, okay," he said to her, "I know. They told me. Is your husband here?"

As Donna turned to get her husband, Jon, she blurted out, "How bad is it?"

"It's bad," Egelhoff told her.

Donna knew right then that her gorgeous daughter would never again run through the doorway where the officers now stood. She'd already guessed the answer when she asked, "Is she dead?"

"Yes," Egelhoff said.

Donna was stunned. The officers took over and ushered her into the house, where Jon Woods was standing at the top of the stairs. Egelhoff will never forget the haunted look on Jon's face as the news sank in, nor can he put out of his mind what Catherine's father did next. Walking down the steps, Jon went to a picture of Catherine hanging on a wall. For a minute or two, he just stood silently looking at the photograph and then suddenly, shockingly, he threw Catherine's picture to the floor and cried out, "Why was she dating that shit-head guy?"

Egelhoff understood Jon's anguish once they finally reached Detective Ryan in New York. Ryan filled the family in on some of the details. The person who had found Catherine and reported her death was David Haughn, but there was some confusion about the particulars: Donna remembers Ryan telling her that David had found Catherine when he returned home from work, not as he was about to take her to work. But there was no confusion about the person police were at that very moment questioning inside the Nineteenth Precinct or about the prime suspect in her death: David Haughn.

For the next two hours, the officers offered as much support as they possibly could to Catherine's parents. Donna was distraught. She recalled the last time she'd spoken to her daughter, just the day before. The conversation was pretty mundane, and Donna was the one who'd ended it.

"Well, I think I'm out of conversation, Catherine, you know?" Donna told her.

"Yep, me, too. I love you, Mom."

"Love you, too."

Now Jon Woods was very worried about his wife's state of mind. Fearful that she might be suicidal, he asked the officers to stay until the family's pastor could arrive. As for him, he struggled to maintain his composure, but when asked to recall what he was told that evening about his firstborn daughter's murder, he says, "I think once I heard that she was dead, I was gone, in shock, and I have trouble remembering some of the conversation."

Jon's relationship with his oldest child had always been close but complicated, in part because of his nearly single-minded devotion to the marching band and the university, where he is also a music professor. The grueling band schedule ruled family life: football games in the fall, basketball all winter. There were band practices, band performances, band festivals, and band camps. The schedule rarely gave way for family events, not even for the birth of children. Jon likes to remind people that Catherine's birth certificate lists Madison, Wisconsin, not Columbus, as the place of her birth: a twist of fate that occurred when Donna unexpectedly went into labor while Jon was a guest conductor at a band festival at the University of Wisconsin. Ever the loyal Buckeye, Jon ends the story with, "And the band director out there never forgets to remind me that she really was born a Badger."

Early on, much to Jon's dismay, Catherine showed little interest in the "family business." Instead, Jon remembers the day when three-year-old Catherine announced that she had three goals in life: "one was to be a dancer, the other to be an ice skater, and the third was to ride horses."

Dancing won out. Still, Jon continued to push Catherine to play an instrument. "She accommodated us by playing the horn in sixth, seventh, and eighth grade, but when we hit ninth grade, that was the end of the baritone horn. And she decided, you know, dance was it."

With the same intensity her father gave music, Catherine threw herself into dancing. Throughout high school, she showed little interest in dating or other typical teenage activities, spending the hours after classes and most weekends either practicing at the studio or performing for a local dance company. And like her father, she came alive in front of an audience. "On the stage she glowed," Jon said proudly, "and she projected and held the attention of people. I'd say God-given talent was there."

Catherine would spend hours studying the moves of dancers in the movie version of the musical *Chicago*. And at one point, she posted on her bedroom wall a line from the musical *Rent* that seemed to sum up her aspirations: TO DANCE! NO WAY TO MAKE A LIVING, MASOCHISM, PAIN, PERFECTION, MUSCLE SPASMS, CHIROPRACTORS, SHORT CAREERS, EATING DISORDERS.

But Columbus is not the place to be if you dream of becoming a professional dancer. Other than teaching, there are few opportunities for professional dancers there. For most young women, the dreams of dancing on Broadway go the way of Barbie dolls and other toys: discarded with youth and replaced with more realistic pastimes. But Catherine wouldn't give up on her dream. During her senior year of high school, in early 2002, she suddenly announced to her parents that she was arranging her classes so that she could graduate early and move to New York City. At first, Jon and Donna wouldn't hear of it. Catherine wasn't even eighteen. They pleaded with her to go to college first. Ohio State has a top dance program, they told her.

But Catherine wouldn't budge. She had money saved, she told them, and was determined to move with or without her parents' permission. "She was going to go dance without going to college first because her body was aging," Donna says, wearily repeating the argument that Catherine gave her, "at seventeen and a half, her body was aging. At seventeen and a half, her body was going over the hill fast. . . ."

There was no stopping Catherine. In early May, she went online and found a room to rent in an apartment in Brooklyn. And on May 21, 2002, she moved to New York. But as her parents had correctly predicted, New York City is no place for a young girl all alone. It's a tough town, and although the crime rate has been plunging for a decade, you need to know your way around. Catherine did not know her way around and, worse, she did not look like or have the manners of a native. The women in New York—especially the attractive ones—have a force field of defensiveness they throw up whenever they go out in public. It's hard to get their attention, much less approach them. Their iPod earbuds securely in place, eyes forward, never making contact with anyone—that's the way of the world for young and beautiful New York women. Catherine wasn't like that. She trusted people, and it didn't work out.

That first trip into New York lasted less than a week. According to a police report, Catherine was sexually assaulted and raped that very night, by the thirty-four-year-old man who rented her a room in his Brooklyn apartment. The landlord was arrested and jailed. Catherine Woods went back home to Columbus. Charges against the landlord were later dropped when Catherine refused to testify against him.

But she didn't give up. Her dream was too strong. By that summer, she was already making plans to move back. Why would she want to return to a place where she had been assaulted? Newspaper columnist Mike Harden believes that like so many other children of accomplished parents, Catherine was struggling to find a way to get out from under her father's shadow.

"I think coming from a family that has such a background in music and entertainment," Harden says, "you strive awfully hard to secure your little niche of recognition within the family." Catherine wanted to come home a star on her own terms, and as her eighteenth birthday approached, her parents knew they couldn't stop her. This time, however, her father found her a small but secure apartment of her own in Manhattan, and over the July 4 weekend, he and Donna drove their daughter to New York City. At the time, they had only high hopes for Catherine. "I can still remember that trip," Jon would later recount. "Approaching the city and seeing the Statue of Liberty and seeing the skyscrapers and the skyline of New York City and this is where she was going to make her home. It wasn't easy for us to drop her off there and put her on her own, but we did, and she sure loved it."

Three years later, on a cold November day, Jon Woods would make that same trip to New York, this time to bring his daughter home one last time.

Sometimes, sadly, dreams do die.

7

Interrogation

Back in New York, David Haughn was deep inside the age-old Nineteenth Precinct, on East Sixty-seventh Street, between Third and Lexington avenues. He was taken immediately to the main interview room, which doubles as a lineup room when circumstances warrant. The room is bare-bones—a door, a bench, a table, and a one-way mirrored window. The station house and the room could easily have been a set for the TV show *Law & Order*.

This little room was about to become David's home away from home. Detective Goetz remained at the crime scene, but several other detectives were ready, willing, and able to begin the interrogation, each of them convinced he'd be the guy to wrangle a confession from the nervous country bumpkin who seemed too timid—or was it too guilty—to make eye contact. Any of them would have bet money that David had killed Catherine. He was just so skittish, and gave off such an odd vibe. But the detectives had no idea about David's background, about the years he and his younger sister spent in foster care, thanks to a mother deep into the drug culture. They also didn't know that a hard life had made David a survivor, someone who did not judge others. That quality of acceptance had made him especially appealing to Catherine and Megan, who both followed a muse that was more than a little unconventional. David was kind of like a big dog, but without a bark or a bite.

But the cops didn't know any of that at this point in the investigation. All they saw in front of them was a big lug.

Before the interrogation was through two and a half days later, some seven or eight detectives had wandered in and out of the interview room, each getting a shot at David. Then they questioned him again to see if he would change any detail of his story, looking for that one crucial discrepancy that would sink him.

But David was not changing his story. He was nervous—as anyone would be under those circumstances—but he was also exceedingly cooperative. He waived his right to a lawyer and later—after news of the murder hit the media—he even turned away a lawyer who was trying to get in to represent him. David was as cooperative as they come: He let the cops take whatever they needed (a DNA sample, fingerprints, shoe prints). When they wanted to get a sample of what was under David's nails, he held out his hands. When they needed photographs of him with his clothes and jacket on and off, he stood up and followed instructions. When they wanted photos of him bare-chested and then naked, he stripped.

They insisted on knowing everything David had done on that Sunday, from the time he got up until the time he claimed to have wandered back into the bloody bedroom to find his ex-girlfriend murdered. They told him—warned him—not to leave out anything.

So David did as they asked. He took the cops into his world, back to the beginning of his day, starting when he got off his overnight doorman shift at seven that morning. As soon as he got off, David said, he went and sat in his car, pulled out his notebook and pen, and began listening to a CD called *Smoke Box*. "A guy I know produced it for me so I could write the words for it," he told the cops.

He said he kept writing until 7:45 a.m., at which point he shut off his car, walked through a garage that went from Eighty-seventh to Eighty-sixth Street, and went to the apartment he shared with Catherine. "When I went into the apartment, the dogs got all excited and started making a lot of noise, so Catherine woke up," he said. "She asked me to go and get her an apple. I told her I'd get her one."

David took the Labrador and Josie out for their morning walks and went into the Gristedes supermarket across the street from their building. He got Catherine the apple she wanted, washed it for her, and delivered it to her as she sat up in bed. The morning was mundane; it was just a day in the life. David told detectives how he took off his uniform and ate his cereal. It was time for him to go to bed, but Catherine's day was just beginning . . . well, almost beginning. After eating her apple, she was still tired and asked David to set her alarm for 9:20 a.m. She went back to sleep, and David headed for the futon in the living room.

The next thing he knew it was 4:20 p.m., time to walk the Lab again. Catherine was gone—he said he had no idea where. "She didn't say, and I didn't ask her," he told the cops.

It was part of their new arrangement. They were just roommates and could come and go as they pleased. David just hung around watching ESPN and thinking about how hungry he was. There was nothing to eat in the apartment. He decided to get some food and walk Josie, and just as he was about to leave, Catherine called him on her cell phone; she was nearly home. So David walked Josie toward Second Avenue, because he knew Catherine would be coming home that way. They met at the corner, hugged, and then walked toward the apartment. Catherine told David she was hungry, too, and asked him to buy her a Smart Ones Chicken Santa Fe frozen dinner and a bag of chips from Gristedes. He did so, and also bought himself a steak and rice taco from Taco Today, on First Avenue. When he got home, David put the frozen dinner in the microwave, in-between bites of his taco.

Catherine was getting ready for work, and David alternately watched television and began "messing with my beat machine."

He went into a lot of detail about the day, especially about what happened next. "Catherine was walking back and forth from the bedroom to the bathroom," he said. "She was only wearing her panties as she walked back and forth. The outline on the panties was black, and I think they had pink and red flowers on them. She was a real pretty girl. At one point, she was standing in front of the mirror."

David, who'd lived with Catherine for three years, still couldn't take his eyes off her. "I wish we could freeze-frame this," he told her. "You look so beautiful, just like a picture."

Catherine smiled. "Thanks, David. That's a cute thing to say."

David got up and "the next time she came out of the bedroom, I met her by the door and we hugged and started kissing. As we moved back into the bedroom, the hugging and kissing became more intimate. I pick her up and set her on the edge of the bed. I pull my penis out of my zipper. She pulled her panties to the side and said, 'We have to hurry.' We start to have sex. It didn't last over five minutes. Right before I finished, I pulled out. I came in my hand. I leaned down and kissed her. I went to the bathroom and washed my hand off. The last time [before this] that we had sex was on Halloween. Normally, I did not come inside her or on her. She didn't like that. Sometimes, we would use a condom, but not always.

"I came out of the bathroom, and she was still getting ready to go to work."

"I wish I didn't have to go to work tonight," she told David.

It was a sore point between them. He gave her as much as he could for the rent and expenses, but it never seemed to be enough and he felt guilty about it. Maybe if he made more money, she wouldn't need to work so much.

"I'm sorry, baby," he told her.

"It's not your fault."

Not knowing what else to say, David told her he'd get the car so she could just hop in and wouldn't be late. "I left the apartment and didn't lock the door. Sometimes we didn't lock it when one of us was there," he said. He estimated the time he left the apartment as twenty minutes earlier, which would have put the time at approximately 6:40 p.m.

David says he cut back through the garage to get his car but then remembered he'd left some CDs near a desk in the basement of the building where he worked as a doorman. While there, he said he spoke to a co-worker named Ali and the building supervisor, a guy named Joe Tabone. David and Ali both wanted off the same time during Christmas holidays, and Joe was telling them he couldn't let them both go. Joe also said that it was the best time of year to get tips from all the residents and that both of them would get more tips if they were around. They agreed to talk again, and David left to go to his car, parked right across the street.

How much time had he spent talking to Ali and Joe?

"I was there five minutes at the most," David told the cops.

He says he got back in his car, put on a Beastie Boys CD, and started driving around the corner to get Catherine. He again told the police how he tried to call her but, getting no answer, went in to find her dead in a pool of blood in her bedroom. That's when he called 911.

The statement seemed complete, but there was a big problem, at least for David: He'd implicated himself in Catherine's murder by telling the police that he had been out of the apartment for only twenty minutes. Because he called 911 just before 7:00 p.m., that would mean that he had not left the apartment until around 6:40 p.m. Andrew Gold, the most reliable earwitness because he was looking at a digital clock at the time, told cops that he and his girlfriend, who could verify her end of the conversation, had definitely heard the screams coming from apartment 2D a few minutes past 6:18 p.m. Using David's time line, that would mean he had been in the apartment when those screams started. And if that was true—well, as cops say, then David was "looking good" for Catherine's murder.

Cops also wondered if David was telling the whole truth about that last sexual encounter. Had he tried to initiate sex but she'd rebuffed him? Was he more upset that Catherine had broken up with him than he was letting on? Was that when he'd lost his temper and raped and killed her?

David had put himself inside the apartment during the murder *and* had given the cops a possible motive.

As detectives at the "one-nine" pieced together the information, they relayed it back to Detective Goetz at the scene, and Goetz sent men out to see if they could verify David's story. The crucial witnesses would be Joe Tabone and Ali. Had they seen David at the building as he'd said? And if so, what time was he there? Any security video cameras on the block would have to be checked, as would the workers in Gristedes. Did they recall seeing David? Did he have any receipts to prove what he was saying? This was the bread and butter of police work—verifying the story of a possible defendant.

There was a lot of work to do, a lot of directions to go in. And in the middle of the interrogation, David had matter-of-factly dropped a bombshell. When police asked about Catherine's job and why David was driving her to work at 7:00 p.m. on a Sunday evening, David didn't hold back. The beautiful and talented Catherine Woods, who had come to New York to dance on Broadway, had secured a different sort of job. She was dancing all right, but not in legitimate theater. She was paying the rent and making ends meet by dancing topless at the notorious Flash Dancers Gentlemen's Club on Broadway, between Fifty-second and Fifty-third streets.

If you've ever seen the Bada Bing Club in *The Sopranos,* you have a pretty good idea of what Flash Dancers is like. For one thing, the club is not secluded in some corner of the city; it's right there on Broadway. Inside, there are a lot of pulsating lights, and naked women gyrating to loud, pounding beats. Generally, the women, who tend to be far more attractive than you might expect, start off their dancing in slinky evening gowns. But those soon drop to the floor, and then the women peel off the layers until all that's left is a thong. There's a lot of teasing directed toward the men sitting at the edge of the stage, and a lot of large bills migrate from hand to thong.

The cops questioning David looked at one another. They knew that once the media got hold of this little nugget, the murder of Catherine Woods, already a red-hot story, would take off into the stratosphere.

8

All News All the Time

The background music of New York City, and one of the root causes of the intensity that drives New Yorkers, is the nonstop drumbeat of news. With *The New York Times,* the *Daily News,* the *New York Post,* at least five local television news divisions, and two daily all-news, all-the-time radio stations—1010 WINS and WCBS 880—it's no wonder New Yorkers end up feeling a little frazzled by the end of the day. It takes a fair amount of effort to *avoid* knowing about the fire that killed three in Astoria or the jackknifed tractor trailer on the BQE. In New York, there's always something happening, some man-made crisis somewhere in the five boroughs and nearly six hundred times a year, that crisis involves murder.

The reporters who cover cops and crime are the ER doctors of the media. They work in the most stressful environment of all their colleagues, because crime happens 24/7, and the race to be the first can make or break a career. *New York Post* veteran police reporter Larry Celona doesn't have to worry about any one story breaking his career. The barrel-chested Celona, who drives a black Ford Explorer with an NYPD permit that allows him to park just about anywhere, is a native New Yorker, born and raised in Brooklyn. With his gruff manner, he looks like a cop, and his no-BS style has endeared him to many of New York's finest. He's been on a first-name basis with New York's police commissioners for two decades now, and has gotten so many scoops over the years that his place in the city's pantheon of established go-to guys is secure. One of the reasons for Celona's success is that he never rests. He's always on the job, looking around for those tiny nuggets that other reporters can't get because they don't have the same sources he does. Celona surrounds himself with cops, on and off the job; he enjoys their company—and Sunday, November 27, was no different.

Celona had worked that day and had knocked off around 7:00 p.m., but instead of going home to his Bay Ridge co-op, he headed, like any cop might, to La Traviata, an old-school Italian restaurant on Montague Street, in Brooklyn Heights. The restaurant was managed by a former cop, and Celona was meeting some police buddies there for dinner. "We were sitting around talking and eating when I got this 'slip' about a murder on the Upper East Side," he said.

The office of Deputy Commissioner, Public Information, better to known to one and all as DCPI, is located in police headquarters, manned around the clock by detectives who put out the word on recent crimes of interest. In the old days, before computers, cops would send out a "slip" on teletype machines. Veterans like Celona still refer to them as slips, even though the information on Catherine Woods came over Celona's BlackBerry in the form of an e-mail. The problem, as reporters see it, is that the detectives in DCPI put out the basics and that's it. They're notorious for giving out as little information as possible. To find the story behind the story, you need police sources, cops who'll tell you the real deal off the record, and Celona had plenty of those.

Celona looked at the information about Catherine Woods's murder, but at that point it consisted of only "young female DOA" and an address. After an initial call, Celona had a feeling the story would be big. Like Detective Goetz, he knew that despite the general perception of New York as Murder Central, there just aren't that many murders of young women on the Upper East Side. He phoned the *Post* City Desk and told them to send a reporter to the scene. In the meantime, Celona reached out to his sources. He knew a cop who knew a cop, and before long Celona knew that Catherine had been twenty-one, beautiful, and a dancer from Ohio. He also found out that her father, Jon, was the leader of the famous Ohio State marching band. With that information, the City Desk quickly placed a call to a freelancer living in Ohio, whose job it was to knock on the Woodses' front door.

Celona tried to finish his meal at La Traviata, but the story kept calling. Soon enough, he was hearing that Catherine was a stripper. He checked with detectives at DCPI, but they refused to confirm the information, at least partly out of respect for Catherine's family. That did not, however, deter Celona. "I heard she worked at Flash Dancers, and of course I know someone there, too." He chuckled.

He called Flash Dancers and was able to confirm that the police were sniffing around as well. He made more calls and, before long, got the confirmation he needed—Catherine Woods had indeed been working as a topless dancer at Flash Dancers under the stage name Ava.

Larry Celona finished his meal.

9

Unimaginable

At eleven-thirty that night, the phone rang in the home of Mr. and Mrs. Robert Pettigrew, of Worthington, a suburb of Columbus, Ohio. It was late for a Sunday night, and Emily, the Pettigrews' twenty-one-year-old daughter, wondered who could be calling at that hour.

"Hi, Emily, this is Donna Woods. May I speak to your mother?"

"Sure, hang on, Mrs. Woods. I'll get her."

Emily had known Catherine since first grade—"we were both the shy kids"—and was one of Catherine's closest friends. Still, this call was unusual; Mrs. Woods almost never called Emily's home, and never this late. Emily told her mother she had a call, but there was something in Mrs. Woods's voice that made Emily stay on the line listening in while her mother picked up the extension. Donna told Emily's mother she had bad news and wanted to make sure the Pettigrews heard it from her before word got out. She thought it best if Mrs. Pettigrew broke the news to her daughter. Donna

Woods then told Mrs. Pettigrew what had happened in New York, that Catherine had been murdered.

"When I heard those words come out of her mouth, I just fell to the ground," Emily said. "I thought, 'No way, this can't be true.' I said to myself, 'I must be dreaming. There's no way that this could ever really happen.' I mean this was a safe part of town. No way could this happen to her."

Emily refused to believe it. Catherine dead? Catherine had been a big part of Emily's life forever and, as long as she'd known Catherine, she'd known how much Catherine wanted to make it as a dancer in New York. "We always said she had an older soul. She was more interested in things that some high school kids never even thought about," Emily said.

"In elementary school, I told her I wanted to be an interior designer, and she wanted to be on Broadway. We'd have fantasies, like I was going to decorate her apartment in New York and then she'd have all these Broadway people over and they'd say, 'Oh, who decorated your apartment?' And then she'd be like, 'Oh, my best friend Emily did.'

"She was the most beautiful person I ever knew, inside and out."

After processing the unthinkable, Emily began calling Catherine's closest friends. One of those she called was Megan Wilkins, who had spoken to Catherine just minutes before she was killed. Even though it was late on a Sunday night, Megan was on her way to the Ohio State University library; she was planning to stay up all night to write a paper she'd been putting off. "Emily was crying," Megan said. "And she just said that I needed to come over immediately, that it was an emergency."

Megan figured "maybe there was trouble with her and her boyfriend or maybe her parents," but Emily sounded so distraught that Megan immediately drove to the Pettigrew house. Ten minutes after the call, Megan pulled into the Pettigrews' driveway. Emily and her mother both came out of the house crying, rushed up to Megan, and told her what had happened.

"What? I just spoke to her," Megan said. "Are you sure you have the right person?"

No one knew any details at that point, but Megan's first thought was that there'd been trouble at the club, that Catherine had been killed at Flash Dancers. Like the rest of Catherine's closest friends, Megan knew how Catherine had been earning money. In fact, Megan knew better than anyone. The previous summer, when she had stayed with Catherine and David in New York for nearly three months, Megan had worked with Catherine, dancing topless.

Megan, a buxom blonde, could see that Catherine was earning fantastic money at the club, and she thought it was too sweet an opportunity to pass up. Catherine gave her the ground rules: Each dancer actually paid the strip club a "house fee," between $100 and $150 a night, and in return the club allowed them to dance and keep the tips, which could be very lucrative. Megan says there were times when Catherine made five thousand dollars in a single night. "She was a very beautiful girl," Megan said. "The money gave her freedom, which is what she wanted."

Megan was intrigued and accompanied Catherine to work one night when the club was hiring new dancers. The audition to become a topless dancer was almost a joke, Megan says. "You go up onstage and, depending on which club it is, they'll have you dance for one or two songs, basically just to make sure you're not gonna fall."

Megan insists that neither of them was involved in anything beyond giving men lap dances, even though at Flash Dancers, Megan and Catherine would sometimes accompany men into a more private room, dubbed "the Blue Room" because of its blue couches. In New York, club patrons are forbidden from touching the dancers. "It's like two thousand dollars to be in there for an hour, and the girl gets a thousand of that," Megan said. "Whoever can afford to take somebody in that room can tip a whole lot more."

The way Megan describes the Blue Room, it doesn't sound all that exciting, and for her, it probably wasn't. For an inebriated businessman, however, sitting next to a nearly naked beautiful young woman wearing only a thong, the air was surely a bit more charged. "The Blue Room has a blue leather couch, and there's a security guard in there with you to make sure nothing happens," Megan said. "There's a TV with cable on it, and there's like a foot massager machine. Most of the people that come into these clubs are just lonely and they really just want somebody to talk to."

Megan said she enjoyed her summer dancing in the club with Catherine. Megan says that it was just a job for both of them and that they made sure to hang on to the easy money. "Catherine, she was a huge saver," Megan said. Catherine used the money to keep up her dance lessons and even began studying voice twice a week. "She was constantly singing around the house," Megan said, laughing at this memory of her friend. "Her favorite was Ani DiFranco, and she loved this song she has about a cockroach. She'd sing that song over and over because Ani DiFranco's voice goes up and down, and Catherine needed to learn those different notes. That was the only song she wanted to sing, and David got kind of annoyed because she'd sing it over and over again."

As Megan and Emily huddled together that night talking about Catherine and what possibly could have happened, they both began to wonder about David. They couldn't reach him and didn't know he was being questioned by police, but they knew he and Catherine had broken up and had been having typical relationship problems. For a fleeting moment, they wondered if David could have had anything to do with her death, but both friends dismissed this notion. After all, Megan said, "I have never seen a couple more in love."

10

The Slain Stripper

On Monday morning, November 28, 2005, New Yorkers woke up to the latest of the city's many iconic crimes. Every New Yorker knows them, the stories with the handy nickname or catchphrase that makes them immediately recognizable—the "Son of Sam," the "Preppy Murder," the "Central Park Jogger." Catherine Woods was about to become the "Slain Stripper." One of her friends pointed out that the stories could just as well have identified her as "Aspiring Broadway Dancer," but that would not have sold as many papers. Reducing someone's life to a few recognizable words that sizzle and sell papers is what tabloid headline writers do. It's not fair and it's not pretty, but that's the way it is.

Instantly, the murder of Catherine Woods became the story of the small-town good girl gone "bad" (never mind that Columbus has more than one million residents). No one came right out and said that Catherine had paid with her life for the sin of topless dancing, but the implication was there. To the headline writers,

Catherine had been dancing all right—right on the edge of morality, and she'd fallen off.

But the first front-page headline of the *New York Post* actually was not so aggressive. It read: "Beauty Slain: Dancer Savagely Stabbed in Upper East Side Apt." The joint byline was Larry Celona in New York and Matthew Marx in Columbus, Ohio. Considering the story hit the stands just about twelve hours after Catherine was murdered, it was very accurate and surprisingly complete. Upstairs neighbor Andrew Gold was quoted, as was Catherine's father, Jon, who said his daughter "was chasing her dream, which just ended." Residents of the building were quoted as saying they were "shocked" by the murder, and a resident at the building where David was a doorman said, "He's the nicest guy, a really sweet kid."

The third paragraph contained the information that would keep the tabloids salivating: "[Catherine's] boyfriend told cops she was an exotic dancer, police sources said."

The very next paragraph noted that Catherine's parents in Ohio said that Catherine had appeared in an Off-Broadway production called *Privilege*. What the Woodses said they didn't know then, and what even *Post* reporters did not realize at the time, was that, yes, there had been an Off-Broadway play called *Privilege* but it was staged in 2002, not 2005, and it wasn't the same Privilege where Catherine worked. It was yet another strip club by the same name, located on Twenty-

third Street and Eleventh Avenue, where Catherine
danced before Flash Dancers.

Five hundred miles away, in Columbus, the reaction to
Catherine's death was, well, different. There were no
sexy pictures of her plastered on the front page of the
only major newspaper in town. No lurid headlines. Columbus remained true to its small-town attitude.

Ben Marrison, the editor of *The Dispatch,* admits
that in the early hours of that first day, he resisted the
story because he thought the tabloids had it all wrong.
This was Jon Woods's daughter, after all. Stripper?
Impossible. "This young woman comes from a proud
and respected family," he told Bob Ruth, the crime reporter assigned to the story. "She wouldn't possibly
have been involved in anything like that."

But Ruth knew better. "There are eighty thousand
people in New York just like her," he told his boss,
"and not all of them can make it on Broadway." By
afternoon, Ruth had confirmed the story, and Marrison
felt he had no choice but to run it.

If New Yorkers revel in sordid stories, Columbusites
are repelled by them.

When the first story about Catherine's topless dancing ran in the *The Dispatch,* the paper was bombarded
with angry letters and e-mails from readers accusing
the paper of violating the privacy of Catherine's family.
"I feel that the story went into unnecessary details that
were no one's business," one reader wrote. Another

asked, "Do you people have souls? Don't you suppose that the NYPD has told the family all of this privately? And if not, is it necessary they know anything other than that she is dead and was murdered?"

The reaction was not surprising to columnist Mike Harden. Harden is what you might call "the conscience" of Columbus. He's lived there all of his sixty-five years, and for nearly thirty of them he has written his warm, folksy metro column. At times, you're unsure if you're reading about Columbus or the fictional Mayberry, RFD. Harden is so much a part of the small-town atmosphere of Columbus that he's been known to show up at community meetings with a German chocolate cake, and not just any cake, but one he'd baked himself. Like his New York counterpart, Jimmy Breslin, Harden says what he thinks, and his reaction to Catherine's murder pretty well summed up how a lot of people in Columbus felt: "We reacted in the manner that we did to Catherine Woods's murder because there was a sense of family about it. This was one of our own. We were affronted by the indignity that someone that we cherished and might send off with our best hopes could die in such a brutal manner."

Harden was upset by his ruthless counterparts at the big-city tabloids, who he says found something "obscene about Catherine's life, when the only obscenity we see is her death."

11
Paul's Catherine?

Sometime between five and six o'clock that same Monday morning, an attractive middle-aged woman named Ivette Cortez was preparing for work up in the East Tremont section of the Bronx, a working-class neighborhood. "My routine is always I have the radio on," she said. "I listen to the news, and they mentioned a dancer, Catherine Woods. In the back of my head, I'm like 'Catherine?'"

Ivette knew a dancer named Catherine, a young woman her son, Paul, was dating, "but for some strange reason at that moment I couldn't remember her last name. So I just made a mental note to call Paul."

Still, the radio report had bothered Ivette; she left the house feeling uneasy. Why couldn't she remember Catherine's last name, and why did she think the dead woman could possibly be *Paul's* Catherine? But a mother's intution is a powerful thing. On the way to the subway, Ivette passed a newsstand. Her stomach dropped. The dead dancer was Paul's Catherine, and her photograph was on the front page of the *New York*

Post. "Her face was there," Ivette said, her voice cracking. "I still can't talk about it. It didn't make any sense."

She bought the newspaper, and as she scanned the story, one gut-wrenching sentence stood out. The police were holding the woman's boyfriend for questioning. "I didn't know what that meant, if they were holding Paul," she said.

She was, however, going to find out. She frantically dialed Paul's cell phone, but the call went straight to voice mail.

Down in Manhattan, at the Equinox fitness club on East Eighty-fifth Street, Ivette's son Paul had just finished a training session with a client named Brian Sampson. The two had chatted about the Giants football game from the night before, a late game that Paul had watched at a friend's house. Brian was a little surprised that Paul was so interested in the game. He'd never known Paul to talk about football at all. He didn't think too much about it, but it stuck in the back of his mind.

By 8:00 a.m., Paul had finished training Brian. "I had a little break in between my first two clients and I went to check my voice mail messages. I didn't charge my phone from the night before, so I just called from the club," Paul said. "I got a voice mail from my mom, and she just sounded really distressed, just like, 'Please call me when you get a chance.' I know my mom and I know her voice, you know? So I called her."

"Mom, what's going on?" Paul asked her.

"Where are you?" she asked, silently thanking God that Paul was not the boyfriend mentioned in the newspaper, the one the cops were questioning.

"I'm at the club. What's going on?"

"Can I come meet you? I'm going to be there in whatever time, just tell me."

"I have one more client left," Paul told her. "I guess I'm done in an hour. You can come in an hour."

Twenty-four-year-old Paul Cortez, Ivette's youngest of three children, was especially close to his mother. Paul had a father and stepfather he spoke to regularly, but it was Ivette who had *raised* Paul. Along with his brother and sister, Paul and his mother had shared a small apartment on Park Avenue and 179th Street in the Bronx. Ivette was a single mother who had worked hard to get off public assistance and into a good-paying job, so she'd be a role model for her three children. She'd succeeded in getting secretarial jobs at Chase bank and later at Bronx-Lebanon Hospital. They were good jobs, but money was tight.

Private school in New York, where annual tuitions are in the range of thirty thousand dollars, was not even a consideration for Ivette's children, but early on it became an option for Paul, when he caught the eye of his teachers. There was just something about the precocious, intelligent, and good-looking kid with the big smile. His teachers wrote one glowing recommendation after another, and by sixth grade, Paul was awarded with a scholarship to The Buckley School, in Manhattan. For high school, he went one better. He gained admittance—again on scholarship—to one of the best private schools in the city, Poly Prep Country Day School, in Brooklyn. Aside from having tested well, Paul was an accomplished athlete and was awarded the scholarship for his wrestling prowess. Poly Prep was a great opportunity, but going there wasn't going to be easy. Paul could handle the schoolwork all right; it was the commute that was a killer.

Getting from the Bronx to Brooklyn by bus and subway is not easy—you can fly from New York to Washington, D.C., faster. Still, Paul made the most of it, waking up at 4:30 a.m. every day, and then heading out in the dark for the two-and-a-half-hour commute—each way. Students with less willpower and determination would have quickly given up. "There were days where he would barely get enough time for just a few hours' sleep," his mother said. "I know there were days that he slept and missed his stop."

But Paul kept at it, even though he lacked the basic resources the rest of his classmates took for granted. One day, Ivette says "a big, old box" was delivered to their apartment. Inside was a computer, a gift from one of Paul's teachers. "It seemed so inappropriate and I couldn't understand why my son was getting a computer from this instructor," she said. "And he [the teacher] told me quite frankly that Paul was the only child in the school that was hand-writing his reports.

And then it dawned on me—no wonder it takes him forever. I just didn't realize that everybody else had what we didn't have."

Paul thrived at Poly Prep, but by the end of his freshman year he was less than thrilled with his wrestling career. He wanted to give up wrestling to follow his heart and study acting and the theater. But would the school allow him to keep his scholarship? By then, the teachers at Poly Prep knew Paul was something special, and they agreed without hesitation. It was the right choice for everyone. Paul went on to excel at acting, and was the lead in one play after another, whether it was a musical or Shakespeare. He was a natural, full of charisma. You couldn't help but stare when he was onstage. He was very handsome and well-spoken, and seemed much more skilled than those around him. In his senior year, he won an honorable mention award in Theater from the National Foundation for Advancement in the Arts, one of only fifty-three students selected from fifty-five hundred nationwide to win the award. When he was only seventeen, he won a role as a tough young punk opposite veteran actor Eli Wallach in a short film called *The Devil's Twilight,* which ran on PBS. It was no surprise when Paul later got a scholarship to Boston University, where he again excelled in student productions and spent his junior year abroad at the London Academy of Music and Dramatic Art. He eventually graduated with a BFA in theater arts.

Ivette Cortez was beyond proud of her son. "He's done so much for our family," she said. "He has been, quite frankly, our Renaissance man. We were poor, we didn't have much, but Paul always had goals and the ambition to strive for them. He was the first in our family to go to a private school, to learn Latin and French, to go to a wonderful university, graduate from there, be onstage. He has his music, he dances. He just does so much with his life. He actually embraces Shakespeare and the classics and things that, quite frankly, most of us in our family just don't understand. He has that love for all of these things and he has such a great spirit, always wanting to be able to do for others, to help others. He has a great sense of spirituality that even as a child he's always had. It's something that always came out naturally for him."

After college, Paul moved back to New York and eventually got his own small apartment in Manhattan. Like Catherine, he had his own dreams of achieving success, and his mother thinks that was the attraction between them. "I think Paul saw a lot of himself in her," Ivette said. "It was obvious that she was pursuing a dream and she had great tenacity and was trying to work very hard and do whatever it took to be able to dance onstage, to pursue her love. I think her spirit is what touched Paul."

Paul says he caught the acting bug very early on, sometime in junior high school, when he was in a production of *Guys and Dolls*. "I'd been in productions before, but it was the first real one that I was in and the director, he told my mom, 'Your son has the potential to really be something big on Broadway.' "

Paul went to auditions in New York—including one for the rock musical *Rent*—but he said he became frustrated because casting directors wanted to typecast him as a Latino. At the same time, he began getting more and more interested in Eastern religions, and his dream shifted somewhat. He was trying to find his way, and as he did, Paul leaned on his poetry, turning some of his poems into songs, and eventually became one of the songwriters and the lead singer for a hard rock band called Monolith.

Playing one paying gig a month is no way to make a living in the big city, so Paul began working odd jobs that fit in with his personal philosophy. He worked the reception desk at the Bikram Yoga studio near Union Square, because he was a devotee of yoga and meditation. One of the perks of the job was the opportunity to attend yoga classes for free. Bikram yoga is often called "hot" yoga because the room is heated to over a hundred degrees. Some hate it and never come back after the first session, while others become fanatics, taking one class a day for thirty days straight without a break. A ninety-minute class in hundred-degree heat can make you feel like you've run a marathon, but it can also get you in fabulous physical condition. Classes in Manhattan are filled with professional dancers and young hardbodies.

Paul had always been in great shape, but the Bikram yoga toned his body even more. He soon became a personal trainer at various health clubs around the city. With his shoulder-length dark hair, Latin looks, and winning personality, he was a magnet for women wherever he worked. It's no surprise that he had plenty of female clients, which kept the gym management happy and gave Paul plenty of opportunity to meet his pick of interesting women, who didn't mind one bit if their workouts came with something extra—a handsome flirt who flattered them with attention. Paul talked a good game and exuded a guru's aura. He was a dashing, romantic figure—intelligent, educated, and insightful. And he was never shy about mentioning that he practiced meditation and yoga and liked to write poetry and lyrics. He went out of his way to let his clients know he wasn't just another gym rat.

A lot of women flocked to Paul—but not Catherine. Paul had previously worked at the New York Sports Club on East Eighty-sixth Street, where Catherine worked out, and one day, in August 2004, one of the other trainers at the club pointed Catherine out to Paul. For whatever reason, Paul had never noticed her, even though she always seemed to be at the club practicing her dance moves.

"That girl in there," the club manager said, "she's always dancing and she's really beautiful. Why don't you go talk to her? Try to, you know, sell her something."

It was Paul's job to sell personal training packages to people at the gym, and Catherine seemed a natural since she was always there anyway. "So I go in and we started talking and I began telling her my history as a dancer," Paul said. "I told her I could help her train. I was trying to show her this move with my leg and she just started laughing because I guess I came off as kind of arrogant, like I was trying to show her how to dance and she was so great at dancing. I really couldn't show her anything.

"She made it clear that she wasn't interested in any packages but she started asking me what I did and if I was still into dance. I told her not at the moment but I was doing music and I actually had one of my solo CDs with me and I told her I was in a band and did some solo work. I gave her one of the CDs and asked her to listen to it. I've had other dancers create projects from my work and I thought maybe she'd be interested in doing something like that. So I gave her the CD, and it had my picture and my phone number on it."

Thinking back, Paul smiled at the memory of that first meeting. "She was beautiful, yes," he said, "but she was also playful, and that's what I really liked about her. She was really open, and you could see compassion in her eyes."

Paul didn't think Catherine was all that interested in him, and didn't think much about the encounter until the next day, when he was in rehearsal with his band. He got a phone call with a 614 area code that he didn't recognize. He let the call go to voice mail. After rehearsal, he checked his messages and heard a familiar woman's voice: "Hey, my name is Catherine. We met yesterday. Give me a call if you want to hang out."

Paul turned to his lead guitarist, Alex Rude, whose real name is Alexis Casella. "Hey, this beautiful girl I met yesterday just called me."

"Go for it, man. Call her."

Paul dialed the number, and after exchanging some pleasantries with Catherine, he said, "So, when do you wanna hang out?"

"What are you doing now?" Catherine asked.

"Well, nothing. I'm done with rehearsal."

"So, why don't we get together now," she said.

"I was blown away," Paul said, thinking back on the conversation. "I'd never really had someone be that interested in me like that."

They got together that day, and Paul was head over heels about Catherine even though she told him that she was living with David. "She said she was in the process of breaking up with him," Paul said. "She couldn't just throw him out because she still had feelings for him and cared about him. The only other support he had was back in Ohio. She said she felt extremely guilty kicking him out and having him go back to Ohio when he had these aspirations in New York. She just said the relationship was extremely rocky, that she was trying to get David to move out so she could have her own place."

At that point, Catherine and David were living in a tiny studio on East Eighty-fifth Street. She soon moved to the one-bedroom apartment at 355 East Eighty-sixth Street, but instead of making sure David got his own place, she allowed him to move there with her. A lot of guys would have been upset at this, but in Paul's eyes, it was further confirmation of Catherine's generous spirit. "She was open and compassionate and very beautiful," he said, "very sensitive, very giving, very big heart. Her heart was so big with animals and people on the street, the homeless, and cabdrivers. She was always giving them extra tips. She was just such a beautiful person. I think that's why I fell in love with her.

"We started dating after that initial time and I think we saw each other like four times a week. I think we called each other almost every day. It was just kind of instant, but we didn't start officially dating until the end of October [2004] or early November, somewhere around there."

Paul says they shared their first kiss as they sat on a bench in Washington Square Park one night after attending a dance performance at the Joyce Theater in Chelsea. "It was such a great time," he said. "She loved it and I loved it, and I think she enjoyed that she could actually go out with someone who appreciated things like ballet and modern dance."

It was a not-so-subtle dig at David. Next to Paul, David, sweet as he was, came off as something of an uneducated lug. Paul had not met him at that point, but he'd heard all about him and probably had a hard time understanding the attraction. He knew Catherine felt sorry for David, but to Paul, David didn't seem too serious a rival. Still, David was living with Catherine, and Paul was not. Paul admitted the situation was awkward. More often than not, he met Catherine not at her apartment but at diners and Starbucks outlets all over Manhattan.

Paul was serious about Catherine. That much was clear to those who knew him. "He saw her not just as a girlfriend but as someone he really connected with spiritually," said Paul's close friend Jaki Levy, who had dinner one night with both of them. "They had a very deep connection, and I saw he really cared for her. The way he spoke about her, the way he thought about her, the way he acted around her, was markedly different from what I've seen before.

"When they were together, they were both really radiant. They were electric. It was a real chemistry between them. When I first saw her, I actually thought she was pretty young. I'm like, 'This is Catherine? Really?' But when I saw them interact, I'm like, 'Wow.' "

Even Paul's mother knew her son was serious about Catherine when he brought her home to meet Ivette. "It just happened to be the beginning of spring," Ivette said. "I'll always remember it because although it was a little chilly, we went to the Bronx Zoo because Catherine had never been to the zoo. And we had a beautiful day, just kind of walking through it. I realized that this was someone that Paul felt very close to. And we came home to my house and, you know, in my household, you get fed of course, and she didn't eat very much because I didn't know she was a vegetarian. I made beef stew, but luckily the rice and beans kind of hit the spot.

"She was a nice girl, and Paul didn't bring many girls to the house."

Paul loved nearly everything about Catherine, but he drew the line at her topless dancing. He considered the job "soul-sucking" and admitted he hated the thought of her doing it, both for how it might hurt her self-esteem and because it was dangerous. He constantly tried to talk her out of it, but she would not be deterred. She saw it as a way to make money while still allowing plenty of time to go to auditions and practice dance. Paul says she told him, "I don't want a job to consume all of my time, and I know that if I do this thing twice a week, I can earn more than enough money to support myself."

Every time Paul raised the topic and tried to get her to stop, she got upset. "I know what you're saying," she told him, "but it really isn't any of your business. This is my life and I'm gonna be careful and nothing's gonna happen to me."

The disagreement became so serious that Paul once broke up with her, but he couldn't stay away and began calling her again. Clearly, she was not going to stop. "She was a very headstrong young woman," he said. "She did what she wanted, and that was that."

Paul said he and Catherine eventually made a "pact." "I said, 'Every time you work, when you get off, you have to call me so I'm not worrying about you.' And she was like, 'Okay, that's fine.' Sometimes, I would have to train someone at like seven in the morning and she would call me at four-thirty, five in the morning to let me know that she was safe. It was more important to me than getting a couple of extra hours' sleep. Sometimes I would sleep through it and I would just call her later."

It was, Paul said, the only way he could make peace with her job.

12

Complete Shock

After finishing with his last client that Monday, November 28, 2005, Paul hurried to pack his gear. He was concerned about the call from his mother. There was something in the tone of her voice. "As soon as I got outside of the club, my mother was there and she had a newspaper with her," Paul said.

She showed Paul the newspaper and broke the news. "She just told me that Catherine was killed the night before and I just, I just buckled. I remember sitting on the stoop right outside of the club and I just couldn't believe it. I was in complete shock."

The previous day, Paul and Catherine had made plans to get together, but she'd been too busy with her friend Christina. He called her a lot that Sunday, so much that she seemed annoyed by it. She called him back a couple of times but was short with him. Now, here in the newspaper, was the hard truth that he'd never see her again. "The only thing I remember seeing in it was David's name and being like, 'Oh my God, this happened.' "

At that point, Paul was nonfunctioning, but Ivette grabbed a passing cab and they rode up to Paul's studio apartment in the old Spanish Harlem neighborhood of 106th Street and Lexington Avenue. "I was just bawling, and my mom was holding me and telling me it was going to be all right."

After he settled down a bit, Paul saw that he'd missed a phone call. He checked his voice mail. It was a New York police detective, telling him they wanted to talk to him about Catherine. His mother encouraged him to talk to the police, tell them everything he knew. Paul called the Nineteenth Precinct and wound up talking to Detective Michael Ahearne.

"Where are you?" the detective asked.

"I'm at home."

"Okay, sit tight. We're gonna come up there to get you."

Within the hour, two police detectives knocked on Paul's door. It was now 11:00 a.m. Not even a full day had gone by since Catherine Woods was murdered and everyone was still a suspect. Paul invited them in, and the two detectives entered cautiously. His place was a mess, with clothes strewn all over. There was just a mattress on the floor; it was more of a crash pad than a home. Paul introduced the detectives to his mother, and then they got right to the point. "What's your relationship to Catherine Woods?" one of them asked.

Paul explained how they'd been dating for a little over a year. The detectives asked a bunch of basic ques-

tions, including whether Paul knew that she was working at a strip club. "I was still hysterical at that point
and still in shock," Paul said. "I remember just bab-
bling—I don't even remember exactly what I said—
but Detective Ahearne kind of calmed me down a little.
He sat me down at my kitchenette, he asked me a few
more questions, and then requested that I go with him
back to the precinct."

Paul agreed but asked the cops if his mother could
ride along with them. They said sure, and Ivette rode
with Paul in the back of the police car, comforting him
as he cried on and off as they made their way to East
Sixty-seventh Street.

When Paul and his mother walked into the Nineteenth Precinct, David Haughn was still there being
interrogated. Paul said he thought he was there to provide information about David and Catherine. The cops
asked Ivette to wait in one room while they took Paul
to another.

"Can my mom be present, just to be kind of a witness?"

"No, she has to wait outside," Ahearne said.

In the room with Paul were three detectives:
Ahearne, Peter Pannuccio, and Thomas Ryan. "They
sat me down with my back facing the door and they
were kind of surrounding me," Paul said.

He might have been feeling closed in, but he didn't
reach for a lifeline. The cops asked Paul if he wanted a
lawyer, but he said no. He would speak freely. The detectives asked him how he'd heard of the murder and

then, after a few basic questions, got right to the point: "Did you kill Catherine Woods?"

"No."

"You know you're a suspect in this, right?" one of them said.

Paul says he was shocked. "No. I thought I was just coming of my own volition."

"No," the detective said. "We have to question you about everything."

Over the next five hours, they questioned Paul closely about Catherine, about their relationship, about David, and especially about where Paul had been the previous night around the time of the murder. "I mean, at this stage, I was still in shock," Paul said. "I was scared, for sure. I didn't know what was going on, and it was just crazy. It was just crazy.

"They kept asking me, 'When was the last time you spoke to her?' And I was like, 'Well, I was in my apartment. That was the last time I spoke to her.' I told them everything they asked."

Four or five hours went by and there were many more questions. Paul kept adding details about his day. He'd gone to work in the morning at the Bikram Yoga studio, and had tried a few times to get in touch with Catherine, his on-and-off girlfriend for the past year or so, but despite a loose promise to get together, Paul said they had not seen each other that day. He told them about another woman he had met that Sunday, a woman by the name of Stephanie Bucci, a client of his at the health club. He'd tagged along while she ran some errands—accompanying her to PC Richard, an electronics store, where she purchased a humidifier, and making a few other stops along the way, once at a grocery store and then at a local Barnes and Noble.

Paul said he then made a few more attempts to call Catherine, and they'd talked briefly, but the call had been disconnected. He was concerned and tried calling her back a number of times, but he said he finally gave up and called some clients he was training the following day. After that, he met a male friend at a bar, where they watched football, went to another friend's apartment to watch more football, and after that, Paul said, he went to bed.

The questions kept coming, until the detectives seemed to run out of things to ask. "All right," Ahearne said. "Now everything you just told us, I want you to write down for me in a statement."

"I just told you everything that I know. I was hoping I could go home," Paul said. "Isn't that enough?"

"No, in order for you to leave, you have to write up a statement so we have it on record."

Paul claims that at the point, Ahearne backed off a bit and said, "Just write down the important parts that you think you can remember. It doesn't have to be so detailed. We were taking notes."

"So I did what he said," Paul said. "I basically wrote down the parts that I thought were important."

Paul was emotionally overwrought, tired, cranky, and hadn't had anything to eat for hours. "I told them everything they asked me," he said. "I answered truthfully. I remember at that point just being in a haze. I had just found out that someone that I loved dearly was killed and that I was a suspect for it as well. I didn't know what to do or what to think or what to really put in. I wanted to put in things that I thought might be helpful for their investigation."

Paul said he just wanted to get out of there and quickly wrote up a three-page statement, but because of circumstances, he said, "I left out a lot."

In the handwritten note, Paul detailed his relationship with Catherine and how troubled he was by the life she'd been living with her former boyfriend, David, with whom she'd been cohabitating when Paul first met her. "She told me she was basically supporting him, while he went out, made music, smoked pot, and then came back home to 'veg' out and watch TV," Paul wrote.

He admitted that Catherine's topless dancing had taken its toll on their relationship. She'd had a run-in with a customer at least one time that necessitated her calling Paul to come to the club to pick her up. He'd worried about her safety and had wanted her to stop, but she'd refused. Paul wrote that they'd have arguments and their relationship was "a little distant." Just six weeks before her murder, he thought she was acting "weird and argumentative. I asked her what was wrong, and she said that she didn't want to talk. I checked her phone to see if it was a problem with her stripping or if there was someone else. She then found out I was checking her phone and was mad at me and said she couldn't trust me. I said the same to her and we split off; after several days we said we should be friends possibly working on a relationship. We talked still. She told me of the guys she had met, like this guy 'Joe' who had met her at Flash Dancers."

"Joe." The detectives had not heard that name before and wondered if there really was a "Joe." Whatever. It was another lead they'd now have to run down. Paul wrote in his statement that "we were still hurt by not being together though we both knew we needed to take some time apart. The last time I saw her was this Saturday 11/26/05 at Equinox."

Paul said that he and Catherine had talked about getting together that Sunday, the day she died, but that when he called her around 5:00 p.m., "she was very short with me and seemed preoccupied. Then her phone got disconnected. She called me back and said we should talk later because she needed to get ready. I knew something was wrong so I called back several times. I thought she was just mad at me again but I didn't know. I was at home when I called her and, when she hung up, I started calling clients for appointments, friends to talk about Thanksgiving, and then I called my friend Spence to hang out with him."

Paul went on to detail his Sunday night, the night of the murder. He'd gone to a bar called The Back Page, on East Eighty-third Street, to hang out and then accompanied Spence Lebowitz to the home of another trainer at the club, Rob. There, they watched the Jets lose "a heartbreaker." Then, Paul said, he went home.

He had to get up early to train a client named Brian Sampson at 7:00 a.m.

The last sentence reads, "The next morning about 10:30, I found out from my mom Catherine was Dead."

The detectives read over his statement, and Paul realized he'd forgotten to write down the part of the day he'd spent with Stephanie Bucci. The detective told him not to worry about it. They had taken notes and had her name.

Then it was time to get some physical evidence. The detectives asked if they could swab the inside of Paul's mouth to get his DNA. Paul agreed. They also took his shoeprint. In an oversight, they did not ask Paul for his fingerprints. "If they wanted my fingerprints, they could've gotten them," Paul said. "I was handling a lot of things, the swab for the DNA, the envelope, but they didn't ask to ink me or anything like that."

At that point, Paul said, Detective Goetz came into the room. "Did you guys check his hands or his body?" he asked the other detectives.

Paul said the detectives looked "sheepishly" at one another. Goetz was upset. "He looked kind of frustrated," Paul said. "He was like, 'Show me your hands. Both sides. Now take off your shirt. Take off your shoes and everything.' He was inspecting everything, and he didn't see anything."

The only thing of interest on Paul's well-toned body was a small nick or blood blister on one hand that he said was the result of his finger getting pinched while adjusting weights for a client. Although Paul said the cops took Polaroid and digital photos of him without his clothes on, those pictures never surfaced. The cops thought they'd gotten all they could from Paul. "Okay," Paul remembers one saying, "I think we're good."

Detective Ahearne and another cop drove Paul and his mother back to Paul's studio apartment on 106th Street. In the car, they told Paul they were still interested in seeing his MetroCard. MetroCards, which replaced tokens on New York City's mass transit system some years ago, record every subway and bus ride on their magnetic strips. Detectives had begun using them to corroborate or disprove a suspect's story, and now they wanted Paul's to see if they could track his whereabouts.

Paul checked his pockets. "I think I left it home," he told them. "I don't have it with me."

While Paul's mother went out to get him some food, Paul and the detectives searched his home for the MetroCard. Paul gave them the full run of his small apartment. "They were looking throughout my stuff at home, going through my apartment, my garbage, through the hamper, underneath the bed. I was just kind of shifting everything and I was looking for it with them and I think we found a MetroCard and I gave it to them and they left," Paul said.

The detectives had Paul's permission to search through his apartment, and if they'd seen anything incriminating, they would surely have taken it or gotten a proper search warrant. But they found nothing of value. Not one item of clothing had visible bloodstains on it, not even Paul's leather jacket, which he wore constantly in the cold winter months. The cops saw no boots in his apartment, bloody or otherwise. They saw no traces of blood at all.

After they left, Paul and his mother sat huddled in his apartment. It had been a long and draining day, and they were hoping against hope that the worst was over.

13

Frustration

At that point, Goetz was getting frustrated. Within hours of Catherine's murder, detectives had hauled in two of Catherine's closest male friends, both of them claiming to have been her boyfriend at one time or another. Either could have killed her but neither seemed like a murderer, and neither had scratches or obvious bruises.

Like David, Paul was almost too willing to help the detectives. He agreed to answer questions without a lawyer present and had even brought his mother along. Goetz liked Ivette. Cops often make quick judgments about people, and just talking to Paul's mother, Goetz felt that she'd raised her son the right way. He had no criminal record and had gone to a good college. That was harder to do than it seemed when you grew up poor and Latino in New York. Paul had allowed the detectives to take all the physical evidence they wanted. In effect, he'd agreed to a search of his apartment. The cops had seen nothing incriminating there.

"Paul Cortez is to me very talented, very well educated. He seemed to be a very, very intelligent person," Goetz said.

In truth, David seemed a far better suspect. Paul had come and gone from the station house while David was still being questioned in another room in the same building. Detectives couldn't ignore the fact that David had put himself inside the apartment at the same time some of the neighbors heard screams. And he did have motive. In fact, Paul could've been David's motive. Here David was living with this woman he obviously cared for and she was off meeting this good-looking guy who was far more educated and polished. It was easy to picture the beautiful Catherine with a guy like Paul but a lot harder to picture her with an unsophisticated guy like David.

"There were times when he was being interviewed that he would say, 'I didn't do this and I'll help you any way I possibly can,' " Goetz said.

But Goetz did not get promoted to detective by accepting the word of every suspect who said he was innocent. "You can't believe him," he said. "I don't know him. I just met him that night. I only knew him as David Haughn who lived with Catherine Woods, and she's now dead."

Detectives pushed David hard. They told him he was facing a long prison stretch for what he'd done. "I'd heard twenty-five years to life and I was thinking in my head, 'Wow,' " David said. "I really didn't understand why this was happening."

No doubt, David was feeling sorry for himself. He'd

finally found the love of his life—a beautiful and talented woman who cared for him deeply—and now she'd been murdered and he was being accused of killing her. "I really didn't understand why this was happening, but at one point I thought, 'Well, maybe this is the way it's supposed to go down for whatever reason.' I really felt at one point, 'I'm gonna take this.' It was just almost like I had lost her and she was like my everything. So, at that point, I didn't have nothing to lose. I thought that was what was going to happen and I just kind of mentally accepted that. It wasn't that I was going to take the rap. I just felt like I didn't have nothing to lose."

But something inside David pulled him back from the edge of confessing. In his mind, he had not killed Catherine, he said, and he wasn't going to take the rap. "I said [to myself], 'This isn't right. This isn't. There's no way, I'm gonna lose the closest person to me and then they're gonna punish me for it? I don't know that's right.'

"I told them, 'You have the wrong person. I would never hit that girl. Not at all. I loved her. I would have done anything for her.'"

Behind the closed doors of the precinct, Goetz was under a lot of pressure to go ahead and arrest David for killing Catherine. Goetz's bosses thought David "looked good" for the murder, but though Goetz didn't trust David blindly, his instincts told him to hold off rushing to make a collar. David just didn't seem like the guy. He was too sincere, too confused, too innocent. Sure, his times were off, but if he *were* guilty, why would he put himself inside the apartment at the time of the murder? It didn't make any sense in light of David's constant denials.

Also, it was clear from the crime scene that Catherine had fought for her life. She had defensive wounds on her hands, and the bedroom was covered in blood. David didn't have a nick on him. He also had almost no blood on his clothing, except for the bottom of his jeans where they'd touched the floor, and a spot on the thigh, where he'd wiped off Catherine's blood. It didn't seem possible that he'd had enough time to kill Catherine, change his clothes, get rid of them, and call the police.

Nothing was feeling right here, and Goetz and the other cops couldn't ignore Catherine's choice of jobs. Maybe one of her gentlemen friends down at Flash Dancers—Paul had said she'd mentioned a guy named Joe—had taken too much of a liking to her and had been stalking her.

There was a lot more ground to cover. They had to find this guy Joe, who might or might not exist, and they had to verify everything David and Paul had told them. One of them may have been lying, but why lie if you're innocent?

14

Tabloid Heaven

Reporters at the New York newspapers had plenty to write about that Monday and Tuesday. Catherine Woods's death was fast becoming a winning trifecta of sex, murder, and salaciousness. The *Post* and *Daily News* were in tabloid heaven. The story was tailor-made for New York's rough-and-tumble newspapers, which even in normal times show no respect for decorum. The *Post* especially does not hold back. Everyone in New York knows the paper's most famous crime headline, which was written after a man took hostages in a topless bar, killed one patron, and cut off his head so the victim could not be identified. The *Post*'s headline the next day: "Headless Body in Topless Bar." Not only was it funny, it was dead-on accurate.

It was no wonder then that there seemed to be an almost gleeful tone in the coverage accorded to the Catherine Woods murder. It was an elbow to the ribs, as in, "Hey, get this. Some hick chick from Ohio thought she'd make it big on Broadway and instead wound up dancing topless. Ain't that something?" The story was all over the papers, television, and radio, and there were times when bad information was passed up and down the media food chain.

The newspapers milked it for all they could, even thoughtfully running sidebars about all the good girls who had turned to topless dancing as a way of making ends meet. Typical was the *New York Post* story headlined "Gals' Big Dreams and Sleazy Money in the Secret World of N.Y. Strip Joints."

By Tuesday, the follow-up stories on the murder itself were coming fast and furious. That day's headline in the *New York Post* was "Slain Stripper Led Double Life." The subhead read, "Told folks back home she was acting in play." For the first time, the story mentioned Paul Cortez, though not by name. The report noted that David "had pointed the finger at Woods' current lover, a 'professional dancer,' who was also questioned and released."

It also detailed how Catherine had fooled her parents into believing she'd had a role as an understudy in the Off-Broadway play *Privilege* when in reality she'd been dancing at a topless club by the same name. Jon Woods didn't say much about that lie at the time, but a month later, his wife, Donna, was still upset about it: "I'm really angry at her for telling us that."

Reporters, no doubt upset by the assignment, fanned out to Privilege and Flash Dancers to talk to strippers who might have known Catherine. A lucky few got quotes. The *Post* talked to an alleged club manager at Flash Dancers named Penny, who told them, "She talked a lot about her family. She was nice and quiet. She didn't drink."

Catherine's father, Jon, the well-known director of the Ohio State marching band, flew to New York that Monday night. Jon was not in the city long. He identified his daughter's body, made arrangements for her to be flown back home, and left, but in those few short hours, a reporter from the *Daily News* managed to get a brief interview with him. "She really met the challenge of moving to New York. It took amazing courage," Jon Woods is quoted as saying. "She was a natural dancer who flowed with the music. I hope they get the right person."

He never indicated in the newspaper story whether he knew that Catherine was a topless dancer or not. He did say he'd visited her in New York a few times, once when she'd suffered a small trauma, but he called it "nothing major." As it would turn out, Jon was not telling the whole story, at least not to nosy reporters.

On Wednesday, three days after Catherine was murdered, the sordid tabloid tales took a dramatic turn. For the first time, both the *New York Post* and the *Daily News* ran stories that mentioned Paul Cortez by name. It was clear that someone in law enforcement had decided to squeeze Paul to see how he reacted under pressure. Information was leaked to reporters, not all of it accurate.

"Slain Dancer's Muscleman Beau," screamed the *New York Post* headline, with the subhead "Cops told he roughed her up." Above the headline, photos of Paul and David framed Catherine's smiling face. The lead got right to the point: "The exotic dancer who was slain in her Upper East Side apartment had an on-again, off-again romance with a hunky personal trainer who once allegedly got rough with her, *The Post* has learned."

Cops had been told, according to the paper, that "the Manhattan man allegedly threw the petite, classically trained dancer against a wall during a fight." As it turned out, that was not true. Paul did later say that he grabbed Catherine's arm at one point, but to this day no one has ever definitively come forward to say that Paul, a seemingly peace-loving, meditative practitioner of yoga, ever laid a hand on Catherine in anger. But that hardly seemed to matter.

Wednesday's *Daily News* led with the headline "Dead Dancer Had Two Partners." The subhead read, "Slain stripper in love triangle." Catherine was shown arm in arm with David, with the image of Paul popping up in an insert on the bottom of the page making the triangle complete. The story was getting a bit more scandalous every day. As far as the tabloids were concerned, the only thing better than a topless dancer who hid that fact from her Ohio family was a topless dancer who hid that fact from her Ohio family while "trapped in a love triangle."

Everyone now had a role in this melodrama: David was the "wannabe rapper" who performed under the stage name "City," while Paul was described as "a slight but muscular yoga and Pilates instructor with chin-length hair." In fairness, the article did quote friends of both men saying they were good people, and it detailed Paul's impressive educational background.

But another new fact emerged in the *Daily News* story that was true and very important: Someone, the article said, had called Catherine "seven times in succession minutes before her throat was cut." The report did not mention who made those calls. The calls had been leaked but not the name of the caller, at least not yet.

The aggressive New York press seemed to enjoy toying with Paul's reputation. He became the new way to advance the story. Reporters took special delight in describing him as a long-haired yoga teacher, even though he was only a receptionist at a yoga studio. The press couldn't help itself. New York's tabloid reporters are not known for their devotion to all things metaphysical. To them, there was something effeminate about yoga, something foreign, and now they had one of those effeminate boys in their sights as a potential murderer. They were having a grand old time at Paul's expense.

That morning, Paul came out of his apartment to find the press surrounding him, pointing cameras, and shouting questions. "Just give me some time," he said, sobbing and running back inside.

That was not going to happen.

Inside the CBS broadcast center on West Fifty-seventh Street, CBS News correspondent Erin Moriarty was paying special attention to every last word of the tragic murder. Moriarty, an on-air reporter for *48 Hours Mystery,* was fascinated by the sad tale of Catherine Woods. It came with the turf, but this time there was something more—this one was hitting very close to home. Like Woods, Moriarty had been raised in Columbus. She went to college at Ohio State University and graduated from OSU's Law School. Her family still lives there, and in some ways Moriarty's never left. Though she's lived in New York City for a couple of decades, her voice retains distinct traces of Ohio. Spend any amount of time with her and you'll hear a lot about Columbus. She visits regularly, is a donor to her former college, and was even the graduating class's commencement speaker in 2004.

Moriarty, who is married to a former University of Notre Dame football player, has season tickets to Ohio State football games and tries to go to a couple of games every year. She knew all too well who Jon Woods was and how important the Ohio State University marching band was to the culture of the city. She'd seen them perform many times. The story was upsetting to Moriarty because she knew that the Woods family was in the eye of an emotional hurricane. The media had no doubt staked out their home, waiting for quotes and whatever tidbits they could get.

Because of her connections to Columbus and Ohio State University, Moriarty was reluctant to get involved with the story. But she is also an intense and competitive reporter, and she thought, in this case, she had the sensitivity that was needed to get beyond the story's scandalous nature. She called Susan Zirinsky, the executive producer of *48 Hours Mystery*, and told her she wanted to pursue the story.

15

Cell Sites

Behind the scenes, Detective Goetz and his investigators were busy checking a key element of Paul Cortez's statement. He'd told cops, and put in his written statement, that he was home on Sunday night when he repeatedly dialed Catherine's cell phone number. But the police had subpoenaed Paul's cell phone records, and they told a different story.

Cell phones, like MetroCards, have become a new investigative tool, a way of checking the alibi of a suspect. MetroCards will reveal which subway line a suspect took and when, but as cops studied the magnetic tape on Paul's MetroCard, it was obvious that it was the wrong MetroCard. It had not been used on the day in question.

Paul's cell phone, on the other hand, had something to say.

Anytime someone makes a cell phone call, the phone signal seeks out the nearest cell site, or cell tower. In a densely populated city like New York, there are thousands of cell sites all over the rooftops, but they're not obvious. They are intentionally designed to blend in with the surroundings, and most people don't even notice them. They're not big towers, like a radio or television station might have. Rather, they are relatively small, white, rectangular screens that look a lot like solar panels. They're usually in small groups of four or five to a rooftop. Once you become aware of them, you start to see them everywhere. The cell site that picks up your phone call when you dial tells where you are located when making that call. It acts like a GPS, or Global Positioning System; once you get the phone records, it's easy literally to track someone by his cell phone calls.

If Paul was telling the truth about being at home when he called Catherine, experts said his calls would have been picked up by the cell site at Third Avenue and East 105th Street. That site did indeed pick up Paul's calls, until 5:14 p.m., but then, suddenly, at 5:27 p.m., a call from his phone was picked up at the cell site at 50 East Eighty-sixth Street, between Madison and Park avenues. It seemed Paul was getting closer to Catherine's apartment. The next ten calls to Catherine and others, made between 5:36 and 6:33 p.m., were picked up by the cell site at 354 East Eighty-fourth Street, between First and Second avenues. Catherine lived on East Eighty-sixth Street, between First and Second avenues. The calls around the time of her murder indicated that Paul was very close at hand.

"When I received the information regarding his cell phone use, I realized he was lying," Goetz said. "He wasn't on One Hundred and Sixth Street, where he claims he was. He was somewhere right in the vicinity of Eighty-sixth Street. David Haughn was not ruled out at that time, but now you had another person of interest [Paul] who you know lied to you at the very beginning of the investigation. My feeling is if Paul Cortez had nothing to do with this, then he had no reason to lie."

Meanwhile, David's alibi had checked out. Detectives had talked to his co-worker Ali and his boss, Joe Tabone, both of whom corroborated David's story: He had stopped there before picking up his car to get Catherine that fateful night. What's more, Ali and Tabone were able to clean up David's time line when they said he'd been with them longer than five minutes. With the new time line and the phone records, cops figured that David had left Catherine's apartment sometime around 6:10 p.m., gone to talk to Ali and Joe, then to his car, which he'd driven around the corner to pick up Catherine. Just before 7:00 p.m., David was on the phone with a 911 operator.

There was approximately a thirty-five-minute gap during which Catherine Woods had been murdered, more than enough time to kill, according to Detective Goetz. "Somebody who's filled with anger, in the manner in which she was killed, it could take thirty seconds," he said. "It could take five minutes depending on how much she struggled, and there was definitely visible signs of a violent struggle. Does that mean it took ten minutes? No. It could have happened so fast, and that's why the struggle was so violent, because somebody wanted to get in and get out and not be seen. But I'm speculating. There's only one person who knows."

If Paul had been close to Catherine's apartment, as phone records indicated, what was to stop him from committing the murder? There were still many questions, such as how he got past two locked doors and how and where he'd cleaned up. Additionally, no one had come forward to say they'd seen Paul in the neighborhood, but there was a lot more investigating that needed to be done.

Investigators still had not looked at all the street security cameras to see if they could spot Paul in the neighborhood.

The decision was made—Goetz and the other detectives would ratchet up the pressure on Paul Contez. By Thursday, "sources" were telling Murray Weiss, police bureau chief of the *New York Post,* that Paul was the one who'd made the seven cell phone calls to Catherine just before she was killed, and furthermore, those same sources were saying that Paul was much closer to her apartment than he'd told cops. The headline to Murray's story became " 'Phony' Slay Tale: Stripper's ex nearer than he says during 7 calls, cops think."

A photograph accompanying the story showed a "forlorn"-looking Paul Cortez—and no wonder. The story revealed "that several ex-girlfriends of Cortez told detectives the aspiring actor-singer appeared to have rejection issues."

Paul's friends rushed to his aid, telling anyone who would listen that the Paul being described in those stories was *not* the peace-loving Paul they knew.

16

Out of Character

"I wish people would look beyond the headlines and really look at all the facts and really give a chance for all the facts to come out accurately," said Paul's good friend Jaki Levy. "I don't think anybody really understands what went on, what their relationship was, how he lived his life. He is such a peaceful person."

The goateed Jaki had met Paul when both were eighteen years old and attending a summer theater program at Carnegie Mellon University, in Pittsburgh. He and Paul struck up a friendship that endured through college and beyond. "We share a really good sense of humor," Jaki said. "We'd tell each other stupid jokes, adolescent jokes." They went to a lot of plays together, and Paul often would hang out in Jaki's dorm room. After they graduated, they even wound up working at the Union Square Bikram Yoga studio together.

Before Paul's name hit the newspapers, and before Paul had a chance to tell Jaki in person about Catherine's death, Jaki had called the Bikram studio early in the week to check on his work schedule. The gossip was flying. "I heard that someone in the yoga studio was a murder suspect," Jaki said. "I said, 'A murder suspect?' I went through every single person in the studio. The manager, the entire staff, the teachers, and then I started going through the students. I'm like, 'Gosh, who could it be?' Out of all the people in the yoga studio, Paul was actually the *last* person I thought of.

"He's just so gentle, he's so caring, so concerned with other people and just his own personal well-being. He wouldn't put himself in that kind of situation to compromise or hurt another person, to do that kind of thing. It's just a total shocker."

Jaki, who had been introduced to Catherine by Paul, was truly astonished when he read the vicious way the young dancer had been murdered. There was no way, Jaki said, that Paul could have had anything to do with the horrible way she'd died. "To lash out in anger? To cut someone's throat like that? It's too grisly. I couldn't imagine him doing something like that," Jaki said. "I just couldn't. It's not what I know of him. It's not what I've seen of him. It's not what I understand of him."

Jaki says he knew Paul as well as anyone and had spoken with him on the day of the murder, at three o'clock and then again at eight, and Paul was not angry or upset before or after Catherine's murder. "He was pretty casual," Jaki said of the latter conversation. "We had a light conversation for less than five minutes. I was like, 'Hey, what's going on?' and he was like, 'We'll get together tomorrow.' It was just pretty casual. I remember him being grounded and peaceful, clear-minded and positive. If I could say one thing about the conversation, it was that he was positive, a positive well-being, a positive attitude."

After Paul's name was revealed publicly and he began to get hounded by reporters, Jaki invited him to stay at his apartment. Paul accepted, and Jaki said Paul "was grieving for Catherine. He was very disturbed by what had happened."

Jaki didn't back down and asked Paul the hard question: Had he had anything to do with her death? "It was really difficult for me to ask him about that, and he said, 'I could never do something like that. I loved her so much.' It was depressing to me, too, because I could see what he was going through," Jaki said. "I could see how devastated he was, to lose someone and also to be suspected of killing her. It was really heavy. I believed him. I really did."

The two friends discussed who might have killed Catherine, and to them, the answer was obvious: "Both of us immediately thought, 'Oh, David. David did it,' " Jaki said. "He left his car. I mean, come on, what a story. Like, that's ridiculous. He was there, he used the apartment, he comes back, and she's dead? I mean that's crazy. I mean you know you can make a case for David [being the killer] if you want. Pile up whatever fights they had, whatever misunderstandings. Why was she dating Paul when she was living with David?"

It seemed like a clear motive to them, but in the days after Catherine's murder, Jaki and Paul began to realize what a complicated person she really was. They had a lot of questions, especially about David. Catherine said he'd moved, but clearly he hadn't. Why had she lied, and what was the true nature of their relationship?

Jaki recalled one of their conversations: "I remember Paul saying specifically, 'You know, I don't even know if what Catherine had told me is the truth. I don't know if what Catherine was telling me is actually what happened.' I remember he told me that a few days after she was murdered. And I remember he was so conflicted about that, because he couldn't go to her and say, 'You know, look, what happened? What was this about? Look, what really was your relationship with David?' "

At one point—it was Wednesday night, just three days after the murder—Jaki looked in on Paul, who was getting ready for bed. He asked if he needed anything and he could see that Paul already had his shirt off. "I looked at him and I saw his body was totally clean," Jaki said. "His arms were totally clean. His hands were totally clean. No scratches, no bruises. There was nothing to indicate that he was the one who'd slashed her throat. There was nothing on his face, nothing on his arms, nothing on his hands that made me think that he had been in a struggle."

Jaki was convinced all the reports were just flat-out mistaken. It was inconceivable that Paul was a killer.

Jaki wasn't the only one who felt that way.

17

The Lizard King

Those who know Paul Cortez well say that after college he was trying to decide between two paths: his music and his spirituality. "I remember," says Jaki Levy, "Paul and I were walking down the street one day and he said to me, 'My whole purpose in life, either I want to be a rock star or I want to be a spiritual guru.' And I'm like, 'What?' What a stark contrast, and it was kind of half-joking, half-serious. He was just so on the opposite ends of the spectrum, but he was really enigmatic that way."

While it may have seemed a strange juxtaposition to Jaki, it wasn't so odd to Paul, and in fact, with his long hair, magnetic personality, killer looks, and leather jacket, Paul was not unlike a modern-day Jim Morrison, the dead lead singer of The Doors, who left behind a treasure trove of journals filled with his poetry and writings. Paul may not have done it intentionally, but he seemed to be almost modeling his persona after Morrison, the Lizard King, who was at once both macho and spiritual.

In his post-college years, Paul was going down the same path. He was singing and writing music for the band Monolith, but aside from the rehearsing and his work as a personal trainer, he was on a full-time spiritual search, and wrote his thoughts and poetry down obsessively in one journal after another. He was meditating, practicing yoga, and reading the Eastern spiritual text the *Bhagavad Gita* almost obsessively. Although always insisting he was a Catholic, Paul carried the book everywhere and recommended it to nearly everyone he knew. Paul was getting deeper and deeper into Eastern religious philosophy.

In the summer of 2005, a wandering Tibetan monk whom Paul admired was visiting a home in upstate New York, and a group of followers, including Paul, traveled there on successive weekends to meditate and pray in the holy man's presence. The house where the monk was staying belonged to Marguerite Shinouda, an acupuncturist who also offers Chinese herbs and Reiki treatments to her clients. Long-haired and attractive, Marguerite looks and talks with the enthusiasm of one who believes she has found a better way, and that way involves following Eastern philosophy and healing practices. She is bright and lively, has an open face, and was quite taken with Paul.

"He's wonderful," she says. "He's funny and warm and helpful. He's very gentlemanly. He wouldn't let me carry anything heavy, and he's a flirt."

The weekend retreats, Marguerite says, "were very intense times" during which she got to know Paul quite well. "Everybody there was great, but Paul was especially sweet and wonderful and helpful. I probably spent more time with Paul than I did with my best girlfriend, because we'd be up at four or five in the morning singing and meditating. . . . It was day after day, and then the next weekend and then the next weekend again. He often slept on the floor because there wasn't enough room, and he was a perfect gentleman."

Marguerite, who is her in forties, said that when she first met Paul, she was initially "intimidated" because "he's a nice-looking young man." Soon enough, she said, she realized how gentle he was, and the two became friends and stayed in touch.

In early November 2005, just a few weeks before Catherine was murdered, Paul again traveled to Marguerite's house, this time for what is known as a *satsang,* or "a gathering for truth and unconditional love," according to Curt DeGroat, who was then a teacher of metaphysics at the Academy of Natural Healing on New York's Upper West Side. There were a dozen or so people present at the *satsang,* but Paul stood out, according to Curt.

"My impression of Paul was just someone who was extraordinarily loving, more than most people," Curt said. "It was the one thing that most people would say who knew him, who even saw him for just a moment in those gatherings. It's also something that the teacher remarked upon, that Paul had a special love for people and this would be something that he would use in his life later, as he developed spiritually to help people.

"His energy, the vibration that I felt from him was very open, very loving, very generous. He was very quick to put others ahead of himself. He was helpful."

At that point, in November 2005, Paul and Catherine were in the midst of one of their breakups. Paul had invited her to this gathering, but she'd refused to accompany him. Paul spoke about her to the group. "One thing he said about Catherine is that she was the most beautiful person he had ever met," Marguerite said. "He just glowed with love when he talked about her. He said . . . he was worried for her because she was in a dangerous situation, and I think he was really trying to be the hero on the white horse and save her, and I think he was distressed that he couldn't."

"He felt that Catherine was in a very negative environment and he wanted to help get her out of that," Curt said. "He didn't feel it was right for her to be there at all."

Curt is quick to say, however, that though Paul was concerned he was not fanatical about saving Catherine to the point where he would have murdered her for not listening to him. "He's not that type of fanatic that would do that type of thing," Curt said. "When you meet a religious fanatic, you can tell right away. They're wired to a high-pitched intensity, and Paul's not like that at all. I can't imagine Paul getting to that level of intensity to do something like that."

"He told us that Catherine was a good person," Marguerite said, "and he was trying to understand how she ended up in this situation. Trying to understand is a different thing than wanting to hurt her because of it. He definitely wanted to help her. He was deeply sad about breaking up with her, but I think was settled in his being that this is what needed to happen. He said something to the effect of 'We love each other but we just can't trust each other anymore' because of some things that had gone on back and forth. But he was trying to stay friends with her."

During the *satsang* session, Marguerite says she saw proof of Paul's continued commitment to Catherine despite the hard times. "There was a girl that he was flirting mildly with, a very pretty blonde, and this woman wanted to know if Paul was available," Marguerite said. "She wanted to know if Paul was just flirting or what? Paul said, 'Maybe soon, but I'm not ready yet. My heart's still full with Catherine, but maybe soon.'"

Three weeks after the *satsang,* news that Paul was suspected of murdering Catherine hit Marguerite like a bolt from beyond. She does not watch news or read newspapers, and so she had no idea of the trouble Paul was in. "Curt called to tell me about all of this, about Paul being accused," she said. "I was just blown away. I just couldn't believe it. If you listed a thousand people that might have done a crime, Paul's name would never have come to mind. So when Curt told me, it just floored me. I just absolutely knew it wasn't true, so it was like, 'How do we help?'"

Marguerite said she was disgusted by Paul's treatment at the hands of the tabloid press. "It was unbelievable," she said. "It was like sharks smelling blood in the water. They just found a story that was hot and juicy and they just ran with it with complete disregard to the facts. They've portrayed him as some long-haired Lothario and yoga boy and all sorts of bizarre epithets. Nobody bothered to find out who Paul really was, just as they didn't seem to bother to find out who Catherine really was. They just went with this hot story of a stripper and a hot-tempered Latino lover and never bothered to find out who the people really were."

At one point, Curt even spoke to the *New York Post* to try to make them aware of how special Paul was, but his attempt to reason with the newspaper backfired. The copy editor who wrote the headline picked out the one quote that would, at the same time, make Curt look ridiculous and Paul even more guilty: "Stripper Had 'Bad Energy': Suspect's complaint to guru before slay."

Marguerite reached out to Paul. "I knew the press was hounding him. I knew they were awful, so I invited him to come stay at my home, which is a couple of hours upstate, to just get away. I never questioned whether he was involved for a second. It was like, 'Come stay with me.'"

18

Nothing Gold Can Stay

In Columbus, Jon and Donna Woods had endured the toughest week of their lives. Ugly rumors about Catherine's life were being circulated, and her death was being transformed into a circus in New York.

"The New York tabloids portrayed Catherine in a very different way than I feel she really was and that certainly made me angry," Jon Woods said.

But he had the support of his community, and that was a very special feeling. Jon said at one point he stopped in a drugstore for some medicine and the pharmacist and some people there who recognized him offered their condolences. Jon began talking about Catherine's terrible treatment in the press. "The police say they don't know where these stories are coming from," he said. "Where do they get them?"

The pharmacist stopped Jon in midsentence and said, "You know what, Dr. Woods? It doesn't matter."

Donna tried not to let the gossip bother her but she admits that it sometimes did. "I feel in my heart that we had a wonderful daughter who lived twenty-one years and who was a beautiful person," she said. "I don't have to justify my daughter's life to anybody, but it affects me, it affects me a lot."

But on Friday, December 2, it was time to put the ugliness aside. Catherine was finally back in Ohio, her body having been released by the New York City medical examiner. It came time for her funeral, and a huge memorial service was planned at the Linworth United Methodist Church. Jon Woods would eulogize his daughter, and providing him strength would be the famed Ohio State University marching band.

But there was still one matter that needed to be taken care of before the service could go on: David Haughn, Catherine's on-again, off-again boyfriend, and still a suspect in her death, sent word through Catherine's friend Emily Pettigrew that he'd like to attend the service. Jon and Donna did not want David there. Despite all the rumors about Paul Cortez, there was no proof Paul had killed their daughter. It was possible that David was her killer, so the Woodses asked David not to attend the service. But it was also possible that David had had nothing to do with Catherine's death, and the Woodses knew how much he loved her and how much Catherine had loved him. So they made David an offer: If he wanted to have some time with her alone, they would allow him to come to the church early, when the media and the mourners would not be around.

David accepted. "I respect Catherine's parents so much that I would do anything they would ask. If that's what they thought was the best thing to do, that's what I would do," he said. "So I was able to go there early in the day and have my time with her."

The service began later that day. Two dozen students from Catherine's high school came, each of them bringing a single rose. Befitting Jon's position in the community and on campus, the president of Ohio State attended; in fact, pretty much every top-ranking university administration official and many of the professors were there. The entire marching band would be there for their leader, despite the fact that it was finals week and everyone was reviewing for exams. That meant a great deal to Jon. "Every one of them came," he said proudly. "Every one of them wanted to wear their uniform. We have two uniforms that we wear, and our game-day uniform is what they agreed upon wearing."

Danielle Curren and Katie Miller, two of Catherine's close friends from the Mary Rose dance school, performed a short dance number, and of course Mary Rose Bushroe, Catherine's dance teacher, who'd known Catherine most of her life, was there. Catherine's four closest friends—Megan Wilkins, Emily Pettigrew, Kim Carvey, and Sahaja Parsa—each got a chance to say a few words. Two framed portraits, one of Catherine and her family, and one of Catherine alone, wearing a red dress and looking as beautiful as ever, were set up onstage.

Mike Harden, the *Columbus Dispatch* columnist, wrote a beautiful story about the service the following day.

Laughter, an absent friend for six days in the anguished hearts of Catherine Woods' mourners, floated across the grieving assemblage at Linworth United Methodist Church like a scarf pulled aloft by the wind.

It came as the slain dancer's father, Jon Woods, recalled a discussion, years ago, with his daughter's first-grade teacher.

"She said she had a problem with Catherine," Woods recounted. The teacher had asked the youngster to select a song for the day.

Catherine, who ate, slept and breathed the Ohio State marching band her dad directs, piped, "How about 'We Don't Give a Damn for the Whole State of Michigan'?"

Woods, his back to the band whose members knuckled away tears when their director wrestled with emotion, said of his daughter, "It is not how long a flower blooms, but how beautiful."

Yesterday, he bid adieu to the 21-year-old Catherine, whose body rested in a rose-banked oak casket, as she always had signed off in her phone calls to family from her apartment in New York City: "Love you." . . .

Toward the end of the service, the familiar brass chimes that ever precede the

OSU alma mater rang out and one, then two, then dozens and hundreds rose to sing a refrain in which one line had never seemed quite so sad: "with joy which death alone can still."

After the casket was eased down the aisle—after the mourners retreated to whisper condolences to Catherine's father and mother, Donna, and her two sibling—family friend Bob Pettigrew observed, "Some of us keep our dreams under our pillows because we are afraid that if we take them out and face them, we might lose them.

"Catherine had her dreams right where she could take them out every day."

"She was a golden girl," a former classmate said after the service, summoning a line from the poet Robert Frost, and "nothing gold can stay."

Jon and Donna had Catherine's body cremated after the service and her ashes remain in the family home on the mantelpiece beside two of her dance shoes. The girl who so desperately wanted to run from Columbus in life will now forever be at home in death.

Donna explained it this way: "We want to keep her close."

19

Video Proof—Not

The same day that Catherine was laid to rest, one of the most damning articles about the possible guilt of Paul Cortez ran in the *New York Post*. It would have been understandable, at that point, if a regular reader of the *Post* felt that Paul had already been tried and convicted.

That Friday's *Post* story was headlined "Vid I.D. in Stripper Slay—Ex Spotted Outside Her Pad at Death Hour: Cops." The first paragraph of the report, written by Murray Weiss and Dan Mangan, summed it up: "Police have video proof that an estranged lover of slain stripper Catherine Woods was standing just outside her Upper East Side building at the time the 21-year-old brunette was brutally murdered, *The Post* has learned."

Even Paul's longtime friend Jaki Levy was shaken by the story. "I haven't seen the footage. I doubt the paper has seen the footage," Jaki said. "Unless that reporter watched it and said, 'You know, I've seen Paul before and that is, without a doubt, him. There could be no other person that could be.' There's nothing convincing me that that is him without a doubt from what I've read. It would concern me, yes. Would it raise doubts? Possibly. Would it convince me that he did it? No."

The *Post* story, as it turned out, was dead wrong.

Cops had no such video of Paul standing outside Catherine's building at the time in question. But it almost didn't matter. Paul was losing the public-relations battle, and he was upset that the police had zeroed in on him despite his cooperation.

That whole first week after the murder, while the newspapers were having their fun and Catherine was laid to rest, a team of forensic detectives—the Crime Scene Unit from the NYPD—was busy scouring the crime scene for physical evidence. They had been there as early as 8:50 p.m. on the night of the murder and had been a constant presence in and out of apartment 2D all week. While Detective Goetz and his team were dealing with the human element outside the apartment, it was up to the forensic detectives inside the apartment to find any irrefutable evidence the killer may have left behind.

One of the most important members of the CSU team was Detective John Entenmann, a thirteen-year veteran who had taken advanced courses in fingerprinting and bloodstain analysis at the FBI Academy and the Miami-Dade Police Department, respectively. It was Entenmann's job to survey the entire crime scene in and out of the apartment. He wound up taking 102 photographs that first night, everything from the out-side entrance of 355 East Eighty-sixth Street to Cather-ine's bloody body lying on the floor. He was looking for fingerprints but also taking careful notes about any blood-transfer patterns he spotted inside the apart-ment. A blood-transfer pattern occurs when a hand or item of clothing covered in blood comes in contact with a wall or other surface and leaves a telltale mark, a transfer.

The first paramedics inside the apartment had moved Catherine's bed away from the doorway and stood it up against a wall so they could get in to treat her. Entenmann surveyed the scene, took photographs of the way it looked when he got there, and then gin-gerly moved the bed off the wall and back onto the floor. Luckily, the bed had been leaning in such a way that only the top of it had touched the wall. That left a void—space between the standing bed and the wall—where Entenmann noticed a transfer pattern when he looked with his flashlight. After moving the bed onto the floor, he took photos of the wall behind the bed.

Entenmann's eye went to the items in the room that would obviously be of value to the investigation: the bootprints the killer had left on the bedsheet and the back of Catherine's tank top, the individual hairs on Catherine's leg and abdomen, and a small tuft of what appeared to be light-colored hair between the fingers of Catherine's bloody left hand. David Haughn had short light-colored hair. Paul had long dark hair, as did Catherine. These hairs would later become the subject of much argument, but in the crime scene photos taken by Entenmann that night, they are clearly visible.

In the kitchen sink, Entenmann found a Good Cook stainless-steel knife. It had a serrated blade that was more than four inches long and a black plastic handle. The knife was forwarded to the medical examiner so he could compare it to Catherine's stab wounds. It turned out not to be the murder weapon.

Once photos were taken of the crime scene as it existed when police found it, Entenmann began dusting the room for latent fingerprints. *Latent* means "hidden" or "invisible" in fingerprinting parlance, those prints that cannot readily be seen. Entenmann took out a feather duster, dipped it in biochromatic fingerprint powder, and began dusting any surface where he felt a latent print could be raised. This powder is what leaves behind the telltale black dust seen in crime shows when something has been fingerprinted. Generally, an investigator will want to dust where people are known to place their hands—doorknobs, bottles, mirrors. If Entenmann found a latent print, he would pull out special fingerprint tape, place it over the print, and "lift" the print. Then he would place that fingerprint onto a special card made for that purpose and send the card downtown to what the New York cops call SAFIS, short for Statewide Automated Fingerprint Identification System.

Entenmann took his time, carefully moving through the apartment, but ultimately he lifted only one latent print. It was on the broken guitar lying next to Catherine's body. That print later proved to be of no importance to the case, but of course Entenmann didn't know that then. After nine and a half hours in the apartment, he left, but not before noting and photographing a blood-transfer pattern halfway up one bedroom wall that appeared to be a partial palm print.

Two days later, Entenmann returned to the apartment with the chief medical examiner's Crime Reconstruction team for a blood-pattern analysis. Entenmann needed the team's help to enhance some of the blood patterns he'd seen the first time he was there. To do so, the team sprayed walls and surfaces with a chemical known as leucocrystal violet. The chemical, which leaves a distinctive purple color, reacts with hemoglobin, an iron-containing protein pigment found in red blood cells. If a criminal cleans up a scene by wiping a bloodstain, the original stain may be invisible to the eye, but when exposed to leucocrystal violet the trace hemoglobin would suddenly appear. That day, the Crime Scene Unit sprayed the bathroom, the kitchen, and the hallways of the apartment, where blood was not readily apparent. A few spatters of blood showed up here and there, but they were largely immaterial.

Once the blood analysis was done, Entenmann instructed cops from the Emergency Service Unit, or ESU, to cut out a section of bedroom wall where he'd noticed a handprint and a section of floor where he'd noticed a bootprint. This had to be done after all the other tests were completed because the dust created from cutting out those sections would settle onto the crime scene. The ESU cops literally cut out those sections of wall and floor with electric saws.

While much of what Entenmann did in those few days ultimately had no bearing on the case, the section of the cutout wall where he noticed that handprint would become crucial. There are basically two types of fingerprints: latent prints, which are not visible to the eye, and patent prints, which can easily be seen by anyone. On the section of wall that Entenmann ordered cut out, the partial handprint was a patent print and was apparent and visible. But the fingertip portion of that handprint—and this is the important distinction—was a latent print and was *not* visible to the naked eye. Because the patent handprint was in blood, it was clear that it had been left on the night of the murder. But the fingertip portion, the latent print, was not as easily dated. As Entenmann himself later said, "Latent prints can last a long time." In fact, he didn't even know that a latent fingertip print was there until much later.

After it was cut out of the wall, the Sheetrock with the patent handprint was sent to an NYPD forensic scientist named Alex Chacko, who holds two master's degrees, in engineering and physics. Chacko handles about forty fingerprint cases a month, and a few days after Entenmann had the section of wall removed, Chacko opened a red cardboard box in his office to examine that piece of Sheetrock, where he saw a bloodstain but no visible prints. The first thing Chacko did was to look at that Sheetrock with an alternate light source, examining the section of wall with ultraviolet and infrared lights, but he did not see any prints. He then used a chemical called amido black, placing it directly on the wall section and then washing it away. Amido black will react with a protein present in blood. In fact, this later became an important point. Does the amido black react with any protein or just protein present in blood? Much later, at trial, Chacko would answer that question this way: "The amido black reacts with the protein to give a better print. Before, when I looked the first time, I did not see any print. I saw only the blood-like stains, so I used the amido black. Once I used the amido black, it enhanced, it showed a black-purple color, so I believe that is blood."

Chacko had to apply the amido black twice, and the result, he says, is that he could now see a purple-colored latent print where none had been visible before. It was a print of someone's left index finger. The amido black had made the print visible to the naked eye. Chacko admitted at trial that while he believed the print to have come from a bloody finger, he did not perform any test to confirm the presence of blood in the print.

Chacko photographed the print with a digital camera, transferred the image to a computer, and used a software program called MoreHits "to make it more clear and more visible." The program is said not to change the original print but rather to enhance the contrast and thus make it a better print. The print in question was enhanced twice by Chacko, who then sent his work to his supervisor for review.

At that point, this single fingerprint—apparently part of a handprint left on Catherine's bedroom wall—continued its travels through the NYPD system, going next to One Police Plaza, the vaunted NYPD headquarters building just to the north of the Brooklyn Bridge.

There, a photograph of the print enhanced by Alex Chacko arrived on the desk of Annabelle Branigan, who has worked twenty-one years as a fingerprint technician, the last five and a half in the Latent Print Section. It was Branigan's job to analyze the fingerprint found on Catherine's wall. (Branigan never saw the wall from which the fingerprint was lifted, only the photograph taken by Chacko.) She did so by looking carefully at the print's "ridge characteristics." As is well known, no two people have the same "ridge characteristics."

Branigan typically looks at fingerprints through a magnifying tool called a fingerprint glass. The job is one of comparison and expertise, comparing two fingerprints to see how many "points" or "characteristics" are the same. Each fingerprint has different "whorls" or "hooks"—shapes and patterns that make it distinct. Once you match up eight similar points on two fingerprints, those prints, by some definitions, can be said to be a match. But to be certain of the match, Branigan says she tries to match up ten or more characteristics.

Branigan began comparing the fingerprint against other fingerprints sent to her by detectives. She compared and eliminated the fingerprints of Catherine Wood, David Haughn, Catherine's neighbor Julia Jeon, and the responding paramedics. Branigan also entered the fingerprint into a database of known criminals, but no matches were found.

She did not, at that point, have an inked fingerprint card for Paul Cortez. Detectives had neglected to ask for his prints the day he was questioned. What Branigan did have was a copy of a typewritten epic poem Paul had given to a female acquaintance the day of Catherine's murder. Paul had handled the sheets of paper extensively. Branigan checked the fingerprints on the paper with the one from Catherine's wall, but there was a big problem—incredibly, out of all the fingerprints on the poem, not one was of Paul's left index finger. Branigan could not make a comparison without a print from that finger.

20

"The Guy's Crazy"

Despite all the information—good and bad—being disseminated by New York's tabloid newspapers, the detectives were keeping plenty of details to themselves, information that only the principals knew. They would later come to light at trial, but back then Goetz and his detectives were still attempting to understand the complicated relationships of everyone involved, and who knew what when. Had David known that Catherine was dating Paul? Had she been dating Paul or had she considered theirs, as many of her friends suggested, a platonic relationship? Had Paul known that Catherine was still living with David? And how much more had the Woodses really known about their daughter's lifestyle than they were letting on?

There was, for instance, a key story that Paul had told detectives—a story he'd told before to others—that clearly indicated that Jon and Donna Woods had known that their daughter was a topless dancer.

The incident happened in early April 2005—Paul says the date was April 1. Paul was living in the Bronx with his stepfather at that point and on the verge of getting his first apartment, the studio up on East 106th Street. He was to finalize the deal, pick up the keys, and sign the lease as soon as he got up that very day.

But Paul's sleep that night was interrupted when he was awakened by a phone call, sometime after midnight. It was a distraught Catherine on the line, and "she was crying," Paul said.

Paul had been in a deep sleep but awoke immediately. "What's going on?" he asked her. "Are you okay?"

"No," Catherine told him. "Please come, please come here."

"Where are you?"

"I'm at the club," Paul says she told him.

"Where's that?"

She told Paul she was down at Privilege, the strip club at the corner of Twenty-third Street and Eleventh Avenue, on the West Side of Manhattan.

Paul caught a cab to the club, but once he got there it wasn't so easy to get inside. With his long hair and casual clothes, Paul was not the kind of customer the club normally let in, especially one who was agitated and wanted to see a particular dancer. "There was a big bouncer at the door with a nice suit, and I just had on jeans and sneakers and a sweatshirt, and he wouldn't let me in," Paul said.

He dialed Catherine's cell phone but couldn't get through, and then he called the house phone. The so-called "house mother" who picked up told Paul she had no idea where Catherine was, that she'd left her alone for a moment and the girl had disappeared.

"Well, is she okay?" Paul asked. "She called me hysterical, crying. What's going on?"

The house mother said she didn't know anything else. Paul's stomach dropped. "I had never gotten a call like that from her," he said. "I'd do anything to help her, and I guess she knew that."

Paul tried again to get past the bouncer, but again he had no luck. The bouncer said there was no dancer there by the name of Catherine. Paul kept calling Catherine's cell phone and the club's house phone until he spotted Catherine coming out of the club. "I had never seen her like that," he said. "She was just stumbling and just kind of off-balance, and her eyes were like pinwheels. She looked like she was on drugs or really drunk.

"She started breaking down crying on my shoulder, and I had to calm her down. At first she just didn't speak. She was just sobbing. So I asked her, 'Do you want to go home? I'll take you home.' She was like, 'No, David's there.' And I was like, 'So what?' But she said, 'He doesn't know [that she was dancing topless].' "

Catherine told Paul that she thought one of the customers had slipped a date rape drug into her drink when she wasn't looking and had in fact raped or molested her—she wasn't sure. "She told me she blacked out and the next thing she knew she was sobbing in the bathroom and one of the girls was holding her and helping her," he said. "She said she felt herself and she didn't feel right."

Catherine was nauseated—light-headed and disoriented. Paul suggested they go to a hospital, but Catherine refused. She also did not want him to take her home, and since Paul did not yet have his own apartment, he suggested they go to a hotel. "Because of her condition, we were rejected at the first three," he said, but somewhere in Times Square—he doesn't remember the exact location—they got a room, and Catherine promised she'd go to a hospital in the morning.

"I did what I thought was best at that point. I carried her to the tub and started washing her off," Paul said. "She was just crying and saying things like 'I deserve this' and 'I'm so stupid.' And I was just trying to comfort her. I told her that no one deserves this and that it would be okay.

"In the morning, she was very embarrassed and felt better. I was like, 'Let's go to the hospital because if you say what happened is what really happened, I want you to be checked out.' She didn't want to go because she had dealt with this sort of situation before—being raped—and there's a lot of paperwork involved and they call your family. She didn't want that to happen, to make it a big deal. She didn't want to file a police report or anything."

Paul's story does ring true, because Catherine had allegedly been raped once before, in Brooklyn, the day she first arrived in New York. It stands to reason that she probably knew about all the paperwork involved, and because she'd been a minor living alone, the police in Brooklyn had probably had reason to call her family. In fact, the Woodses later admitted that they knew of the Brooklyn attack.

Despite that earlier experience, Paul said he eventually persuaded Catherine to go to the Emergency department at Roosevelt Hospital. "I knew her personality, like she wanted to sweep it all under the rug, so I took her phone from her and I said, 'I'm gonna call everyone that you care about, your dad and your mom, and tell them what is going on. This is ridiculous, you have to take care of yourself,' " he said he told her. "And she was like, 'Okay, okay, I'll go.' "

When she wasn't paying attention, he copied some of the numbers from her cell phone into his phone in case she changed her mind.

Paul did escort Catherine to the hospital, but before she could be seen, he had to leave to go sign his apartment lease. No one has ever found a record of Catherine being examined that day at that hospital, so it's likely that she skipped out and went home soon after Paul left. The next day, the two of them got together to discuss the incident, and according to Paul, he confronted Catherine, giving her an ultimatum.

"I can't have anything like that ever happen again. This is too much," he said. "You have to find a new job, do something else that isn't as dangerous, or I can't be with you. I can't deal with this stress."

According to Paul, Catherine said, "I love you so much, but it's unfair for you to make me choose. I really need this money. This is my job." Catherine told him flat out that she planned to go to work that night and was putting the attack behind her.

"Well, then, we can't be together," Paul told her. "You just had this crazy thing happen. How can you do that?"

But she told him she was still stripping because she was "on schedule." She was saving her money and planned to quit in the near future.

"She wanted to go back to work like nothing had happened," Paul said.

After they separated, Paul wouldn't leave the situation alone. Concerned for her well-being, he carried out his threat—he called Catherine's father in Columbus.

"I tried to be very calm about things but also let him know that this was an urgent situation, that his daughter had just been involved in something that was a big concern to me, and I let him know who I was and that I had been seeing her and that we were dating and I basically told him what happened the night of April first," Paul said.

Jon Woods later confirmed the phone call and said he thought Paul "was very impressive on the phone.

"Paul introduced himself and told me he was calling because the night before he had been called from a place called the Privilege to come and get Catherine," Jon said. "He told me that he went there and got her. He said that she was drugged. He was concerned because her eyes weren't focusing and was very worried and that's the reason for [his putting her in] the bathtub and, when she didn't seem to be responding, he took her to a hospital."

The two men now disagree about some of what was said over a series of phone calls back and forth that day. Jon Woods says that Paul told him that Catherine was doing drugs, had done pornography, and was prostituting herself. Paul says that he told Mr. Woods that Catherine had told Paul she'd done those things in the past. In any event, it's no surprise that Jon and Donna Woods were extremely upset by the information, but Jon said they had no hard feelings toward Paul. "As any concerned father would, I thanked him," Jon said. "He was very pleasant on the phone, and I thanked him for the information. . . . This was shocking news to us because we had never seen any signs [that Catherine was doing drugs]."

Jon and Donna had visited and stayed with Catherine for a week in New York the year before, and she'd been in Columbus, but they'd never seen any sign of drug use. "She was very strict about her diet, about exercising, keeping in condition, because she came to the most challenging place in the world for dance," Jon said.

As soon as Jon hung up and discussed the conversation with his wife, he called Privilege and asked the person who answered if they knew if a Catherine Woods worked there. Of course they said no because they didn't know her by that name. He then asked if they knew Eva or Ava, and again they said no, but even Jon admits he's not sure whom he spoke to. "It could have been the cleaning woman," he said.

He then called Roosevelt Hospital, but couldn't get any information. They would not even confirm Catherine had been a patient.

Paul had told Jon that Catherine planned to return to the strip club that very night. Jon asked him to try to stop this from happening, so Paul called the club himself and talked to Chloe, the house mother. Chloe remembered his calls.

"He said, 'My name is Paul. I need to talk to her.' He said she needed to come back to him. She needed to stop what she was doing. Her family was really mad about her doing what she was doing.

"He says to me: 'Her parents are really mad about her.' When she came back, I'm like, 'Catherine, what is going on with this boyfriend of yours? He's calling me. You need to tell him to stop calling me. I don't know what's going on here.'

"And she said to me: 'Don't worry about it. The guy's crazy. I'm not seeing him anymore. It's just that he won't leave me alone.' "

Meanwhile, Jon Woods did what any father would do. He got on the next plane to New York to confront his daughter and check her state of mind and body. He asked her point-blank about everything Paul had said. "I said that I was told that she was involved in prostitution, and she said she was not," Jon said.

She also denied taking drugs, but Jon and Donna Woods admitted to CBS News correspondent Erin Moriarty that they never confronted Catherine about her topless dancing. They seemed most concerned about prostitution and drug use; once it became clear that Catherine was not involved in those activities, they never asked her if she was stripping.

"She didn't volunteer, and we weren't making an issue of, 'Where are you working?'" Jon said.

It's possible that, like a lot of parents, they didn't want to know about something they couldn't control. It seemed their line in the sand was her alleged prostitution and drug use, and once she denied those charges, the Woodses were satisfied.

Catherine told her father straight out that Paul was a liar. "She just said she was very upset that he was calling her incessantly and calling her at work to get her fired, and that she was going to get a restraining order," Jon said.

Catherine had said some of the same things to David, but there is no record or evidence that she ever got a restraining order against Paul or anyone else.

After talking to Catherine, Jon began to see Paul in a different light. He chose to believe his daughter and told Paul that Catherine had "said his accusations were not true and that there was no further need for discussion. I think maybe he might have called me once after that to see if there was any change, and I said, 'No, this is a dead issue now.'"

But it was not a dead issue for Catherine, who was beside herself with anger at Paul.

"Oh my God, was she mad," Paul said, laughing

nervously when he thought about Catherine's reaction. "She was really mad. At first she was really mad and didn't want to speak to me."

Paul said that Catherine called him and said, "I hate you. You betrayed me," and then slammed down the phone. Catherine completely broke off contact with Paul. He said that she dropped him for about three weeks, but then she relented. "We got into contact with each other again and she told me that she realized that what I was doing was trying to help her and she was sorry for saying the hurtful things that she said to me," Paul said. "We realized that we loved each other. We were always thinking about each other, and we got back together."

But to Paul's dismay, Catherine continued to live with David. The two men in Catherine's life had still never met, but that was about to change.

21

Go Away

By mid-June 2005, Catherine had apparently forgiven Paul for calling her father, and the two of them were back in touch, according to Paul's version of events. At least they were talking, he said, but then, one morning, after he had finished training some clients, he called her and she seemed upset.

"Are you okay?" he asked her.

"Yeah, you know," Catherine said. "I'm okay, I'm just . . . fine."

Paul wanted to keep the conversation going, but at that point his cell phone battery ran out. "So I figured, okay, let me just go to her place," he said. "I'd done that before. I'll try to get her to come out and eat with me. We'll just go out and talk about things, see how she is."

The relationship was still strained, but Paul was nothing if not a talker. He was the kind of guy women claimed they wanted—he *always* wanted to talk about the relationship and where it was going, more so, it seemed, than Catherine.

At that point, even though he and Catherine had known each other for almost a year, they were still meeting at coffee shops and other locations because David continued to live with Catherine. Paul says that Catherine never explicitly told him not to show up at her place, but it was understood that she didn't want him there, not as long as David was around. She always made very clear to Paul her love for David, whether he was her boyfriend or not.

Paul had always honored her wishes, but for whatever reason, on this day he decided he was through playing by her rules. He went directly to her apartment building and rang the buzzer to her apartment.

Through the intercom she asked who it was, and when he answered, Catherine immediately told him to "Go away."

But Paul was not going away. He rang the buzzer again. "It's Paul, your boyfriend," he said this time.

"Get out of here," Paul says she told him.

Paul says he buzzed one more time, and then someone, probably not Catherine, pressed a buzzer that unlocked the outdoor gate.

Up in Catherine's apartment, David was angry at whoever was leaning on their buzzer. "I didn't know who it was and I was kind of confused," he said. "I told her I wanted to go downstairs to find out who it was, possibly to confront the person, and she told me not to."

But David wasn't listening to what Catherine wanted. "I stepped out, went into the hallway, went downstairs, and when I went to exit out the building, I passed a guy who I thought might have been Paul in the hallway," David said. "I kept going and went out the front gate. I just decided to take a walk for a second. I was just kind of confused as to what was going on. I walked maybe halfway down the block and came back to the apartment."

Paul, in the meantime, had avoided David on purpose because, he said, he didn't want a physical confrontation. Paul claimed that Catherine had told him that David sometimes flew into rages and once broke a lot of dishes, but Catherine's friends say she had never said anything like that to them. In any case, on this day, as David passed within inches of Paul, Paul thought it best to lie low. "He looked pretty pissed," Paul said. "I remember moving away from the door entrance so he could get past me, and I was on guard just in case."

Paul went upstairs, but before he had a chance to say anything, he claims that Catherine confronted him. "What are you doing here?"

"My phone died and I wanted to see if you wanted to hang out," he told her. "Was that David that just left?"

"Yeah," Paul said Catherine told him. "We were just arguing. I was telling him to pack up his stuff."

Paul said he could see that David's clothing was on the bed and that Catherine was folding it as they talked. Catherine had often told Paul, according to him, that David was mooching off her and not contributing to the household expenses. "Why didn't you tell me what was going on?" Paul said. "I would have left you alone."

"I didn't want to worry you," he said Catherine told him.

"Then, all of a sudden," Paul said, "I hear some knocks on the door. She's like, 'Oh my gosh, it's him. Wait here.'"

Paul said he sat on the futon in the living room while Catherine and David had a hushed conversation just outside, in the hallway. David said that Catherine told him, "I need to take care of something." He said he tried to get into the apartment, but Catherine blocked the door. "Just wait out in the hallway for a second," he said she told him. "It's just something that I have to take care of."

Paul watched the whole scene from the living room. "She was trying to pacify him a little, and then I thought, 'It's stupid to be in here: What am I doing just waiting inside? I'm gonna go talk to this guy, see what's going on,' so I just left."

Catherine tried to close the door and keep the two men apart, but Paul said he told her, "It's okay, it's okay."

He asked David if they could talk, while Catherine was begging them not to fight, according to Paul. Even Paul says that David told her, "I'm not gonna fight."

David agreed to talk to Paul, and they left the apartment building and began walking west on Eighty-sixth Street, toward the Lexington Avenue subway station.

David asked Paul his name and how long he'd known Catherine. "He asked if I was having sex with her," Paul said.

Paul said yes.

"Wow," David said, "she got me good. I bet you she's been saying some really nasty stuff about me."

"She basically told me you don't contribute at all and, you know, you've lost that spark with her," Paul said.

Paul admits that David never once got angry, just "somber." Paul told David he'd known Catherine since August 2004, and David told Paul that he'd had sex with Catherine in the intervening year as well. It was that remark that later made Paul go home and write in his diary, "Catherine turned out to be lying to me."

Paul was emotionally wounded by meeting his rival in the flesh, as was David, who essentially confirmed the story just as Paul had told it. "We didn't get into an argument," David said. "We kind of talked it out, and I remember once we got to the subway, he actually told me if I needed anything to call him, and that was the last time I saw Paul."

David returned to the apartment, where a worried Catherine was waiting. "She asked what we talked about, and I told her him saying that they were dating, and she said that that wasn't true about them having sex. She said it wasn't true. She was also telling me, 'You know this guy is crazy. This guy is crazy. Don't listen to him.'

"Something inside me just told me to believe her, and that's what I did," David said.

"I went home and told myself to just leave this situation alone," Paul said. "It's best not to be part of this whole mess, you know? I didn't call her for a couple of weeks, but eventually we got back together again. She told me that David would do anything to keep her and that he was lying to me [when he said they'd had sex]. She said that he was trying to ruin our relationship."

Paul said that about a month later he received a phone call one night from a guy who said, "Is this Paul?"

"Yeah, who's this?"

"It doesn't matter. Where's my girl?"

"Is this David?" Paul asked.

The caller didn't acknowledge that he was David, and Paul says he doesn't know for sure. He said the unknown caller started threatening him, and Paul hung up. "Then he called me back and this time the [number] wasn't blocked," Paul said. "It was his actual number, and I told him, 'How dare you call me to find her?' "

David later admitted that he had called Paul that one time and "confronted" him. David said he was upset because he could tell from Catherine's cell phone that Paul had been calling her a lot, even though Catherine, according to David, had said that her relationship with Paul was over.

Paul said he told Catherine about the call from David, and she said she'd talk to David.

Was Catherine keeping both men on a string for her own purposes, telling each what she wanted him to hear? Whatever her reasons, both David and Paul were still in her life until the day she died. So was a third suitor, the man Paul knew only as Joe, from Flash Dancers.

22
"Joe"

Detective Steven Goetz was more than a little curious about the identity of Joe from Flash Dancers, especially after Paul Cortez told detectives that Catherine had mentioned Joe as someone new and special in her life. Detectives didn't know much more than his first name, until they began to go through Catherine's cell phone. As they checked the numbers, they saw that Catherine had called a Joe Cabrera at 8:55 p.m. the night before she was murdered. Although much of the evidence was pointing toward Paul Cortez, Goetz couldn't afford to ignore a lead that might come back to bite him in the ass at trial. A good defense attorney would make a compelling case that an unknown stalker who'd seen Catherine dance at a strip club had waited outside Catherine's apartment until David left and had then gone in to kill her.

Goetz called Cabrera, and he agreed to come to the Nineteenth Precinct to tell what he could about his relationship with Catherine. Cabrera was flashy and handsome, with more than a passing resemblance to

That '70s Show actor Wilmer Valderrama. Cabrera, who lived in Washington Heights, told Goetz that he met Catherine on the night of October 21, when he and some friends were celebrating a birthday at Flash Dancers. The men watched her dance up onstage, and then, as is the custom at strip clubs, Catherine and other dancers who had finished their routines mingled in the audience to see if anyone wanted to buy a lap dance.

Catherine was a beautiful woman with an innocent look who enjoyed taking off her clothes onstage, and to a lot of men, *that* is a winning package. Joe and his friends didn't need much convincing to buy several lap dances from her. It might seem hard to believe that a conversation could take place in that bump-and-grind atmosphere, but Cabrera said that he and Catherine chatted amicably while she danced nearly naked just inches from his face.

"You seem to be too intelligent to be working at a place like this," he told her.

"I've got bills to pay just like everyone," Catherine said.

She must have liked something about Cabrera because she told him a little about her life—how she taught young kids to dance—and gave him her e-mail address. Cabrera e-mailed her a few nights later. On Monday, October 24, he wrote:

> Hi, I just wanted to say it was great meeting you . . . I hope I get to see you again. I'll look for

you and your "love" tattoo . . . have you decided
what your Halloween costume will be?
Joe

Catherine seemed to be equally taken with him because she responded the next night.

Hey you!
It's nice to hear from you and am happy to know
you guys had a good time . . . I sure did. It's always nice when there are people in the club that
I don't have to pretend to enjoy. It sure makes
my job easier! . . . no Halloween costume
yet . . . last night I worked I had several people
suggest I be a school girl, several suggest I be a
Hula dancer . . . and there was one vote for
being "a pussy cat." Very funny. Perhaps drunk
strip club attendees are not the best people to
ask for advice?

When Catherine responded to Cabrera's initial
e-mail, he seemed a bit shocked but very happy.

It's so great to hear from you. I wasn't sure if I
was going to get a response. I'm sure you had
so many people falling for you (and believe me I
see how that's not hard to do) that it must get
tired . . . I felt totally captivated by you . . . I'm
partial to the whole school girl look which I can
only imagine would look so sexy on you but I'm

sure that whatever you decide on, it won't be
staying on for long.:)
J

Catherine eventually was so trusting of Joe that she
included her cell phone number in one of the e-mails,
and the two of them got together in early November at
a café in Greenwich Village. They flirted, and Joe
wanted to know if Catherine had a boyfriend. She told
him no but that she was close to an ex-boyfriend. She
didn't reveal his name or tell Joe that she still lived
with him. Joe for his part said he had an on-again, off-
again relationship with an "older lady." He and Catherine spent two and a half hours at the café and then
shared a cab uptown. Catherine may have trusted Cabrera, but she wouldn't let the cab drop her off in front
of her apartment building. She got out at Eighty-sixth
Street and First Avenue, while Cabrera stayed in the
cab and then took it farther uptown to his apartment
in Washington Heights. At least based on what he told
police, Cabrera apparently did not know Catherine's
address. In fact, he told them he hadn't even known
her last name, until he saw her photo in the newspapers.

In a wistful tone, Cabrera told Goetz that their date
was the only time he'd seen Catherine outside of his
visit to Flash Dancers. Catherine told Cabrera that she
was exploring alternative religions and had attended
Wicca meetings in the East Village with her friend
Christina, another dancer from the club. The day be-

fore Thanksgiving, Cabrera left Catherine a voice mail wishing her a happy holiday and expressing his good wishes.

It was to be the last Thanksgiving of Catherine's young life and she seemed to be sending mixed signals to this third man in her life. Later on, what she did and did not do that week, the phone calls she made, and with whom she spent time would be analyzed by detectives, lawyers, and a jury. They were all trying to find out the same thing: Had there been a misunderstanding that led to murder?

23

Thanksgiving Week

In the week leading up to Catherine's murder, Paul Cortez was eager for her to spend Thanksgiving with him at his mother's house in the East Tremont section of the Bronx. It was a family affair, and Paul's two older siblings, father, stepfather, and various aunts and uncles would be there. It promised to be a fun time, as it always had been.

"All the discussions I had with him [that week] seemed to be going well," said Paul's mother, Ivette. "We were planning Thanksgiving. I was expecting him to be there, and yes, he was hoping to bring Catherine along and one of his other close friends [Jaki]. I told him to just let me know. Got to make sure we have plenty for everybody."

At that point, Paul was convinced—because he said Catherine had told him so—that David had finally moved out of her apartment. But she was not telling Paul the whole truth. David *had* moved out of her apartment for two weeks in the fall, but now he was back living with her. It was true they'd agreed *not* to be a couple, but Catherine, as all her friends said, had a soft spot in her heart for David, and she could not bring herself to kick him out. He remained in the apartment, albeit sleeping on the futon, not in Catherine's bed. Later, Paul, who says he spoke frequently with Catherine, would admit he had no idea that she was once again living with David.

On the day before Thanksgiving, Paul was spotted with a woman who either was Catherine or who looked a lot like her at the Equinox fitness club on East Eighty-fifth Street.

Equinox is one of the most upscale health clubs in the city and does not take kindly to untoward behavior. At around 4:30 p.m., the woman entered an upstairs studio, where she began stretching and doing ballet exercises, according to witnesses Annabella Davis and Astrid Wilson. Astrid was training Annabella in the room. Five minutes later, Paul walked in and greeted the woman with a hug. The hug became a kiss, then an embrace, and finally Paul and the woman were groping each other with gusto. The couple seemed on the verge of having sex. Annabella was disgusted and told them to "get a room." It's doubtful they heard because their embraces and kisses had become even more heated. Finally, Annabella turned to Astrid and said, "Can we get out of here, please? This is getting gross."

Astrid encouraged Annabella to file a complaint, and she did. After Catherine's murder, the complaint was reported by Equinox executives to the police. At that point, the executive reported that the woman was Catherine Woods. But this was never confirmed.

One of the enduring mysteries of this story is the nature of the relationship between Paul and Catherine. He claims theirs was a torrid love affair, complete with wild ups and downs. His friends, including Jaki Levy, and his mother say Paul and Catherine seemed like a couple in love, that they'd seen them kissing and holding hands. But friends of Catherine's dispute that she was in love with Paul or even that she considered him a boyfriend. They say she mentioned Paul only as a friend and did not speak of him at all in the months before her murder. Megan Wilkins, who lived with Catherine and David from mid-June to mid-August 2005, said she saw Paul only once in those two months.

"He may have been in love with her," Megan said. "She was just his friend. I think he just got it in his head that he wanted to be more than friends."

Megan gets indignant when it is suggested that she might be wrong. "That gets me mad. It's insulting," she said. "Catherine was my best friend. I would have known—she would never lie to me. I think he just let this fantasy run amok in his head."

Catherine's lifelong friend Katie Miller agrees. She talked to Catherine "about boys" just a week or two before the murder. Catherine mentioned a few men in her life, including a guy named Joe. But not once did Paul's name come up. "He was just not a part of her life," Katie said.

Paul's bandmates in Monolith never saw much of Catherine, either, although she did attend one of the band's concerts, in August 2005. Alex Rude, the lead guitarist, met her once while bass player Ilya Hamovic, who lived with Paul from April to June in 2005, says he never met Catherine, though he heard a lot about her. She and Paul were, Ilya said, in constant touch over the phone.

But Paul, of course, tells a completely different story: He says he and Catherine were a couple in love going through a rough patch. In fact, there are at least three text messages sent from Catherine to Paul in the days leading up to Thanksgiving that all end in the words "I love you."

Paul said that he and Catherine were together at Paul's apartment the night before Thanksgiving, and that she helped him get ready for his singing performance that night. Paul's band, Monolith, had a gig at a club called Rear, on Fourteenth Street, and Paul said that Catherine applied heavy eye makeup to give him a more dramatic look. "She did my eyes kind of like outlined, kind of like an Ozzy Osbourne kind of rock, a Gothic kind of thing," Paul said. "She pulled back my hair, and I had my leather clothes on and it looked really cool."

But Catherine did not appear that night at Paul's show. He claims it's because he asked her not to come. "When you perform in rock shows, there are girls there and I didn't want her to be around and watch me kind of flirting with other girls and stuff like that," he said.

Does it sound plausible that you'd spend hours with your girlfriend carrying on in public, have her help you prepare for your show, only to then ask her not to come, especially if you were as in love as Paul claims he was? Paul tells different stories at different times. One time, he said he asked Catherine not to come to the show because of the groupies, but he told *48 Hours Mystery* that he asked Catherine not to come because he knew the show was not going to be good.

He was right about that, according to his bandmates, who said Paul's terrible performance that night convinced them they should fire him from the band. There was a concern that Paul might be drinking or using drugs. "That was the last nail. He sang the wrong lyrics to songs," said guitarist Alex Rude. "He was slurring his word, his eyes were dilated. He was wearing sunglasses at one o'clock in the morning. He introduced all three of us by completely wrong names."

Ironically, one of the other reasons Paul's bandmates wanted to get rid of him was because, they say, he simply was not aggressive enough to be the lead singer of a hard rock band. Alex thought Paul was very talented in many ways but ultimately didn't have what it took to lead a band like Monolith. "He's always been a very laid-back person, very Zen-like somehow," said Alex. "There were many times I wish he was more aggressive in the way he was singing and stuff. And it was really difficult to get him to be like that and perform like that."

What is known for sure is that Catherine did not

appear at Monolith's show on the night before Thanksgiving. Paul claims he suggested a late-night rendezvous, "and she was like, 'I don't know. Call me. I'll see if I'm up.' "

They did get together after the show, according to Paul, and went back to his place. The next day was Thanksgiving, and Paul said that Catherine broke the news that she would not be going to his family's Thanksgiving gathering.

"I think I'm going to spend time with David," she said.

"Are you sure? I think Jaki might come by, too."

But Catherine *was* sure. She was going to spend the holiday with David, her erstwhile boyfriend. She told Paul she didn't want David to have to spend the holiday by himself. That had to annoy Paul, but he claimed he understood. "I let her have her freedom," he said. "I didn't want to constrain her in any way. I wasn't upset like I was mad at her but I was upset in the sense that I wanted that family dinner to be with her and, you know, have her get something good to eat, have some jokes, and be in a good atmosphere. I wanted to give her that."

Paul tried to keep up appearances, but his mother could see he wasn't himself the moment he arrived at her house for Thanksgiving. "He was sad when he came into the house," she said. "And I'm sure Catherine was probably part of that. But it was Thanksgiving. The house was full. There was food all up and down in the kitchen. He was having a grand old time. It was a good day and when he left, I gave him a shopping bag full of food, leftovers. No one would have ever said anything was wrong."

At Catherine's apartment on Thanksgiving Day, David was the cook, preparing a big turkey dinner in their tiny New York City kitchen. It was a fun day for the two of them. "She was real hungry [by 3:00 p.m.] and kept trying to peek into the kitchen to see what I was making," David said. "And I said, 'Be patient, I'm almost finished.' I remember even as I made the plates and got everything ready, she's was pouting in the living room, saying, 'I'm hungry,' just being silly like she always was. And I remember once we sat down and started eating, well, she was small but she could out-eat me anytime. She finished her whole plate and it was a big plate piled high. I was only half finished, and she's like, 'Are you full?' and I said, 'I'm getting there,' and she starts picking at my plate. It was funny, very funny."

Later, Catherine and David went to see the movie version of the Broadway play *Rent* before going back to the apartment to while away the rest of the day.

Paul said Catherine called him sometime late that afternoon to tell him she was sorry she'd missed his family Thanksgiving, and also, he said, to tell him that she loved him. She also sent him a text message that was later alluded to in court. The message read: "Call me please."

But Catherine also called Joe Cabrera on Thanksgiving night to thank him for his message from the day before. He says she was flirtatious, and they talked for an hour about relationships. Catherine again asked him if he had a girlfriend and he told her again about an older woman he was seeing on and off. Catherine seemed smitten with Cabrera, because she called him again the next day and left a message about their getting together again, sometime in the coming weeks.

If there's one thing that's clear about Catherine's Thanksgiving Day, it's that she was communicating regularly and being flirtatious with three different men. In retrospect, it's hard to understand how she felt about each of them. She'd spent the day with David rather than Paul. Was she pulling away from Paul? Was Paul trying to rekindle a relationship that was actually dead? Judging by the phone records, investigators were beginning to suspect that. Especially toward the end of her life, Paul called Catherine a lot more than she called him.

And then, finally, Catherine had a new guy, Joe Cabrera, whom she had recently met in a strip club. Was she serious about him? None of these relationships seemed all that stable.

Looking at it from an investigator's point of view, it was possible that Catherine might have been playing with fire, especially if any one of these men was the jealous type.

24

Danielle

Paul Cortez knew a lot of people in New York, and as the newspapers ran stories about him day after day, some of his past friends and acquaintances came forward to tell police what they knew. On Sunday, December 4, it was Danielle Mitchell's* turn.

Danielle had been distraught the whole week as she read about Catherine's murder. She thought she might stay out of it but finally felt compelled to come forward. Danielle, a voluptuous blonde with a killer body, was particularly stung by all the tabloid stories, at least partly because they hit much too close to home. Like Catherine, Danielle had come to New York from a small town to follow her own dream of becoming a professional actress, but she, too, had turned to exotic dancing to make ends meet. That's where she'd met Catherine. But even more important, and the reason Danielle wanted to talk to the police, was that she also knew Paul Cortez, she said, "all too well."

* Not her real name.

After thinking long and hard about what she knew, Danielle screwed up her courage, walked into the Nineteenth Precinct, and told the desk sergeant that she was there to tell detectives what she knew about the Catherine Woods case. Danielle, who in an old-time detective novel might be described as "a tough cookie," was haunted by her last interaction with Catherine. It wasn't a big deal, but it bothered Danielle that she'd been a bit mean to Catherine, whom Danielle perceived as a naïve girl who was in over her head in New York.

The last time she saw Catherine, Danielle was walking out of Privilege when Catherine was walking in.

"Oh, you've got your yoga mat," Catherine said brightly.

"Yeah," said Danielle, who didn't slow down a beat.

It was nothing, really, but after Catherine's murder, it preyed on Danielle's mind.

"I liked Catherine," Danielle said. "She was a very open person, and in the stripping industry, you get a lot of egos and snotty girls. She came in just very bright and open and wanted to talk to everybody and make it her community."

Danielle tears up when she talks and thinks about Catherine, no doubt in small part because in hindsight she sees a younger, less jaded version of herself. "She'll never get to do all the things that she wanted to do here, in New York. I came here to do the same things and I went down the wrong path as well, dancing," she said. "Not that it's a bad thing, but it's not what I want my family knowing that I did. If I were to die, I wouldn't want someone to say that about me. She wanted to succeed and be a star. She *was* a star, and now everybody has an image of Catherine as a *'dead stripper'* and I think that takes away from her dreams and her spirit and it just typecasts her. Nobody will ever know anything but that about her now. And I cry because I have an image of her beauty, and it was really powerful.

"She was an amazing person. She wasn't involved in anything dark. She worked at the best clubs in the city as far as classiness. Nothing goes on there. Now when people see the newspapers, they're automatically gonna think she was doing sexual things, and that's not the way it is. That's not what the business is. And I guess my last vision of her is as this very caring person who was really wanting to know everybody."

Danielle said the two of them met on a cigarette break at Privilege, where Catherine introduced herself by her real name but told Danielle she danced under the name of Ava. Danielle admits their conversations were short. They talked about weight issues and Broadway auditions, and the movie business. They never talked all that much about dancing topless. "I think we're all very uncomfortable being there deep down," she said. "I don't think any of us really wants to be there. We just want the money."

Danielle said the money is so good that it's hard to walk away from. "New York is tough, okay?" she said. "You might have all these huge dreams when you get here that you're gonna do it, but it doesn't happen overnight and it's very expensive to live here. Head shots cost money. You have to be training all the time. You've got to be in the gym and you have to take classes, which all cost tons of money. Where are you going to get that money from? I don't think the bill collectors are asking where you're getting the money, you know?

"And you can't tell your family that you're failing because that's the worst thing that you want to do. You can't tell them, 'Maybe I'm not gonna make it.' They're thinking, 'My daughter is gonna be an actress? Why can't she be a doctor or something, something more legit?' That's why [Catherine] didn't want to let anybody know, like I did. You want to make it in the end. I would never imagine that I would be dancing, but your bills call and you're in New York and you think, 'Well, you're a good-looking girl, why not go and try it?' It's good money but in the end you want all this [the topless dancing] to disappear and forget that you ever done it and put it in your tool belt as an experience."

Danielle said that Catherine never once mentioned Paul Cortez. If she had, Danielle would have said something because, in the oddest of coincidences, she had also met Paul, well before Catherine.

Danielle was a constant presence at the Bikram Yoga studio in Union Square, having studied for more than five years. She'd often take two ninety-minutes classes a day, and she struck up a friendship with Paul, who worked at the reception desk. You sweat a great deal in those hot yoga classes, and it's common for people to sit around the reception area and cool down before and after taking a shower. She was sitting there one day when Paul looked over at her and said, "You have the light. I can see it."

She didn't know exactly what he was talking about, and thought it was yet another corny pickup line, but she agreed to go out to lunch with him. She said before any meal they ever ate together, Paul would put his hands together and pray in Sanskrit. They saw each other around the studio a lot, and Paul would flatter Danielle, telling her she had the perfect package of body, mind, and spirit. Not surprisingly, they became friends.

"We definitely spent a lot of time together. I got intimate with him," she said, not in a sexual way, but in their private conversations. "I wasn't physically attracted to him that much. He has a nice body but what interested me was his artistic ability. That was a turn-on for me."

She told Paul about her topless dancing, and as he would do with Catherine, he tried to persuade Danielle to stop. "He was always talking about it," she said. "He wanted to get me out of the business. He'd say, 'Oh, you're so spiritual, why do you want to do that?' And he told me I could live with him, that he could help me out and we were gonna go to yoga training together."

At that point, Danielle did quit stripping, but it had nothing to do with Paul. She quit because she got a film-editing job. "I told him that, and he was proud of me, that I wasn't a stripper anymore," she said, rolling her eyes.

During the time she was on good terms with Paul, she told him what she really thought of the business. "I told him my deepest feelings about the business, and he was very concerned about me. My perfect dream of work is doing something that I love in a business where it's okay to make money and you can also learn a lot. But this [topless dancing] is definitely hard. You drink a lot, and it's hard to have a relationship. You question a lot of things as far as men go."

And that included Paul. Danielle had invited him to her apartment, where they discussed plans to travels to Los Angeles together to become certified as Bikram yoga teachers. At one point, she says, she took a shower and came out wearing only a towel. "We kissed and then he tried to force himself on me and that's when we had a falling out," she said.

Pressed to detail what happened, Danielle thought about it for a moment and blurted out, "He tried to make me give him a blow job, and I wasn't gonna have it. So I told him he could sleep on the couch and that I was gonna go to bed because I had an early day the next day and I had to go to work. And he was really upset about that and every time I'd be almost falling asleep, he'd start singing and chanting. He carried his *Bhagavad Gita* book around with him. He even bought me one. He just had to purchase it for me. He quoted from this book all the time. He even talked in Sanskrit, the Hindu language. And there'd be all these words I didn't understand, and finally I told him, 'Listen, Paul, I don't know what you're saying. I'm not Hindi. I don't believe that stuff. I'm not very spiritual. I might have a picture of Ganeesh on my wall, but I'm not into all that stuff. I don't know what you're talking about.' "

The next morning after the rejection, as Danielle and Paul were walking to the subway, Paul told Danielle that he was still upset about the night before. "He said he couldn't believe that I wouldn't even give him oral sex, and I told him, 'I don't know where you've been. I'm just not feeling that about you.' And he said, 'I'll wait for you. I'll do whatever I have to [to] be with you.' "

For Danielle, it was one in a series of what she said were "red flags" about Paul. She knew that he had told others in the yoga studio about her stripping, because one of the managers told her that he knew Danielle was in "a bad place." That was Paul's terminology for stripping, and Danielle knew right then that he'd been gossiping about her in the studio, and she didn't like that at all, especially since she was planning at one point to take the Bikram training and become a teacher.

Danielle consciously began distancing herself from

Paul, but it only made him more determined; he'd call her even more incessantly. "He would call me all the time and he was creating havoc for me in my personal places, and I just felt like it was time to stop talking to him."

She said that she got a new cell phone number and refused to give it to him.

Then one day, about a month after they'd stopped talking, Paul asked if he could talk to her, and he began confiding in her about another woman he'd met, who was also working as a topless dancer to make money. "I thought he was lying," she said. "I didn't think he could possibly have met a dancer right after me, a month after we'd stopped talking. I just thought that subliminally he was trying to tell me, 'Oh, you're a slut, Danielle,' or something like that. He said he was really concerned about this girl, that she was in a dark place and that she seemed like she liked it a lot because she kept going back.

"And I said, 'Well, maybe she needs money.' And he said she had been drugged and raped there, and I said, 'I'm sorry. I just think that's really impossible because I know from experience that those bouncers are watching you the entire time. There's like a hundred bouncers there. There's no way you're gonna get drugged and raped at a club.'"

Later, when Danielle began thinking about what Paul had said about the rape at the club, it suddenly dawned on her that Paul was talking about Catherine.

What's more, Danielle was dancing at Privilege the night Catherine felt faint and called Paul. Danielle said the incident was nowhere nearly as dramatic as Paul made it out to be. She said she'd heard from the other women also there that night that Catherine was feeling light-headed and possibly had been drugged, but that she definitely had not been raped.

By the time Danielle began reading of Catherine's murder in the newspapers, she had not seen Paul at the Bikram Yoga studio for quite a while and thought he'd quit working there. But the manager, who seemed unusually close to Paul, told her that he still worked there and, in fact, had worked the day of the murder.

Danielle went into a panic because she now realized how much she had in common with Catherine. "Who knows that he didn't want to kill me?" she asked. "I believe he probably did want to kill me the same way because I fit the profile and he knew me first."

Based on what she knew of Paul's obsessive nature, Danielle feared that Paul might still come after her. "I locked my door and I didn't leave. I was paranoid. I couldn't even take a shower. Even now I can hardly sleep. I wake up in the middle of the night. I have a knife next to my bed. My door is bolted with a door brace, and even then I'm still paranoid."

The final straw, she said, is when she picked up the *Bhagavad Gita* one night, the same book that Paul had bought for her. One section in particular stunned her. "I couldn't believe it," Danielle said. "It's about beheading. It's about death and how you shouldn't mourn someone's death, and if you do kill someone, they're taken to a higher level."

It was at that point that Danielle put down the book and decided to talk to the detectives. The whole story had shaken her core beliefs. "It makes me question all the people that I've met. You wouldn't think a yoga instructor would murder you, would you?" Paul was *not* a yoga teacher but that wasn't the point.

Danielle was an interesting potential witness who could testify to Paul's obsessive ways. She'd spent a lot of time with him and seemed to have insight into his personality. About a month after she first walked into the Nineteenth Precinct, detectives asked her to come back. She'd told them that she'd often seen Paul putting his shoes into a cubbyhole near the front of the yoga studio and was sure she could identify the type of shoe he wore.

Detectives showed her photos of all types of Sketchers footwear, shoes and boots, but Danielle said none of them matched the type of shoe Paul had worn. She did say, however, that from the side, one of the boots had the same type of sole and heel as a shoe Paul had worn. But she was sure she had not seen him wearing any of the Sketchers boots.

That was not what detectives wanted to hear.

25

Meeting the Woodses

Inside the broadcast center of CBS News at 524 West Fifty-seventh Street, Al Briganti, the executive editor of *48 Hours Mystery,* was talking to staff producer Patti Aronofsky about the story of Catherine Woods. Patti, a onetime local news producer for WCBS-TV, is a news junkie; she of course knew about the dancer's murder, but she wanted to hear why Briganti thought the broadcast should pursue the story. Because of the way the story was being trumpeted in New York, Patti at that point believed Catherine was little more than a stripper.

Briganti began by telling Patti how important Catherine's father was back in his hometown of Columbus. "He's the director of the Ohio State marching band," Briganti said.

But Patti is nothing if not a native New Yorker, and she didn't know anything about college football or marching bands or why they were considered important to anyone. At that point Patti had never watched a football game in her entire life. But Briganti didn't know that, and he went on, telling Patti about the OSU band tradition where they spell out the word *Ohio* on the field, and then how someone is chosen to dot the *i* in *Ohio*. "It's a very big deal," Briganti said.

Nothing was registering with Patti. Briganti knew he had a dyed-in-the-wool New Yorker on his hands, so he tried another approach. He made the case that Catherine was not *just* a stripper. That had merely been a job to make money. She was really a young artist, a woman with a dream, and her dream had been to dance on Broadway. Her story was like the stories of a lot of young people who come to New York with stars in their eyes. "You know that line," Briganti told Patti, " 'For every light on Broadway, there's a broken heart'? That's this story."

Patti perked up. Now Briganti was speaking her language, in part because Patti had briefly studied ballet at the New York High School for Performing Arts. Briganti was talking about how the piece could be developed using other young dancers who were trying to achieve the same dream as Catherine. Maybe Patti could even go to Broadway auditions to help round out the story. For Patti, this was an appealing idea, and she was sold on the story. She was further convinced after reading a heartfelt profile of Catherine by *New York Times* reporter Jennifer Bleyer. The story shone a light on all of Catherine's accomplishments and her dream; it was entitled "The Pride of Columbus" and ran on the front page of the *Times*'s City Section.

The next challenge was to persuade Jon and Donna Woods to work with the broadcast and provide insight into what they were going through. Because of Erin Moriarty's strong ties to OSU and Columbus, Patti felt the broadcast had a leg up on the competition. That afternoon, she sent a letter to the Woods family.

The letter read, in part:

> CBS News *48 Hours* is preparing a one-hour special on your daughter. We want to tell the story of her life and her dreams. We want to speak with her family, her friends, her teachers— everyone who loved and cared about her. We think her story will touch people across the country.

About a week later, Patti was sitting across from Jon and Donna Woods in a hotel room near OSU's Steinbrenner Band Center. Patti had brought along Daria Karp, a young associate on the broadcast, but there were no cameras. The Woodses had by their side an employee of OSU who knew Erin Moriarty and knew of her connection to the school. The Woodses were, of course, still raw and numb from their daughter's death and didn't say much. Neither did anyone else, according to Daria, who marveled at how Patti took over the meeting. Patti told the Woodses how she knew what it was like to be a young woman dating in New York, how she'd also taken a lot of chances when she was younger. She told them about her own background in dance and how she'd briefly studied at a performing arts high school.

The Woodses told Patti that the tabloid coverage in New York had caused problems for their young teenager, Tori, who was still in junior high school. They made it clear that even if they agreed to be interviewed, they would not allow their two children to speak on camera.

The Woodses obviously were in a lot of emotional pain, but they were taking comfort in the kindness of strangers. They remarked on an e-mail they'd received from someone who'd once seen Catherine perform in front of Central Park's Bethesda Fountain. The author of the e-mail was a woman from Canton, Ohio, who had come across Catherine one autumn day.

> It was not until I saw your daughter's picture in the news that I realized she was the remarkable dancer who performed by the fountain in Central Park. . . . The sun was shining and your daughter seemed to float across the stones. . . . I remembered her vividly because her performance seemed to embody all the spontaneity I loved about the city.

The letter writer knew it was definitely Catherine because of a small item she had with her, a water bottle with the colors red and gray and the initials OSU. As a native Ohioan, the e-mail writer knew immediately what those letters stood for: Ohio State University.

The Woodses also mentioned the *New York Times* profile "The Pride of Columbus." In their darkest hour, they said, that article had reaffirmed their faith in journalism. Patti told the Woodses that this was the direction in which *48 Hours Mystery* wanted to take the story. This had to be the story of a young woman cut down while chasing a dream, not the sordid tale of a stripper.

At the end of the half-hour meeting, the Woodses agreed—from that moment on, they would tell their story to Patti and Erin from *48 Hours Mystery*, and no one else.

In yet another bizarre coincidence that seemed to dog the story at every turn, Daria Karp, the young assistant who sat in on the meeting, later told Patti and Erin that she'd met Paul Cortez but hadn't realized it until after the meeting with the Woodses. It turned out that Daria's freshman roommate at Princeton, a graduate of Poly Prep, had asked Paul Cortez to be her date for the senior prom, even though Paul was then a junior. Daria said her roommate had carried a crush on Paul into her freshman year and, one weekend, asked Daria to accompany her to see Paul perform in the Poly Prep production of *Pippin*.

"He was great, very talented," Daria said. "I could see why my roommate liked him. He had great stage presence but he also had charisma offstage."

After the show, she and her roommate went out to dinner with Paul, and like a lot of women, Daria came away from the evening very impressed.

26
Monica

As Christmas approached, the stories on Catherine's murder slowed down. For the moment, there wasn't much to report. Criminologists were doing their jobs behind the scenes, and detectives continued to talk to anyone who knew Catherine, Paul, or David. The best leads continued to be the bootprints left on Catherine's bedsheet and shirt, and the left index fingerprint lifted off Catherine's bedroom wall. But the detectives were stymied by the fingerprint because they had neglected to get a clean set from Paul while he was still cooperating.

Detectives were sure the killer had left that telltale fingerprint because, although it had not been visible, it seemed to belong to or be part of the bloody palm print that was visible. The cops wanted Paul's print so they could rule him in or out once and for all, but they didn't seem to have a way to get one.

Up to that point, Detective Goetz had never met Jon Woods, but he had spoken to him on the phone.

"And I remember telling Jon, 'Sooner or later, we're gonna get a phone call or somebody's gonna come into the precinct and we're gonna get a break.' And we got a break."

That break came in the form of a young woman we'll call Monica, for reasons that will become obvious. Monica, who has never told her story to the press until now, was twenty-four years old and a senior at a Catholic college in the New York area when she met Paul Cortez. Unlike Danielle Mitchell, Monica was not a hardened New Yorker; she has something of a little girl's voice and comes across as meek. She wasn't wise to the ways of the city—she would visit the city on weekends, and the only person she knew was a girl-friend who at the time was dating Alex Rude, the guitarist in Paul's band. Monica accompanied her girlfriend on New Year's Eve 2004, when Monolith was performing at a club called Continental, on Third Avenue near St. Mark's Place. Monica said she was attracted to Paul right away, and the attraction seemed mutual. When the band took a break, the two would talk. "It was almost like a first date," she said.

At midnight, Monica said it just seemed natural to kiss Paul, since she was looking for someone with whom to celebrate the New Year. The two wound up exchanging heavy kisses in the club's bathroom. "I was feeling loose by then," she said. "I'd had a lot to drink."

She gave Paul her phone number and she and her

girlfriend went home to wait for the guys to call them and come over. By 4:00 a.m., Monica was sleeping. "I just figured he'd met some other girl," she said.

But then Paul did call, and even though she was dog-tired and still drunk, Monica invited him over. As soon as Paul got to the apartment, Monica said he wanted to have sex—right away. "There was no foreplay, no warm-up. I wouldn't say he was violent, but he was very rough," she said, adding that he did not seem drunk.

She agrees that the sex—at least in the beginning—was consensual, even though "it was very unpleasant. The stuff that was happening was something I wouldn't do with someone I just met."

Paul was not using a condom and, according to Monica, initiated anal sex with her, which is something, she said, she did not want to do. She asked him to stop and he did, but then he demanded oral sex. "He was kneeling on my chest and at that point, I just wanted him to leave," she said, explaining that she did provide oral sex even though it was not something she wanted to do but she felt coerced into it. He left soon after.

"The next day, I felt confused," she said. "It was complicated. Something wrong had happened, but it was not rape or assault. I didn't tell anyone because it was too embarrassing."

Nearly a year went by, and in December 2005, while reading the Monolith band website and blog, Monica came across some postings that urged fans, "Don't believe the lies in the *New York Post*."

She had no idea what that meant because she had not heard anything about Catherine's murder. She immediately Googled the *Post* website and read all the stories about Paul. "I was really shocked," she said. At the time, Monica was working with a woman whose boyfriend was an NYPD detective. She told her friend about the New Year's Eve sex with Paul, and the friend told her boyfriend, who advised Monica to talk to detectives at the Nineteenth Precinct.

"I was kind of embarrassed because there were two male detectives, so they asked if I wanted to tell my story to a female detective who worked in the Special Victims Unit," she said.

Monica told the female detective the story "and I thought that would be the end of it." But it wasn't. The authorities were intent on getting Paul's fingerprints and this was a way to get them, once and for all.

The cops asked Monica if she wanted to press charges. "I said I didn't know."

Then they asked if she could get Paul on the phone so they could audiotape him admitting to the assault. "I told them I didn't think I could get him on the phone," she said.

But the detectives would not be dissuaded. The next day, December 19, they arrested Paul and charged him with a single count of sodomy based on Monica's statement. Monica was surprised and then horrified. Her name and address (by then she was living in Manhattan) were leaked to the press, who showed up in force outside her door the next day. "It was horrible," she said. "I didn't want my name in the *Post* that I was anally sodomized. I was not prepared." She refused to talk to any member of the press.

Paul's arrest shocked his family, friends, and supporters. "I was very shaken—very, very, very shaken," said Jaki Levy. "I was very disturbed. I started thinking, 'What's going on here?' I asked Paul about that. He said they went home willingly with each other and she went to go see him at shows afterwards. If someone raped me, I probably wouldn't be very close with that person. I would probably stay away from that person."

Paul's mother had heard the same story. "From all accounts, everybody says the same thing," Ivette said. "It was obvious that she came on to him. She invited him to her apartment, and somewhere along the line, what? It's a rape? They continued seeing each other at the band's shows."

Monica admitted that she did go to two other Monolith concerts, not to see Paul but only to hang out with her girlfriend, the only person she really knew in the city. She said, "I never hung out with [Paul] again. He didn't acknowledge me and I didn't know how to feel about it. He acted like nothing had ever happened."

For the authorities, Monica was clearly a means to an end, and her story gave them a way to get Paul's fingerprints. Events unfolded quickly after the authorities had those prints. The day after Paul's arrest on sodomy charges, Assistant District Attorney Martha Stolley made another dramatic announcement: "There was a bloody fingerprint found at the murder scene that has been matched to this defendant."

It was the first time the authorities referred in public to what would become the infamous "bloody fingerprint." The newspapers and media did the same. But that terminology would later be the source of many a heated courtroom argument. Was the phrase "bloody fingerprint" overstating the evidence?

Hearing that, the average person must surely envision the red outline of a fingerprint in blood on the wall. But that was *not* what cops had found in Catherine's apartment. This "bloody fingerprint" could not even be seen with the naked eye. It wasn't until chemicals were added to it that it became visible. The chemicals, the experts say, react with the protein in blood, so authorities felt it was fair to call it a bloody fingerprint. However, no test was ever done on that fingerprint specifically for the presence of blood. It's a fine distinction. Could the chemical have reacted with a protein other than blood?

Once Stolley made her announcement, Paul's indictment was a formality, but there was a minor hitch: The unions that operate New York City's subways and buses had called a strike and brought the city to a standstill. The DA could not empanel enough jurors to indict Paul for a few more days, but after five days, the strike ended. Two days before Christmas, on December 23, 2005, Paul Cortez was charged with killing Catherine Woods.

The tabloids celebrated Christmas early. Paul was alternately described in the arrest stories as "a long-haired lothario" and "a crazed creep."

As for Monica, she never heard from the authorities again. In the middle of 2006, the sodomy charge against Paul was dropped. Neither the police nor the DA bothered to tell Monica; she read about it in the paper.

The other person more or less forgotten was David Haughn. After leaving the interrogation room days after Catherine's murder, he'd gone to stay with his friend in Suffern, New York. He never went back to work as a doorman, never went back to the apartment he'd shared with Catherine, and he didn't even have his old car, which had been impounded by the police. He moved back to Ohio to live with his grandmother and tried to pick up the pieces of his life. He was depressed, moving from job to job until he finally pulled himself together enough to get work as a forklift operator at a Wal-Mart.

The only time David returned to New York before he was asked to testify at Paul's trial was to pick up his car. He showed up at the Nineteenth Precinct with Megan, Catherine's good friend, and the two had a brief meeting with Detective Goetz. Goetz recalls Megan being testy and angry with the police for the way they'd treated David, but Goetz explained to her that David had to be cleared before the cops could build their case. She seemed to understand, and at the end of the meeting, she gave Goetz a big hug. Then David recovered his car and the two drove back to Ohio.

27

The Confession—Not

"Why I Killed Stripper Beauty: Boyfriend's secret murder diary."

The words jumped off the front page of the *New York Post* on January 10, 2006. In a murder case full of shocking headlines, this "exclusive" was the topper. It alleged, in no uncertain terms, that not only had Paul Cortez killed Catherine Woods, but he'd also written down his confession—"admitted his sadistic crime," as the paper alleged—in a "secret" diary.

The first line of the story by Laura Italiano was: "He had to save Catherine Woods from sin—by slashing her throat," and it went downhill from there, at least for Paul.

Anyone who knew Paul well understood his obsessive need to write down his innermost thoughts. His mother said he'd been doing it since he was a little boy. Paul's friend Jaki Levy was very familiar with the journals. Paul had often let him read them. "I've read his poetry before," Jaki said. "He would talk about spirits and gods. He would talk about the afterlife. He would talk about before life. A lot of these spiritual things. In the *Bhaghavad Gita,* the main character is a warrior.

"It's very, very easy to take a piece of poetry or to take something that is art or whatever it is and interpret [it] in a million different ways. I believe someone went into his diary and looked at it and said, 'Oh, look at this journal entry. This is his confession right there. That's right there.' You can take it out of context. It's very easy to do.

"You know, are the people who created [the video game] Grand Theft Auto murderers? I mean, could they have been rapists? There's a rape in the videogame."

Jaki thought the whole thing was ridiculous. Detectives, however, didn't think the journals were ridiculous, not at all. They were especially keyed up about one phrase buried in the diary. It read: "She wipes clean the shaft that cuts her throat." Authorities thought that was just too close to the reality of how Catherine died. The entry is dated nearly a year before her death, as Paul pointed out.

The same *Post* article about Paul's so-called "confession" made yet another reference to the supposed security camera videotape of Paul "standing outside Woods's East 86th Street apartment." That video was mentioned in story after story, but much later, at trial, it was found never to have existed.

Paul may or may not have killed Catherine, but at that point he was still considered innocent in the eyes of the law. In the eyes of the *New York Post,* though, he was something else—a monster. The *Post* was printing inflammatory material, some of which turned out not to be true.

Paul did refer to the *Bhagavad Gita* in his journals, and one section of that text does in fact refer to beheadings, but it is about a young warrior on the verge of going into battle. A lot of people have read and continue to read the *Bhagavad Gita*, and very few of them are killers. Paul had kept all his journals in his apartment, probably because he felt they had no bearing on the case. As he was later to learn, he was being much too naïve. The journals were not confessionals, but that didn't stop the district attorney from trying to connect the dots between Paul's poetry and Catherine's murder.

The *Post* article created a stir and even prompted a group calling itself the International Society for Krishna Consciousness to issue a statement in support of the *Bhagavad Gita,* which, it said, "advocates the sanctity of all life.

"The *Gita* condemns murder and teaches that even to harm an animal is reprehensible. None of us has the right to cast judgment on or cause pain to another," the statement read. "If Paul Cortez, the alleged killer, was influenced by the *Bhagavad Gita* or Hindu culture, he, like many violent criminals, grossly misinterpreted a sacred text and tradition to justify vile acts. It is certainly no reflection whatsoever on the *Bhagavad Gita*'s 5,000-year-old message of love and peace."

28

Last Visit

Two weeks later, on January 28, 2006, Jon and Donna Woods arrived at the front gate of the building at 355 East Eighty-sixth Street, in an SUV they had driven from Ohio. They were there to pick up their daughter's personal possessions.

Over the previous two months, their lives had been turned upside down, as Catherine's life had been turned into a seamy sideshow. The Woodses had been through a lifetime's worth of emotions in a very short time and had come out onto the other side, clinging to each other and holding their collective breath for what would come next. Driving to New York City and seeing the familiar sights, they couldn't help but think of the time they'd made this trip with Catherine over the July 4 weekend of 2002. It had been the beginning of Catherine's dream, and today would be the final chapter. Someone else would soon move into her apartment, maybe a young woman with her own dream. The cycle that is New York would begin again.

The Woodses' younger children, Stephen and Tori, had not come along, but Jon and Donna were not alone. Meeting them at the front gate was Detective Steven Goetz, who had spoken to Jon several times by phone since the murder. This, however, was the first time the two men would meet in person, and Goetz was determined to make a heartbreaking task go as smoothly as possible. An extremely compassionate man, Goetz is a father himself, and it's clear that he had great sympathy for what Jon Woods was going through.

"It had to be tough on him," Goetz said. "I can't imagine what it would be like to lose a loved one in the manner that he lost his daughter. I tried to comfort them as best as possible."

That he did. Goetz made sure a uniformed police officer was with him that day to guard the Woodses' SUV as they slowly packed it with Catherine's belongings. When they first arrived on the block, the Woodses had parked on the wrong side of the street, and Goetz had the uniformed cop stop traffic so the SUV could make a U-turn.

It was cold and overcast that day, but Goetz wanted to explain a few things to the Woodses before escorting them inside. First off, he told them that he'd moved everything of value out of the bedroom and sealed the room off so they would not have to enter the place where their daughter was murdered. "The apartment is a mess because of us," Goetz said. "When you go in, you're going to see purple stuff all over the walls. That's not blood. That's the Luminol stuff that they sprayed to find blood, and it makes a purple stain. So where all the purple stuff is, don't think that's blood."

Goetz then explained to the Woodses about the state's Crime Victims Compensation Board, and how they could be reimbursed for travel and funeral expenses.

It was time to go inside. Goetz knew it was going to be emotionally grueling for them. "Take your time," he told them. "I've got all day."

The detective, who physically towered over the Woodses, led them inside and up to Catherine's second-floor apartment. He carried the plastic crates the Woodses had brought along.

It was as emotionally draining as Goetz expected. The moment Donna set foot in Catherine's living room and saw some of her daughter's personal possessions, she broke down and began sobbing loudly. "As soon as Donna walked in is when it really hit home," he said. "I gave Jon and Donna a few moments inside the apartment by themselves, and I remember shutting the door to give them time to themselves.

"Sometimes in this job you're a detective, sometimes you're a counselor, and that day I was a counselor. I was there for Jon and Donna and got them through it as best as possible."

Goetz said there was one thing he always appreciated about Jon Woods. "Jon was very good," Goetz said. "He made it clear from the very beginning that he was going to let the New York City Police Department do their job. He had faith in us, and that's what he did."

After a while, the Woodses began to carry items out into the hall, and Goetz carried the crates down to the truck. Eventually, Goetz went into the apartment to help them pack, and as Donna picked through Catherine's clothing, Jon and Goetz discussed college football.

Producer Patti Aronofsky was allowed into the apartment and was helping the Woodses sort through Catherine's possessions. They were looking for a bank statement, because they believed Catherine had been squirreling away her "stripper money." It's interesting that, for all the talk about how much Catherine made dancing topless, she had only $63.11 in her wallet. No other cash was found in the apartment and the sole bank account Catherine's parents found contained a little more than two hundred dollars. If she had any other money saved, it was never found.

In any case, that day at the apartment, Patti did come across several notebooks in Catherine's handwriting that had been left behind by the police. The notebooks were not diaries per se, Patti said, but at least in the short time she had to look at them, she could see that Catherine had been writing down her inner thoughts. A piece of paper fell out of one notebook. Patti picked it up and saw Catherine's musings about a sobering night at a strip club. Given the raw emotions that day, Patti did not want the Woodses to have to read the revealing passage she'd just read and she quietly returned the notebooks to a box where she'd found them and resumed looking for the bank statement. Patti was eager to read more, but out of respect for the Woodses, she felt obliged not to go any further.

Whatever else was in those notebooks is not known. The Woodses packed them up and took them back to Ohio. Whether they ever read them or even are aware of their existence is unclear. It remains a mystery as to why the police did not take them or at least make copies of them, but one detective, when later asked if Catherine had kept a diary, said he wished she had because it would have locked down the case.

The packing continued, and there was a polite silence about the clothing in Catherine's closet, clothing that was clearly intended for her job as a topless dancer—the slinky sequined evening gowns and large collection of high heels, at least one pair in hot pink. Both parents brightened a bit when Donna found two OSU hats in Catherine's closet. Goetz had moved Catherine's stuffed bunny rabbit, Hop-Hop, from the bloody bookshelf in the bedroom to the living room. Donna clutched it to her chest and regarded it sadly.

"She got this for Easter. She would have been nine months old. And she's had it so long," Donna said. "He has survived longer than Catherine now."

Then Jon looked around at the plastic crates and debris of Catherine's life strewn all over the apartment. "This is probably the hardest thing I've ever done. I mean we're really movin' her out of New York now. We're bringing her home."

29

"Fosse Would Have Hired Her"

Before the Woodses drove back to Columbus, they had one more stop to make. Jon and Donna wanted to see the Broadway Dance Center where Catherine had studied and where she'd spent hour upon hour honing her craft. Located on the second floor of a building on Broadway and West Fifty-seventh Street in Midtown Manhattan, the Broadway Dance Center is *the* place for dancers who are serious about their art. Thousands of young men and women from all over the world have trained there and gone on to Broadway, Off-Broadway, and road shows all over the country. You can see them there still, stretching and dancing in front of the big picture windows that overlook the street.

Two of Catherine's teachers there were Debra Zalkind and Diana Laurenson, both of whom have had great success on the Broadway stage. Both teachers thought Catherine had real talent and eventually would have achieved her dream of dancing on Broadway. In fact, Debra Zalkind, a native New Yorker who danced in *Hair* for Twyla Tharp, said she was surprised that Catherine had not already gotten a show.

"She could pick up a combination very fast and turn them into more of a performance," Zalkind said. "I thought she was very professional. I just thought it was just a matter of time that she was gonna come and tell me she got a show."

It's one thing to say that after a tragedy, when everyone is programmed to say something nice, but Diana Laurenson, a veteran Bob Fosse dancer who rules her classes with a no-nonsense style, told Catherine personally, just days *before* her murder, that she had what it took to make it.

"It was the Tuesday before Thanksgiving," Laurenson remembered. "I had actually run up to Catherine after class and asked to speak with her because she stood out in my class. She was a lovely young girl, strikingly, strikingly beautiful, really. And I had pointed her out to a couple of other kids in my class and talked about her.

"I ran up to her and I just wanted to speak with her for a couple of minutes about her plans, whether she was following the right lines of study. Was she taking her ballet classes, and how were her voice classes going? I knew auditions would be coming up. I just wanted to check in with her and ask her how her package was coming together. She assured me everything was going fine. She was working hard.

"And I let her know that she stood out in my class. And if Mr. Fosse were still alive, she probably would have been hired very quickly by him, had she had the chance to ever go and audition for him.

"She had a terrific sense of performance. She had a beautiful look and a great deal of talent. She really did. My class is about performance. She had a sparkle about her. She had an acting base. She brought a life to her dance. She had just something special that set her above the rest of the crowd."

It was the last time Laurenson ever saw Catherine, but she said she takes comfort now in knowing that Catherine heard that from her, that she had an inkling that all the hard work she was doing was not for naught. "She seemed very hopeful, positive," Laurenson said. "She had told me things were going well with her studies. Asked if she was auditioning, she said yes, things are going fine, you know. Nothing negative, everything positive, everything hopeful, everything good."

The two dance teachers said they knew nothing of Catherine's life as a topless dancer, and if they had, both would have told her to quit. "If she would have ever mentioned she was working in a club I certainly would have advised her to get out of it, just because of the element," Zalkind said. "If I knew she really needed money I could have come up with it. Believe me."

Laurenson said many young women go through what Catherine was experiencing. The teacher sees thousands of girls show up every year with the same dream. They soon come face-to-face with the tough reality of living in the city.

"It's a very tough start-up for a lot of the younger

kids to come in," Laurenson said. "I mean you've got high rent to pay, you have to eat. You're taking classes, which are expensive—very expensive. Your dance classes, your voice classes, your drama classes, your head shots and résumés are extremely expensive to get together. You have to do postcards and mailings, and it's a very high-end business, it sure is. If you don't do all of that, you're not gonna get ahead."

Talent alone will not win out, she said. "You need perseverance, a little luck, lots of talent, and hoping that you're in the right place at the right time. Somebody told me a long time ago, when I was starting. . . . You have to put up with a hundred nos before you get the first yes. So count to one hundred at least. And just keep going. It's very difficult, and many people drop out before ninety-nine. There're many talented people that just drop by the wayside before they get their yes. And I tell my kids just keep trying."

Catherine, she said, was still trying. "She was doing fine. As far as I knew she was doing great."

Laurenson said young dancers are forced to take what are known as "survival jobs" in the community, jobs that pay the rent and put food on the table. "Whether you wait on tables, whether you work in a club, whether you work at a catering office or a temp joint, it doesn't affect who you are, except perhaps to add to your life experience. But it certainly doesn't negate who you are or turn you into some kind of monster. It's a job. You pay the bills. That's all."

Like Zalkind, Laurenson said that had she known

Catherine was dancing topless, she would have guided her to a less dangerous job.

Both teachers said they were devastated by how the newspapers were portraying Catherine. "It makes me just so angry," Zalkind said, "because she really was not a stripper. She was a beautiful gal who was studying dance that was looking for a job." Laurenson was adamant that Catherine could not have been using drugs. "Her skin was clear," Laurenson said. She was sure that Catherine could not have kept up her intense practice schedule if she had been abusing her body in any way.

When the Woodses visited the Broadway Dance Center, they spotted a photograph of Catherine on the bulletin board with the words "In Loving Memory." Jon Woods slowly reached out, touched it, looked at the image of his daughter, and then turned away.

Moments later, a young assistant came out to read a letter Diana Laurenson had written to the Woodses. One line stood out: "I still feel a presence of Catherine when I teach class and I think I always will."

Jon and Donna nodded and smiled; they knew what their daughter was really like, but it was still nice to hear.

30

Defending Paul

The Woodses were not the only parents suffering because of Catherine's murder. Paul's mother, Ivette, was living in her own netherworld of emotions. The newspaper stories, with their lurid revelations, had hit her hard, and they'd kept coming for two months straight. But there's no doubt that the worst part for her was Paul's arrest. She'd found out about it when someone called her at four in the morning. It was downhill from there. She said she "never, never" expected Paul to be arrested. "After all those hours in the precinct and everyone being polite and such, and even Paul felt like he was providing valuable information," Ivette said. "He was exhausted, tired, and distraught, but he thought he did the best he could do to help Catherine."

Suddenly, her baby boy, Paul, was being housed in The Tombs, the notorious city jail attached to the downtown criminal court. Although the building has undergone many renovations over the years, it dates back to the nineteenth century, and in decades past, at

Photo of Catherine introduced at trial and shown to Jon Woods, who called it "a perfect representation of my beautiful daughter."

A teenage Catherine Woods. *(Courtesy of Peters Photography)*

Catherine in a red dress. This photo was onstage during
Catherine's memorial service in Ohio. *(Courtesy of Peters Photography)*

Proud parents: Donna and Jon Woods with baby Catherine.
(Courtesy of Jon and Donna Woods)

Jon Woods in his bandleader uniform with daughter
Catherine. *(Courtesy of Jon and Donna Woods)*

Jon and Donna Woods being interviewed after
their daughter's murder by correspondent Erin Moriarty.
(CBS News/48 Hours Mystery)

New York Post headline announcing Paul Cortez's "secret murder diary." The article flatly stated that Paul "admitted his sadistic crime," seemingly convicting Paul a full year before his trial.

First *New York Post* headline the morning after Catherine's murder. Written by staffer Larry Celona, the story was dead-on accurate.

David Haughn *(CBS News/*48 Hours Mystery*)*

David Haughn at the Nineteenth Precinct,
taken by police soon after the murder.

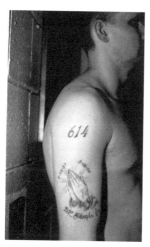
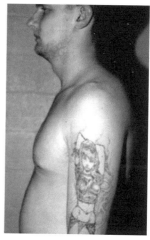

LEFT David at the Nineteenth Precinct soon after Catherine's murder. "614" is the area code of Columbus, Ohio. *(Courtesy of the NYPD)*; RIGHT David Haughn, naked from the waist up, taken by police soon after the murder to determine if he had any cuts or marks on him. None were apparent. *(Courtesy of the NYPD)*

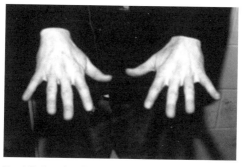

David's hands when police were looking for cuts after the murder. None were found. *(Courtesy of the NYPD)*

Paul Cortez. Paul gave this photo to Catherine as a present. This photo was introduced in court by Paul's lawyers to attempt to prove Paul's relationship with Catherine was serious.

Paul (center) with his brother and sister on Thanksgiving Day, 2005. This photo was introduced by Paul's lawyers to show that Paul was "happy" on this day and not depressed because Catherine had decided not to attend his family's meal.

Paul Cortez in court.
*(CBS News/*48 Hours Mystery*)*

Ivette Cortez, Paul's mother.
*(CBS News/*48 Hours Mystery*)*

RIGHT Catherine's friend Megan Wilkins. *(CBS News/ 48 Hours Mystery)*

LEFT Key witness Spence Lebowitz. *(CBS News/ 48 Hours Mystery)*

RIGHT Paul Cortez's good friend Jaki Levy. *(CBS News/ 48 Hours Mystery)*

Friend Marguerite Shinouda raised money for Paul's defense.
(CBS News/ 48 Hours Mystery)

Dawn Florio, one of Paul Cortez's two lawyers.
(CBS News/ 48 Hours Mystery)

Laura Miranda, Paul Cortez's lawyer.
(CBS News/ 48 Hours Mystery)

Assistant Manhattan District Attorney Peter Casolaro and his "wall of hair." *(CBS News/*48 Hours Mystery*)*

Jon Woods and NYPD detective Steven Goetz outside Catherine's apartment in January 2006 on the day Jon and Donna removed her personal possessions from the murder scene. *(CBS News/*48 Hours Mystery*)*

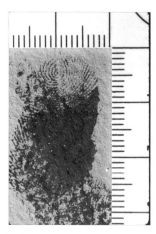

Telltale "bloody" fingerprint found on Catherine's bedroom wall as it appeared after chemicals were applied.

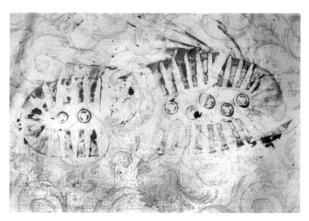

Bloody boot impression left by the killer on a bedsheet in Catherine's room. *(Courtesy of the NYPD)*

Exterior gate leading to Catherine's building.
(Courtesy of the NYPD)

Catherine Woods preforming.
(Courtesy of Jon and Donna Woods)

least fifty souls were lost there, hanged on those very grounds.

Paul had always been a special child, the one who had risen above his working-class roots, but in some ways his arrest had reduced him to just another Latino prisoner in a jail full of them. Paul's mother was determined to get him out of there, but all she could do was find him a great trial lawyer, since there was no bail.

Asked why she thought Paul had been arrested, Ivette didn't hesitate. "Because he loved her," she said, "because he was always there for her. He was always trying to protect her, and everything that he tried to do, they turned it into a negative.

"I didn't really know Catherine, I didn't know what was in her heart," she said. "She had a very complicated life and she was not in a profession that was going to be safe for any young woman. If someone actually abused her in the club itself, who's to say that she wasn't followed home? Who's to say it wasn't the same individual? It just could have been anyone. I can only imagine how many individuals run in and out of those kind of places, and Catherine was so beautiful. I'm sure with her love of dance she must've been something very special, and I'm sure people would have noticed that."

But Ivette could not let her thoughts linger on Catherine. Her focus had to be on her youngest child, whom she desperately wanted to save from a murder conviction. Paul had been charged with murder in the second degree, which carried a sentence of fifteen years to life. He needed a good lawyer. Since his arrest, he'd been represented by a public defender, but Paul's family thought he needed a private lawyer.

The centerpiece of the state's case was Paul's cell phone calls, made just before the murder, and the fingerprint found on Catherine's bedroom wall. Paul felt he could explain the fingerprint, since he said he'd been in Catherine's bedroom many times and perhaps had left it there on a previous occasion. He also had an explanation for those phone calls.

Aside from that incriminating evidence, there were plenty of problems with the state's case, and a fair amount of exculpatory evidence to bolster Paul's claims that he was innocent.

Not a drop of Paul's blood was found in the apartment, even though the place was a bloody mess and even though Catherine had defensive wounds, indicating movements that might have injured her assailant. Not a single strand of Paul's long dark hair was found in the apartment, despite the fact that police said Catherine had fought valiantly for her life. And whose light-colored hair was that in Catherine's bloody left hand? Marguerite Shinouda, the acupuncturist who'd met Paul at a meditation retreat in her home months before Catherine's murder, thought it might be David's. The authorities did not have an answer. The police had not found a pair of Paul's boots that matched the bootprints found in Catherine's bedroom, and no one could recall Paul ever wearing Sketchers boots. Paul did wear a size ten and a half—the size of the boots that had left the impressions—but then, so did David.

And if Paul had committed the crime, how had he gotten out of the apartment building? Not a single witness had come forward to say they'd seen a bloody Paul leaving the apartment.

Still, Paul needed help defending himself. He wanted a lawyer who believed in his innocence. But a private lawyer would cost money, and Paul's family didn't have much. Ivette began checking into how much it would cost to fund Paul's defense with a private criminal lawyer. "They wanted a fifty-thousand-dollar retainer fee," she said, "and that's not including all the fees for the experts and the investigative work and the research that's involved. Then they want another fifty thousand dollars to take it to trial. We're at a loss. As big as our family is, we're trying to scrape out a few dollars here and there, but we can't even make a dent in the bucket."

In the middle of this hopeless situation stepped Marguerite Shinouda. She'd met Paul only a few times but she wanted to help and reached out to Paul's family. "His family are dear, warm, loving people, but they were shell-shocked. They were just stunned," Marguerite said. "They had no skill in knowing what to do, and I'm a very good organizer. I have lots of background in being an organizer and being a go-to girl. I don't know how to do things sometimes, but I just hit the ground running and get things done."

Marguerite's resolve only hardened after she visited

Paul in jail. "I felt in my gut that he was innocent, but I had to see him to be sure, just to be sure," she said. "The first time I went to see him, after he'd been arrested, he kind of disarmed me with his humor that he's never lost in spite of the horrid circumstances.

"He'd had an invitation from a meditation teacher to go to India and meditate in a cave in the Himalayas with him and so, when I saw Paul, I said, 'You know, you should have taken up the offer for the other cave.' And he said, 'Yeah, but this one has indoor plumbing.' "

To Marguerite, it was a defining moment, the fact that he'd retained his humanity when he could easily have been so bitter. She said she was "99.999 percent" sure of Paul's innocence but had to ask him the question. Paul responded with a story about his public defender. "He said his public defender had spent hours and hours trying to convince Paul to take a plea bargain, and he kept telling his attorney, 'I'm innocent.' He says, 'Yeah, yeah, but if you go to court and you get a guilty verdict, you'll spend twenty-five to life so take a plea, just take a plea.' And finally, after three of four hours of the attorney trying to convince him to take a plea, Paul finally found the resolve inside of himself and he just said, 'I will tell the truth and God will do as he wills. I did not kill Catherine.'

"When he repeated that story to me, it had that absolute conviction. I know it was the absolute truth," she said.

Marguerite put together a website to help defend Paul against the newspaper reports and to raise money for his defense. A lot of Paul's friends were willing to help but wanted to be reassured of his innocence, because they'd been getting all of their information from the tabloids. "I spent a lot of time in those first few months calling everybody and telling them what was happening," she said. "I had to tell the same stories over and over and over again. Everybody was in the same ballpark of 'I know, I know, I know he's innocent, but can you tell me some evidence that he is?'

"My phone records showed like five thousand minutes a month of reaching out to Paul's friends and family and telling the same story over and over—'He's still the Paul that you know. He's not evasive, he's not distant, he's not numb. He's sad, he's scared for his life, he's lonely. He's grief-stricken, but he's still the Paul that we know.' "

Marguerite, who has a thriving alternative health care practice, said that some of her friends questioned her sanity. Why was she putting her life on hold to help this guy who might be a killer, a guy she'd known for only a few months? "My friends fall into two camps," she said with typical enthusiasm. "One camp thinks I'm crazy, and the other camp thinks I'm a saint.

"This wasn't something that I planned on. It wasn't like I marked my calendar in December 2005 and said, 'Hmm, find a cause to dedicate your life to,' but when

I saw Paul . . . I don't believe he's an innocent person, I believe he's an extraordinary person!

"He's a special person. You know, he's got some character foibles, so I won't go on and on and say he doesn't, because he is a womanizer and he's stubborn as can be, but he also is warm and generous and insightful. He's helped me many times with personal problems. In his situation, he's given me the best advice anybody has given me, so when I saw him in this predicament, it just called to my heart. There was nothing else I could do.

"I believe in him and I love him and I appreciate who he is as a person, because I know he's innocent."

As she began her search to find Paul a top-notch criminal attorney, Marguerite quickly found herself suffering from sticker shock. "I interviewed fifty lawyers, and in New York City they told me that the average murder defense costs about a hundred to a hundred and fifty thousand dollars. The top, top, top-of-the-line was seven hundred and fifty thousand dollars. That just wasn't going to happen. Paul and I agreed that the most important factor for us was to find a lawyer who believed in his innocence."

As the search progressed, a fellow inmate in The Tombs gave Paul a name: Dawn Florio.

31

Paul's Defense Team

Attorney Dawn Florio is an imposing woman. She stands five feet, ten inches tall and weighs in at a rumored 230 pounds, considerably less than she once weighed. She carries around cans of SlimFast shakes, which she downs whenever she gets a hunger pang. Florio is big and colorful, with bleached blond hair and loud dress suits that are often the talk of her contemporaries. She also wears colored contact lenses that turn her eyes a lovely shade of green. There is nothing quiet about the superconfident attorney, not her car, a luxury red convertible, nor her shoes, which at times are pink mules. But loud people attract attention, and Florio had certainly garnered her fair share.

In September 2005, not long before Catherine Woods's murder, the then-forty-three-year-old Florio was allegedly caught passing steroids and other contraband to a jailed client at The Tombs. She was arraigned on a ten-count indictment in April 2006 on drug sale charges. According to the indictment, Florio passed an alleged gang leader a manila envelope under a table. A corrections officer claims he spotted Florio pushing the envelope to the inmate with her foot. The officer seized the envelope, which allegedly contained two bags, one with ninety-eight blue pills, the other with ninety-five yellow pills. There was also a piece of tissue paper containing one hundred pink pills.

As of February 2008, Florio had still not been tried for the offenses, but if convicted, she could lose her law license. The case was pending as this book went to press.

It's unclear how much of Florio's past troubles Paul knew about when he first met and interviewed her in The Tombs. As time went on, he found out she was in some legal trouble, but it didn't matter. He liked her, and at the time, Florio was sharing an impressive office in the Empire State Building with another lawyer named Laura Miranda, a graduate of Cornell University and an amateur boxer. The two lawyers are an odd sight when together. Florio is big, and Miranda is not. But Miranda is instantly likable and full of fire, and she believed in Paul from the moment she met him. Like Paul, Miranda is Puerto Rican, and felt an instant bond with him.

She said the first time she ever spoke to Paul at The Tombs, she went into a room with him alone and "I never felt uncomfortable. He seems like the gentlest soul out of all the people accused that I've ever defended.

"This case really calls for justice," Miranda said. "We heard everything on the news, and the press had basically tried and convicted him. We met with his mother and then with him, and then I sent him a letter and I said that in the seventeen years I've been practicing as a criminal defense attorney, it is the most peaceful interview that I've ever had. He has just this Zen-like presence about him that I can't even imagine. Dawn felt the same way. How could somebody like this have committed such a vicious crime? It's just not in his character. He's a very sensitive guy. He's very gentle, and we enjoy being with him."

Florio also believed in Paul, but she admitted that it felt like a burden to represent someone she truly thought was innocent. "Sometimes I'd rather not know, because then it puts so much pressure on you if the person is really innocent," she said. "You're like, 'Oh my God, I have to win this case because this person really is innocent.'"

Marguerite Shinouda met the two lawyers and agreed with Paul's assessment: "Laura and Dawn both spoke with Paul at length, and Laura sent a beautiful letter saying, 'That was the most peaceful interview with an inmate I have ever had. I walked out of there feeling like I had just walked out of church because you uplifted me and inspired me. If you choose me as your attorney, I will fight to my utmost to prove your innocence.'"

With the money Paul's family and Marguerite were raising and borrowing, they had barely enough to hire the two women, but somehow they did it. The idea that Paul, at trial, was going to be sandwiched between two women was a side benefit, but an important one. "I think it says that we're not scared of him, that we believe in him," Florio said.

Florio and Miranda told Paul that they had sympathy for the way Catherine had died, and the viciousness of it proved to them that he could not have been the killer. He insisted that they not drag Catherine's reputation through the mud, the way the newspapers had. "Paul doesn't want us to say one bad thing about Catherine," Florio said.

The lawyers claimed that the cops, despite intense investigations, had not found any women from Paul's past whom he had assaulted. That is not quite true, of course, if you believe Monica's story that Paul sexually assaulted her. But Monica's story was muddled because the sex had begun as consensual and because she had not come forward for a year. She was never called to the stand, no doubt because of those very problems.

Florio and Miranda liked to point to the way Paul behaved after a girlfriend from college had slept with his best friend. He was upset but never violent, and he and the woman had remained friends. There was not one reliable witness to say Paul had raised a hand to Catherine, either, and despite what she told some people about him being crazy and obsessed, "at no time does she go to the police, does she make a report that says, 'Listen, I'm being stalked. I'm scared of this guy.' Never does she get an order of protection," said Florio. "So if she was really that scared or that frightened, she would have reached out to someone, and she didn't."

In fact, on the night of her murder, Catherine and David left the front door of their apartment unlocked.

Paul's trial was put off for an entire year, but it was set to begin in late January 2007. Florio and Miranda promised one thing—Paul would take the stand. They wanted the jury to see the real Paul, the way they saw him. As Laura Miranda said, "I've never met anyone like Paul, and the jury needs to actually see him and feel his persona and hear what he had to say. I think Paul's gonna blow them away because he's that compelling. He's that compassionate. He's so peaceful that, when the jury sees him, they're gonna be like, 'This guy could never do it.' "

32

48 Hours Mystery

Behind the scenes, producer Patti Aronofsky and correspondent Erin Moriarty had been working nonstop on the ill-fated love story of Paul and Catherine. With the trial a year away, the decision was made by *48 Hours* executive producer Susan Zirinsky that the interviews and material they'd gathered would run an hour before the trial, and on May 6, 2006, a *48 Hours Mystery* aired with the title "The Last Dance."

True to the their word, the Woodses participated, as did David Haughn, Ivette Cortez, and various friends of Paul's, including his bandmates. The person who refused all requests for an interview was Paul Cortez. It was the prudent thing to do. Surely the authorities would be watching the broadcast to pick up any information they'd missed.

And they *had* missed something.

The police, for whatever reason, had neglected to interview Paul's bandmates—and that was a big mistake. Alex Rude and the others knew something about

Paul's so-called diaries that the cops did not—Paul's journals were in fact part diary, part songbook. Many of the words the cops had thought were diary entries were actually *song lyrics*!

Paul would try out new lyrics and write and rewrite them until they became a song. Members of Paul's band knew about the book the police had called a diary—a red satin journal, bought for Paul by his mother. "It's not a diary, it's where he wrote his lyrics," said Alex Rude. "He had it there every day. That's where he would read from or write into whenever he had an idea."

Alex thought it was "pretty stupid" that lyrics to a song could be used against Paul, not only in the newspaper but in a criminal case as well. "How many bands do we have on the planet who write about killing, murdering, raping?" he asked. "What should we do with them all, throw them in jail? . . . I know better than the police about that book."

One of Paul's songs noted that "the swan is gone," a clear reference to Catherine, and written, according to Alex, after her death. And so what? Alex said. "The best lyrics anyone writes usually come from personal experience somehow," he said. "You lose someone close to you, a lot of people are going to write about those situations. It was kind of a melancholy thing, and he was singing about Catherine and his part in it. I think that at that point he was calling the song 'witch hunt.' That really sums up how he felt about the whole situation and what it means. Somebody he cared for is gone and they're still persecuting him, trying to nail him for this. That's really what it's about."

For his part, Paul was angry because the authorities were picking apart his writing, choosing lyrics that suited their purposes. "They took thirteen different excerpts from twenty-five diaries, each of which are two hundred and fifty pages long," he said. "Some of those writings are from five years ago."

But the cops were adamant; they thought the writings went to the very heart of the case. As one detective told the *Post,* "He's so nuts. It's three weeks after the murder and he's still got a diary in his apartment talking about the murder beforehand, and then talking about how bad he feels afterward—using her name."

Alex thought it was the cops who were nuts for leaning so heavily on song lyrics. "In the paper it said, 'This guy's crazy for leaving evidence around,'" Alex said. "Well, he's not crazy if it's not evidence."

Alex was genuinely shocked that detectives had not questioned him and the other members of Monolith. "They haven't talked to us," he said.

Moriarty pounced: "What does that say to you about the investigation?"

"It's shoddy, at best," Alex said.

"You're concerned because if police haven't talked to you then they may not have investigated enough?" Moriarty asked.

Alex was angry: "They should have talked to us days after this happened."

Why? Because at 6:00 p.m. on the night of November 27, 2005—almost the exact time Catherine was murdered—Paul was expected to be at a band rehearsal but had not shown up.

"Are you troubled," Moriarty asked, "that he didn't come to practice that night?"

"Of course," Alex said. "If he had come there would be no problem. We'd all vouch for him. It would have been no problem."

"He would have an alibi," Ilya said.

"There'd be no charges," Alex continued. "He would have been a hundred blocks away."

When Paul did not turn up—a move that was uncharacteristic, according to Alex—the guitarist phoned him at eight o'clock and asked where he was. Paul told him he'd overslept. Alex accepted his excuse, but he wasn't happy. Paul's performance the night before Thanksgiving had been terrible, and Alex and the others had planned to confront him, to tell him he was out of the band. They never got that chance because of everything that happened in the days following Catherine's murder.

Later, when newspaper reports surfaced that quoted Paul as saying he had been calling Catherine between six and seven o'clock on the night of the murder, Alex decided to confront Paul. "A week or two later, I told him things were getting a little weird. I was like, 'Dude, if you were asleep, how were you calling?'" Alex asked Paul. "He's like, 'I didn't tell you that night I was calling her, because I knew you'd be mad that I didn't come down to rehearsal.' " Alex accepted that story. "That's absolutely true. I'd be pissed off and especially since he was calling his ex-girlfriend," he said.

When Assistant District Attorney Peter Casolaro saw the *48 Hours* interview, he told detectives to go out and interview Alex. Casolaro needed Alex for the upcoming trial to corroborate the fact that, when it suited Paul's best interests, he was willing to lie.

If there's one thing that juries hate, it's a liar.

PART III

THE TRIAL

I feel that we're her voice. I feel a responsibility to represent her and do that in a way that would be consistent with her values, because she's not here to do it for herself.

Donna Woods

33

Jury Selection

By the time Sunday, January 21, 2007, turned up on the calendar, Jon and Donna Woods had gone through every conceivable emotion and had steeled themselves for the murder trial that was now at hand. Jury selection would begin the following day, and the Woodses feared the unknown. "I don't know what is going to transpire in a trial like this, what questions will be raised, what accusations may be made," Jon said. "I loved my daughter. I don't want to be defensive about her. I think she was a wonderful person and she did the best she could with her life."

The Woodses' stay in New York would be much easier than anticipated thanks to an anonymous financial angel. The couple had been worried about the cost of staying in the city for the trial's duration, but that was taken care of when a certain New York sports owner with strong ties to Ohio—a man known for being cantankerous—stepped forward with a very generous offer. He would pick up the tab for the Woodses' stay and arrange for them to have a suite at the New

York Regency Hotel, on Sixty-first Street and Park Avenue. What's more, he'd pay for a driver and a bodyguard. It was a wonderful offer that they readily accepted.

To ease the couple's mind the day before the trial, correspondent Erin Moriarty invited the Woodses to watch the Super Bowl with her. The Woodses, who of course loved football, seemed to lose themselves in the game as they watched Peyton Manning of the Indianapolis Colts win his first Super Bowl. On the surface at least, they seemed to have a good time and appeared to relax.

That would all change the next day, however, because of an unexpected surprise. As the eleventh-floor courtroom of Judge Carol Berkman filled with lawyers, reporters, and the Woods and Cortez families, two people were conspicuously missing: Paul's lawyers, Dawn Florio and Laura Miranda. Everyone waited, with no sign of the defense. Judge Berkman fumed. The previous Friday, Miranda had implored the judge for a delay and more time, which the judge rejected. "I'll have her arrested," the judge declared.

At 11:00 a.m., Miranda faxed a letter to the judge's chambers. She was in Puerto Rico because of a serious illness that had befallen her mother. Florio was missing because of a relative's funeral. "I'm supposed to believe this?" the judge asked. She fined Miranda a thousand dollars and charged her with contempt.

The delay upset everyone—even Paul. He was

forced to sit and wait the entire day in a dingy holding cell behind the courtroom, eating nothing but peanut butter sandwiches.

For the families, the delay was excruciating. Here they were, all geared up after fourteen long months, and now they were left with nothing but their thoughts. At one point, Ivette Cortez approached Jon and Donna Woods, but a court officer intervened. The Woodses were upset with Ivette because of a letter she'd written to them expressing her sorrow for Catherine's death but also making it clear that she felt the Woodses should have brought Catherine home after she was attacked at the topless club in April 2005. Ivette was very sympathetic to them, but the Woodses did not want to hear any more from her. "I understand," Ivette said.

Laura Miranda's absence lasted three days, but finally, on Thursday, jury selection began. It took only two days to seat a jury. Opening statements were set for Monday morning.

34

Mane Man

The prosecutor who would try the case for "the people of the city of New York" was Assistant District Attorney Peter Casolaro, a senior trial lawyer in the Manhattan District Attorney's office and the go-to guy for his boss, Nancy Ryan, head of the Trial Division. Over the years, Casolaro, a "lifer" in the DA's office, had handled an impressive array of high-profile cases, including the infamous Joel Steinberg case. Steinberg had brutalized his live-in girlfriend, Hedda Nussbaum, the star witness against him, and was convicted of first-degree manslaughter for beating his young daughter, Lisa, to death. It was a case fraught with issues, including much of the public's disdain for Nussbaum, who had done very little to save Lisa. That trial had been televised, and viewers all over the country were mesmerized by Nussbaum's severely disfigured face. Somehow, Casolaro tiptoed through all those issues and won a conviction.

But when you ask anyone about Casolaro, the first thing mentioned is his hair. The fiftysomething Casolaro is in love with his thick mane of salt-and-pepper hair and always sports a towering pompadour, the type in style before the Beatles arrived on our shores. "He uses hairspray to hold it together. It's a bit strange," said someone who knows him.

Married to a former public-relations official for the Manhattan District Attorney's office, Casolaro is known for being quirky, and apparently revels in it. While he has his detractors, most speak highly of him. "He's friendly and has a sense of humor and likes to shoot the breeze," said one courthouse veteran.

The Woodses thought the world of him, feeling he was warm and concerned and as inclusive as he could be. The bottom line: To those who like him and those who don't, he's known as a good lawyer.

In the courtroom, Casolaro has a straight-ahead style that possesses all the subtlety of a freight train. He is very confident and barges through almost any argument defense lawyers care to put up. He is no-nonsense, well prepared, and not above an occasional sarcastic aside, especially if it comes at the expense of the person on trial. And one more thing that surely endears him to the enigmatic Robert Morgenthau, the longtime Manhattan district attorney—Casolaro does not give interviews to the press.

On January 29, 2007, Casolaro stood before the jury of eight women and four men and began the case by telling them Catherine Woods's life story. She was, Casolaro said, "a young woman from a suburban section of Columbus, Ohio, with an aspiration to dance on the legitimate stage. She made her way here to New York but like so many others before her, she failed to reach her dream. She was never able to succeed in landing a part in a theater company or in the ballet, but what makes her story uniquely tragic is that rather than losing hope in the dream, she lost her life. Her dreams died on the floor of a small apartment on East Eighty-sixth Street, in a pool of her own blood that flowed from her horribly slashed throat.

"The evidence will show that her life and those dreams ended so horribly not because of any misdeed of her own or any activity that she engaged in but because she was too young and too inexperienced to realize that she would become romantically involved with a twisted and obsessive individual named Paul Cortez, the defendant in this case."

In court, Paul no longer appeared to be the strapping, buff personal trainer "hunk" described in the tabloids. He'd been in jail for a year, at times kept in his cell twenty-three hours a day. There was little chance for exercise or even a chance to see the sun, and he was paler than ever. Sitting at the defense table, he looked meek, mild, and small in stature, even more so sitting next to the much larger Dawn Florio. As Casolaro eviscerated him before the jury, Paul, with his long locks tied back, seemed to get even smaller. He had desperately wanted to get a haircut before trial, but his lawyers would not hear of it. They wanted to make the point that Paul wore his long flowing hair the same way he had on the night of the murder and not a single strand of it had been found in Catherine's apartment.

Casolaro detailed Catherine's routine, how hard she worked out, and the fact that she lived in a tiny apartment. But he knew he had to do more than paint Catherine as a deluded dreamer who had wound up dead. By most standards, even those of New Yorkers, she had led an unusual life, and Casolaro had to make her choices understandable to the jury.

As he knew he must, Casolaro addressed the issue of how Catherine had chosen to make money. "Now, not wanting to financially ruin her parents, who would have the burden of supporting her, she turned in desperation to the most degrading form of dance that exists in our city, and that is what we euphemistically call stripping. There, she made enough money to support herself. However humiliated by her decision to do it, as she properly should have been, she concealed her work from her parents, and all the while she kept trying to find a part on a legitimate stage."

And then it came time to introduce the fact that Catherine had had a male roommate, an on-again, off-again lover. Casolaro knew that when David Haughn took the stand, his persona would not square so easily with the way the DA was building up Catherine. Many people, including her own parents, had wondered why Catherine and David were together, and Casolaro knew jurors would have those same questions: What was this beautiful, vibrant woman doing with a guy like David?

Luckily, David, who would later be called as a witness, was not in the courtroom to hear Casolaro describe him as "a little slow, not very articulate, and kind of lacking in the work ethic and the drive to succeed that Catherine had.

"You'll see that David Haughn is very young, very inexperienced, and very naïve."

But, said Casolaro, Catherine loved David because he treated her in "a simple and kindly way." All in all, the prosecutor's description would not have been different if he'd been describing a nice pet Catherine kept around the apartment.

When it came time to describe Paul, Casolaro painted a vivid picture. He wanted jurors to have a strong image in their minds, and the one Casolaro chose seemed to be modeled after Travis Bickle, Robert De Niro's character in the film *Taxi Driver,* who fell in love with and wanted to save the teenage prostitute played by Jodie Foster. "One thing is clear from the evidence," Casolaro said, and that would be "that the defendant became obsessed with Catherine Woods. For whatever reason, he came to believe that she was the one true love of his life.

"The evidence will show that he would telephone her every day, at all hours of the day and night—two, three, four, five o'clock in the morning—and that he would call her sometimes twenty, thirty, forty times a day. And that if he didn't get her on the telephone, he would call her every minute, eight, nine, ten, twelve minutes in a row. Call after call . . . in late November 2005, Catherine Woods had enough of Paul Cortez's obsession. Especially after she discovered him searching through her cell phone, through her telephone book in her cell phone, finding out all the people she knew and all the people she called, so he could see if she was dating any other men.

"The defendant now came face-to-face with his failure. He wasn't going to possess Catherine Woods. She was going to get rid of him, and the object of his desire would be lost forever to him. The evidence will show that he then began to turn against her.

"His internal rage grew, and unfortunately for Catherine Woods, she was the woman on whom his thoughts of violence turned to action. The evidence is going to show that frustrated and angry at his failure to possess her, the defendant came to the selfish and completely unoriginal conclusion that if he could not possess her, no one would."

On the night of November 27, 2005, Casolaro said that Paul's obsession and rage had reached their zenith, and after watching David leave Catherine's apartment, Paul "rushed inside. He entered through an unlocked door to their apartment. It was not their practice to lock their door, unfortunately, and he trapped Catherine in the bedroom. Now, it's impossible to say at this point if there was any conversation between them, but the evidence is definitive that he attacked her with a knife and, in an absolutely savage fashion, inflicted over twenty wounds on her, including virtually tearing her throat apart with multiple slashes and stab wounds.

"By 6:25 or so, he had killed Catherine Woods and then, just as stealthily as he entered the apartment, he was successfully able to flee it without being seen."

Casolaro warned the jury that there would be no eyewitness to testify that he had seen Paul with a bloody knife, nor would there be any witnesses who said that Paul had confessed to them. Casolaro made Paul out to be something of a master criminal who had nearly gotten away with murder. "Despite his obvious intelligence, which is much greater than David's, for example, and certainly much greater than Catherine's was, he fortunately made several critical mistakes which brought him here today."

In brief, Casolaro ticked off the building blocks of his case: the cell phone calls made from nearby Catherine's apartment, the "bloody fingerprint," and Paul's "own private writings."

With that, the prosecutor sat down and settled in to hear the defense opening statement, which was given by Dawn Florio.

35

He's an Artist

Dawn Florio had barely risen from her seat when she made the jury a promise: They would hear directly from murder defendant Paul Cortez. "He'll stand up, swear to tell the truth, and he's going to tell you that he did not kill Catherine Woods and he loved Catherine Woods and Catherine Woods loved him," she said.

Juries always want to hear from the person on trial, and Florio was going to grant their wish. After all, the defense team felt that the charismatic Paul was their ace in the hole. If they could get the jury to see him the way they did—as a peace-loving person who lived his life according to the precepts of the Hindu religion— they felt they would win an acquittal. Certainly, no one as calm and grounded as Paul would erupt in rage the way the prosecutor said the killer had. Florio wanted the jurors to believe that the prosecutor's scenario was inconceivable, just as it was to most of Paul's family and friends.

The defense pointed the finger of guilt directly at

David Haughn, who in many ways was the opposite of Paul—he was edgy, uncomfortable in social situations, and appeared to have something to hide. His eyes darted around in his head and he had a slight ghetto cadence to the way he spoke. Florio thought he looked like a poor man's Eminem. If the defense could get the jury to consider David as the potential murderer of Catherine, they'd have all the reasonable doubt they'd need. Florio pointed out that David had much more of a motive than Paul. He lived with Catherine, and yet she was dating other men. It was a biblical motive—jealousy.

But Florio had to counter the portrayal of Paul that Casolaro had painted. "The evidence, ladies and gentlemen, in this case will show that there was a love story going on between Catherine Woods and Paul Cortez," she said. "They were both young, so beautiful, talented; they were talented artists who came to New York City to fulfill their dreams.

"Who is Paul Cortez? The evidence will show that he's not twisted; maybe he's gifted, he's artistic, he's very intelligent. He's a very, very peaceful person, a nonviolent person, the evidence will show, and he's a very, very determined person."

Florio went on to describe Paul's impressive background and education. She hoped the jury would see Paul as she did—a working-class hero who had overcome his life circumstances to chase his dream. Catherine, by contrast, had been born with a silver spoon in her mouth.

She told the jury the story that when Catherine was in her most dire hour—after she'd been drugged, molested, and possibly raped at the club Privilege—she'd turned for help not to David or her parents but to Paul. And yes, Paul had gone behind her back and called her father to tell him what Catherine was up to, but that was a good thing. He'd only done it because he cared for her and wanted her to get away from a lifestyle that had already proven to be dangerous. Paul had called Jon Woods that day, Florio said, for no other reason than "out of concern and love for Catherine, not some obsessive behavior on his part.

"The evidence will also reveal that the kind of relationship that Paul Cortez had with Catherine Woods was the kind of relationship that was up and down, up and down, like a roller coaster. They loved each other to death," Florio said.

Some reporters snickered and made sure to write that quote down, but Florio did not acknowledge the verbal gaffe.

She went on to attack David Haughn over and over again, calling him "a mooch" who was living off Catherine. "He also stayed at home and didn't contribute," she said. "You could see the apartment was totally a mess, and it was never cleaned up. It was very, very filthy, and he basically stayed in the house all day and smoked pot."

David had admitted that he and Catherine had had sex not long before she was murdered, but Florio raised the possibility that it was not consensual. After all, some neighbors had heard furniture being moved about and some screams at a time when David may have been in the apartment. "David may have forced her," the lawyer said. "You will also hear that when David came back and found Catherine, who he referred to as 'baby girl'—and you'll hear the 911 call—that he didn't sound upset. He didn't sound devastated. He was monotone, and he really took his time. He was not excited—no emotion. He didn't cry, even when David Haughn was being interviewed by the police, not one tear. You'll hear the testimony through the detectives that when Paul Cortez was interviewed, he bawled like a baby.

"You'll also hear that Catherine was found clutching hair, and that there was a struggle going on. You should pay careful attention to all the details going on in the case. She was clutching hair. She has brown hair. David Haughn has blond hair."

Florio emphasized how much Paul had cooperated with police the day after the murder, when he allowed them to take his DNA, gave them a footprint, and let them look at his hands and arms, which, she told the jury, "had no cuts.

"The evidence will show that it was impossible for Paul Cortez to have committed this brutal, bloody, horrendous murder, and clean up. Because the evidence will show that at no time is there any blood spattering or blood coming out to the hall. Someone had to take their shoes off or clean them off very, very carefully, and all that took time. The evidence will show that

Paul Cortez could not have committed that crime in that time frame, that it was impossible."

And with that, Dawn Florio sat down. Both lawyers had made some good points, and as with most trials, the jury was being pulled in opposite directions by compelling arguments for guilt and innocence. Paul was either an obsessive nut or a loving boyfriend, depending on whom you cared to believe.

But Casolaro wasn't about to have the jurors sit and think too much at that moment. He decided he was going for the emotional punch.

The first witness would be Jon Woods.

Jon looked wary as he began answering questions from Casolaro about his family situation and what he did for a living. He appeared a bit nervous, and Casolaro had to tell him to move back, away from the microphone. Jon described his daughter Catherine and her passion for dance and was doing pretty well until the assistant district attorney asked how he came to know that his loving daughter was dead. As Jon began to describe that horrible night, he choked up. Casolaro had succeeded in getting the jury to feel the human side of Catherine's murder, and that, after all, was the whole point.

In his last question, the assistant district attorney introduced a lovely photograph of Catherine and asked Jon Woods if it fairly and accurately depicted Catherine. Jon answered, "It's a perfect representation of my beautiful daughter."

Attorney Laura Miranda took over the cross-examination and she concentrated on the April 2005 phone call that Paul had made to Jon, when Paul had told Catherine's father about the attack at Privilege. Jon had already recounted the incident on direct examination, but now Miranda wanted to know what Jon had thought of Paul that day when he called. "I was very impressed with what he had to say, and we had a pleasant conversation," Jon said. "I thanked him. He seemed to be a very educated person and sincere and interested, and what I heard, I appreciated the call and thanked him."

It was a point in the defense's favor. Here was the bereaved father of the murder victim saying positive things about the man on trial for killing his daughter.

If even her father thought Paul was impressive, well . . .

36

That Fingerprint

After Jon Woods's testimony, the trial moved into a more tedious yet important phase. Prosecutor Casolaro called Detective John Entenmann of the NYPD Crime Scene Unit to the stand to discuss how he collected the evidence—the bootprints on the bedsheet and Catherine's shirt, the hairs in her left hand, and the crucial "blood-pattern transfer" on Catherine's bedroom wall. "The blood-pattern transfer," Entenmann explained, was what he recognized to be a handprint. That handprint went to the heart of the case because that was where fingerprint experts would later discover a print that matched the left index finger of Paul Cortez.

The more Entenmann testified, the more muddled things became until it was unclear what exactly Entenmann saw on that wall that caused him to have the wall preserved. His testimony got bogged down over the terminology of blood-transfer patterns, *handprints*, *latent prints* and *patent prints*. He testified that the only latent, or invisible, print he lifted in the entire apartment was the one found on the broken guitar next to

Catherine (a print that did not match any of the principals and was not pertinent to the case). Entenmann did not pull any prints from the wall where he saw the blood-transfer, latent (invisible) or patent (visible).

In her cross-examination, Attorney Florio tried, painfully, to clear things up: "[Aside from the latent print on the guitar] you didn't process any prints with respect to any other prints in the apartment, correct?"

"I don't understand the question," Entenmann said.

"Well, did you ever write down in your report that on the north wall there was a latent print?"

"I didn't specifically refer to it as a latent print," Entenmann said. "I referred to it as a hand transfer, which in blood-pattern analysis would be a blood-pattern transfer, which was a hand transfer."

Florio pressed him: "But in fact, you never referred to it in your report as a latent print, correct?"

"It's not a latent print. It's an actual patent print, but I referred to it as a hand transfer."

Even with the benefit of being able to read the testimony multiple times, this exchange makes just about no sense. One can easily argue that Florio should have done a better job demonstrating the apparent contradictions in Entenmann's testimony. One can only imagine what jurors were thinking.

Translating Entenmann, it seems that he saw a bloody patch on the wall that appeared to him to have been made by a hand. He thought enough of it to have it cut out, but looking at a photograph of what that original blood transfer looked like on the wall, it's not possible to see a defined fingerprint there.

Florio did score some points when she later got Entenmann to admit that "latent prints can last a long time." She was trying to get the jury to understand that if a person touched a wall a week before the murder, it was possible his fingerprint would still be there, even if you could not see it.

Casolaro then called to the stand Alex Chacko, the NYPD forensic scientist. It was Chacko's job to enhance any fingerprints sent his way. The proof that Entenmann did not see any fingerprints around the bloody hand transfer is contained in Chacko's testimony, because after the bloody section of the wall was cut out, it was sent directly to Chacko. He says that when he opened the box and looked at the section of wall, "I did not see any prints."

Entenmann was not recalled to explain this contradiction.

Chacko explained that only after the Sheetrock was treated twice with chemicals did a print become visible. When he could actually see the print, he took a digital photograph of it and then uploaded it to a computer so he could apply special software to it. The software enhanced the print even more.

During cross-examination Florio pressed Chacko on what he did and did not see. "So you're saying when you had received that Sheetrock, that you couldn't see any prints?" she asked.

"No," he said, meaning he had not seen any prints.

It stands to reason that if the left index fingerprint was found near the bloody handprint then it, too, was left in blood. That was what the prosecution was arguing. In fact, the chemical Chacko applied to the invisible print, amido black, reacts with a protein found in blood. But Florio's question was: Did the chemical react with anything other than blood?

"Is it possible that the print enhanced with the amido black was not a bloody print?" she asked.

Casolaro interrupted: "I object to that."

"Sustained," the judge ruled, and then said to Florio, "He just gave his opinion that he thought it was blood."

Florio tried again. "So you did not do any test to confirm the presence of blood in the print, correct?"

"No," said Chacko.

The final fingerprint expert to testify was Annabelle Branigan, who compared the enhanced photograph made by Chacko with Paul's inked fingerprints. She said that at least ten unique characteristics matched, and that she had run it by a supervisor, who agreed with her assessment that the print found on the bedroom wall matched Paul's fingerprint.

Florio asked if it was possible for mistakes to be made. "Is it possible that you have ever made a mistake in comparing latent prints?" she asked.

Branigan puffed up and said, "I have never made a mistake in comparing latent prints."

37

Eyewitness?

If Paul did kill Catherine, what did he do with his bloody clothes? Detectives were at his apartment by eleven the next morning and did not see any blood anywhere. They'd examined his ubiquitous leather jacket, but it was clean, or almost clean. A police source claimed that the jacket did have a single tiny drop of female blood but that was not introduced at trial. To help answer this question or at least give the jury something to think about, Assistant District Attorney Casolaro called to the stand Jacques Szwarcbart, a neighbor of Paul's in the building on East 106th Street.

Jacques is a saxophonist and, because of his job, is used to coming home late at night or in the early morning hours. He was playing at a club called the Fat Cat, down in Greenwich Village, on the Thanksgiving weekend of 2005. He'd seen Paul a couple of times before and knew him to live in the building.

"Over that weekend," Casolaro asked, "did you see the person you now know as Paul Cortez?"

"Yes, I did see him."

"When did you see him?"

"I saw him either Sunday morning or Saturday morning, in his underwear, outside the building, dumping some garbage in the cold," Jacques said.

"Do you know for sure which day it was—Saturday into Sunday or Sunday into Monday?"

"I can't say for sure."

"And how far away were you from each other?"

"Well," Jacques said, "we crossed maybe just one yard away from each other because he was right in front of the door, and I needed to go through the door to go back home."

"Now, you say he was in his underwear. Could you describe what articles of clothing did he have on?"

"He just had some boxer shorts and he, to my best recollection, he was barefooted and bare-chested. And that struck my imagination because it was very cold this morning."

Jacques was far from the perfect witness. He could not recall what night he'd allegedly seen Paul dump the garbage and he described Paul as having "very straight" hair, when in fact Paul's hair is very wavy. Still, his testimony probably achieved what Casolaro was hoping—it gave jurors something else to think about. And if Jacques did see Paul, what was he doing dumping garbage in his underwear on a frigid morning?

38

Dozens of Phone Calls

Prosecutor Casolaro next called several employees of different telephone companies to the stand. Phone records, like the fingerprint on the wall, were crucial to his case, and Casolaro spent a considerable amount of time making sure the jury understood the way cell phone calls bounced off specific cell sites nearest to the person making the call. Casolaro showed how Paul's location could be tracked depending on where he was when making a phone call, and it was clear from the testimony that at the time of Catherine's murder, he was in her neighborhood. The experts testified, however, that they could not state exactly where he was standing, just his general location.

But Casolaro had something else in mind—he wanted to show by highlighting the number of phone calls just how many times Paul called Catherine on a particular day. To Casolaro, the sheer volume of calls showed the depth of Paul's obsession.

An employee of T-Mobile noted that on October

19, 2005, fifty-seven phone calls were made from Paul's cell phone to Catherine's. During that same period, she called him three times. A week later, on October 25, 2005, forty-seven phone calls were made from Paul's cell phone to Catherine's, and only seven made from hers to his. On the flip side, Catherine's calls to Paul lasted much longer.

Finally, Casolaro pointed to the calls Paul had made to Catherine on the day of the murder. He called her seventeen times.

"What's the last time that a call is recorded to that number by Mr. Cortez?" Casolaro asked.

"November 27, 2005, at 5:56 p.m.," the witness said.

Catherine was killed somewhere between 6:10 p.m. and 6:50 p.m., and according to Casolaro there were no calls from Paul to Catherine during that time.

However, one call made from Paul's cell phone to Catherine's, recorded at 6:33 p.m., and lasting just one second, became the subject of much argument. While the call appeared on Catherine's list of incoming calls, it did not appear on Paul's list of outgoing calls. The defense considered that call very important because if Paul had killed Catherine or was in the process of killing her, why would he call her? Not surprisingly, for the same reason, the prosecution wanted to discount that call.

Defense Attorney Laura Miranda objected to the introduction of Paul's cell phone bill precisely because that call did not appear.

"I'll explain that, Judge," Casolaro said. "When calls don't connect, they don't appear in the billing records."

Miranda pounced. "So you're stipulating there was a call at 6:33?" she asked.

But Casolaro was cagey. "I'll put it on the record to reflect the call was made. This record reflects that the call didn't connect, Your Honor."

But Miranda objected. "It's our understanding that it does connect and it did connect at 6:33 that day," she said.

"Your Honor," Casolaro said, "their records are their records."

"Well, Judge," Miranda countered, "there were other records as well from this company that demonstrate that there was a connection."

The two sides agreed to disagree and would explain it to the jury later in their closing statements, but that single call would definitely come up again.

Toward the end of the day, a criminalist from the city medical examiner's office testified. She went over the various tests done on material collected from the crime scene. A few important points came out of her testimony:

- No blood in the apartment matched that of Paul Cortez or David Haughn.

- The only thing found under Catherine's nails was her own blood.
- The hairs found in Catherine's hand and sent to the M.E. were returned to the NYPD for further analysis because the M.E.'s office does not do hair analysis.

39

"He Didn't Really Have a Life"

The next day was a Friday and would be one of the most interesting days at trial, though it hardly started out that way. The first witness was a forensic examiner who specialized in footwear impressions. He had examined the bloody bootprints on Catherine's bedsheet and tank top and testified that the prints had to have been made by a Sketchers Cool Cat Bully II boot, size ten and a half, the same size worn by Paul Cortez. It turned out though, that sizes ten and a half and eleven are pretty much the most common sizes in men's shoes, and in fact, David Haughn wore the same size, too. Furthermore, the police had never found a pair of Paul's boots that matched, and he denied having such a pair.

The testimony was more or less uneventful, but then, after a short break, Casolaro stood to announce, "The people call David Haughn."

The courtroom was packed in expectation. David had been interviewed by Erin Moriarty on the *48 Hours Mystery* broadcast in May, but very few people had seen him in person. Everyone was apprehensive to see this guy whom Catherine had chosen to live with and stick by. David was edgy—not at all polished—and it was hard to predict what the jury would make of him. For their part, defense lawyers Dawn Florio and Laura Miranda couldn't wait for him to take the stand. The more suspicion they could divert to David, the better it would be for Paul.

"David is somebody who really didn't have a life," Miranda said. "He was somebody who was living off of Catherine, despite the fact that he was working. And she was upset about that. She was basically saying to him, 'You have to move out.' So I would say he was desperate because, number one, where is he going to move to in New York City that he can afford? And he has no home to go back to."

The idea that Catherine lived with and had David as a boyfriend was astounding to Florio, as it was to a lot of others—including Catherine's parents. Like some of Catherine's friends, they initially wondered if it was David who had killed their daughter.

The outspoken Florio said what everyone was thinking: "What I think is really interesting is Catherine's choice in men. I mean, Paul's refined, educated, and David's like a redneck, you know? I can't even see what Catherine would possibly see in David."

For her part, Miranda thought she understood Catherine's thinking. "He probably did everything for her," she said. "If you look at the time line of that day, she gets up. 'David, I want an apple.' He goes out and buys her an apple. When she says a few hours later, 'David, I'm hungry.' David goes out and buys her food. 'David, can you heat that up for me?' David heats it up. And it's just like, okay, 'David, I want to have sex now but I gotta go to work. Can we make this quick?' So it's like he takes care of her needs."

Twenty-five-year-old David was nervous, as anyone would be testifying at the murder trial of a loved one. From the start, he lived up to his local-yokel billing. Even his answers to the basic questions put to him by Casolaro were clunky. David told the DA that he had a high school education and, when asked his occupation, David answered, "Warehouse."

He went on to explain that he'd met Catherine outside a Columbus pool hall and that he'd been so infatuated he'd moved to New York. He outlined his various part-time jobs—a shoe store, a pet food store—until he secured steady work as a doorman. He explained how he'd met Paul Cortez on that one occasion, when Paul visited the apartment. He was honest about the ups and downs in his and Catherine's relationship.

David moved on to the day of the murder and his description of the murder and his description of the murder scene. The spectators were riveted. "I just remember seeing the walls, seeing the floor," he said. "I had had a house broken into before and it had almost looked like a burglary, how messy things were. Things were just all over the place. And I see Catherine laying on the floor and I just, in my head—I don't know if it's an accident or really what to think—just kind of, just kind of in shock.

"So, you know, my first instinct is to call. There is blood everywhere. I never seen so much blood in my life and I remember calling 911, and I had climbed over the bed to get to where she was. And I remember while I was on the phone with 911 them asking me if I knew CPR. I told them that I didn't and that I didn't know if she was alive or not. And they told me, 'Can you get any movement out of her?' And I don't know if she had a sweater on or what she had on, but I remember I had kind of grabbed like the mid-back of whatever she was wearing and kind of tugged at it to try to get some kind of reaction out of her, and there was no, no reaction at all.

"She was limp, just like laying there, and I was scared to turn her over, and the 911 operator told me not to touch her. And I had told her that, you know, I had tried to wake her or, you know, tried to move her to get a reaction, and I remember climbing back over the bed to go into the living room, still on the phone with 911, and at this point I still didn't know if it was an accident or just I didn't know what happened. I had no clue. And I was climbing over the bed still on the phone, I see a bootprint. And as soon as I seen that, that just, I can't explain, just I remember telling the 911 operator that I had found a bootprint and that I know that somebody did this."

Casolaro led David through the days he spent being interrogated by carious detectives at the Nineteenth

Precinct, each of them trying to break him down, to get him to admit he was the killer.

"Do you know how long you were in the precinct going through this questioning-break-questioning-break sequence?" Casolaro asked.

"I would say at least a day, a day and a half."

"Besides questioning you, did the detectives ask you for anything?"

"Yeah, they brought in—I don't know if it was a DNA person, but somebody who does that type of work, who asked if they could scrape my fingernails, under my fingernails."

"Did you agree to do that?"

"Yeah."

"Did they ask you for anything else?"

"Yes, they asked for fingerprints. They asked for pictures of my hands. . . . They asked if they could take pictures of me with no clothes on, front and back. They did that. I'm not sure what else."

"Did they ask you if they could take your clothes?"

"Yes."

"And did you agree to let then have your clothes?"

"Yes."

"Did they ask if they could search your car?"

"Yes."

"Did you agree to let them search your car?"

"Yes."

"Did they ask if they could search the apartment and your personal things in the apartment?"

"Yes."

"Did you agree to that?"

"Yes."

"Did they ask you for a written statement?"

"Yes."

"Did you agree to that?"

"Yes."

"While you were in there this time, while all of this was going on, did you ever ask for a lawyer?"

"No."

"Did any lawyer try to contact you while you were there?"

"Yeah, but I don't know who they were."

"How many times did lawyers try to contact you?"

"Two or three."

"And did you say you wanted or didn't want a lawyer?"

"I said I didn't need a lawyer."

"Why not?"

"I just didn't feel like I needed one. I felt like I was telling the truth and I felt like that would come out."

David may have been unsophisticated, but at least up until this point, the overall effect was that this was a truthful witness who had nothing to hide. For more than thirty-six hours, he had withstood intense questioning from at least seven of New York's finest detectives—without a lawyer.

But David had yet to be cross-examined.

40

Who's Obsessive?

When it was the defense's turn, Laura Miranda, the little pit bull of the defense team, went on the attack, intent on painting David as a jealous and spurned lover. The implication of course was that David was so angry at Catherine for stepping out on him that he'd killed her in a jealous rage. Miranda suggested that this was the reason David had called Paul at least twice on July 18, 2005.

"Didn't you tell him that he better not be sleeping with your woman?" Miranda asked.

"I don't remember saying that," David replied.

"Well, didn't you threaten him and tell him that he better not see her anymore?"

"I don't remember."

"Well, did you call him to say, 'Hi, how are you doing?' " Miranda asked sarcastically.

"No. I called him to find out why he was calling Catherine's phone."

"Did you know that she called him on July 17th six times? Did she tell you that?" Miranda asked.

"No."

"Did you know that she called him on July 18th as well?"

"No."

"Did you know that she called him on July 19th nine times?"

"No."

"Did you know she called him twice on July 20th?"

"No."

"What about July 21st? She called him thirteen times. Did she tell you that, too?"

"I can't remember," David said. "I just know at some point they were friends, and that was the extent of it that I knew."

"Well, you were concerned that they were sleeping together, right?"

"Not necessarily," David answered.

Miranda attacked David's character repeatedly and got him to admit that he was financially dependent on Catherine. She asked if he'd spent Catherine's money to feed a marijuana habit. He denied it. Again and again, Miranda hammered David with questions intended to show that *he* was the jealous ex-boyfriend.

"Did you know that Catherine was corresponding by e-mail with a gentleman by the name of Joe Cabrera?"

"No. I had no idea."

"And did you know that they had somewhat of a relationship?"

"No," said David. "I didn't know that."

"Weren't you upset that once she started stripping that Catherine would meet someone who had more money than you did?"

"No. I wasn't really upset, but her stripping is not something I wanted her to do, and I felt bad that I didn't have enough money to support us."

"Weren't you concerned not only that you did not like her stripping—weren't you concerned she would meet another guy who had more money than you did?" Miranda asked again.

"No."

Miranda presented David with his statement to police indicating that he had not left Catherine's apartment until 6:39 the night of the murder. If that was true, then he had to have been inside the apartment when neighbor Andrew Gold and others heard Catherine's screams. David said he couldn't remember exactly what he'd told police about the timetable.

It was a formidable cross-examination, and it did make David appear ineffectual and weak. Worse than that, with all of his "I don't remember" answers, David seemed to be hiding something. Some courtroom observers began to wonder if the cops had arrested the wrong boyfriend. "We thought David did it," said one print reporter.

But did the jurors believe that David had been jealous enough to kill the love of his life? The defense needed just one juror to answer yes to that question.

41

Ms. Bucci

As the second week of the trial began, a woman by the name of Stephanie Nicole Bucci was called to the stand. A self-described business consultant, Bucci had the bad luck to have been with Paul Cortez in the hours before Catherine was murdered. Bucci expressed frustration that the trial was dragging her away from her business and taking so much of her time, but a subpoena is a subpoena, and she answered it with her appearance. Bucci was a strikingly attractive woman, reminiscent of Uma Thurman except she was nowhere as tall and not nearly as thin. She'd been a client of Paul's at the Equinox fitness club on East Eighty-fifth Street where the two of them had spent hours talking about their personal relationships.

Paul had trained Bucci for two one-hour sessions a week for six weeks, so she'd heard plenty about Catherine Woods. Bucci described Paul as a "nice guy" who was having some "issues" with his girlfriend.

"Could you tell us what these issues were as he related them to you?" Casolaro asked.

"Mostly that, you know, she was a problematic girlfriend in the sense that she was partaking of activities that he didn't agree with, that hurt his feelings," Bucci said. "He had mentioned to me that she was really into pornography and making pornographic movies."

Jon and Donna Woods tried not to react to any of the harsh comments made about their beloved daughter throughout the trial, but it wasn't easy. Each day, her name and reputation were dragged a little further into the mud. And now the idea that Catherine had been involved in pornography was being tossed around publicly, even though there was not a shred of evidence that it was true. No pornography featuring her or anyone else was found in her apartment and no one has ever come forward with nude photos or videos of her.

Bucci said that while training with Paul, she tried to lend a sympathetic ear. During Thanksgiving week, she said, Paul seemed "upset as usual."

She had never met him outside the health club, but on this occasion she told him she'd be around if he wanted to talk on the weekend. She suggested they get together on the Sunday following Thanksgiving. Sure enough, Paul took her up on her offer and called her. Of course, it was the same time he'd been trying to get in touch with Catherine, who was out with her friend Christina Dupont. Bucci agreed to meet with Paul but told him she had a bunch of errands to run and, if he wanted, he could accompany her. He agreed. Bucci was an important witness because she was able to offer her assessment of Paul's mood on the day of the murder and, not insignificantly, what he was wearing.

The two of them met on East Eighty-sixth Street and Third Avenue. They began walking east toward P.C. Richard, an electronics and appliance store, where Bucci wanted to buy a humidifier. Paul was excited and went on and on about a thirty-six-page epic poem he'd finished writing that morning, a copy of which he gave to Bucci.

"I have a strong background in literature, and he had hoped that I would sit down and review the poetry with him," Bucci said. "I just didn't want to do it," she said. "I didn't have the time. I had my own agenda."

"Do you recall how Mr. Cortez was dressed that day?" Casolaro asked.

"He had on a leather coat, and I know—I don't think it was a collared shirt. I don't really remember the pants, but I know he had on a leather coat."

In answer to questions, Bucci said the two next went into a nearby Food Emporium supermarket, where Paul's cell phone rang. "I don't know to whom he was speaking," Bucci said, "but on his end, he said, 'Hey, I'm in Food Emporium and I'm in the fresh fruit section. And I'm, you know, with this, you know, beautiful blond thirty-six-year-old professional woman. And I'm going to buy—we're going to buy strawberries.

I'm going to take them home and put them all over her body and lick them off.'

"I got very upset over it," Bucci said. "I turned right around to him. I said, 'Excuse me,' I said, 'Paul, you don't say that kind of stuff.' And I got upset. And I could tell that—you know, I chastised him, for he was totally inappropriate and it made me feel very uncomfortable."

She may have been upset, but the two of them stayed together and continued running her errands, next going into a Barnes and Noble. By 4:10 p.m., Bucci said she was back in her apartment, but she spoke to Paul again later, sometime around six o' clock, at which point Paul again apologized for his behavior in the grocery store and told her he was enjoying a book she'd bought for him.

When Laura Miranda began her cross-examination, she immediately questioned Bucci about the strawberry incident and what had happened afterward. "And isn't it a fact that you purchased a book for him in Barnes and Noble?"

"Yeah, I did."

"And isn't it somewhat of an erotic book that you purchased for him in Barnes and Noble?"

The book was *Little Birds,* by Anaïs Nin, well known as a writer of literary erotica; this book is one of her classics. It is a collection of thirteen short stories, and the title short story concerns a male adult who enjoys exposing himself to young girls, or "little birds." In the introduction, Nin writes, "These are my adventures in that world of prostitution."

Miranda pressed on: "And those are erotic stories, basically?"

"Yeah, and they're beautiful stories, and the context was, 'You should read them and then pick up the French version.'"

"This was after Paul had said to someone on the phone that he was going to cover your body with strawberries and lick them off and you thought that was inappropriate, correct?"

"I thought it was very inappropriate, and that's why I bought him the book. I said, 'You need to read the book so you don't do things like put people on the spot. Deal with your issues in private.'"

Bucci was hostile to Miranda, and this attitude came out when she asked Bucci how she had learned that Catherine had been murdered.

"He [Paul] called me and he said, 'This girl was dead.' And I said, 'Well, Paul, she is your girlfriend and you need to go to the cops, and if she was killed on Sunday, this is not good.'"

"And when he called you, he was very upset about Catherine's death, wasn't he?"

"Well, you would—yes, I mean, you would assume that he would be upset."

"No, I'm not asking you if you made an assumption. I'm asking if you heard it in his tone of voice when he spoke to you?"

"Yeah, I heard, I heard a tone of upset in his voice."

"And he, in fact, he also indicated to you that he was upset about her death, didn't he, when he spoke to you?"

"Yes, but he also lied to me because he had spent the whole day down at the precinct and told me that he had not spoken to the cops yet."

"Judge, I would ask that that portion of the answer be stricken since it's not responsive."

"Okay," Berkman said.

Miranda was not too happy with Bucci, either, and seemed to enjoy pressing her buttons, bringing out embarrassing testimony concerning her personal life. Miranda's questions left the impression that Bucci was displeased with her boyfriend and in fact was interested in Paul. What else was this business executive doing with her handsome and much younger personal trainer on the weekend?

"Miss Bucci," Miranda said, "didn't you invite Paul Cortez up to your apartment to eat when you were at Food Emporium together on November 27, 2005?"

"When I was there shopping, I said, 'I'm going to make some eggs and make myself brunch.' And then I felt like that was rude. And I said, 'Would you like to come?' And he said, 'Yes.' And then he got the phone call and said that, and I told him I didn't think it was appropriate for him to come to my apartment after that, and in fact, he did not."

"So he respected your desires, didn't he?"

"Well, he didn't have a choice."

"And didn't you used to flirt with Paul Cortez when you knew him from the period from October to November 2005?"

"Absolutely never did I flirt with Paul Cortez."

"I have no further questions, Your Honor," Miranda said.

42

He Was Holding Her Arm

Despite all the negative stories in the tabloids about Paul's behavior and personality, Casolaro still found it difficult to find someone to put on the stand who had been an eyewitness to any violent behavior perpetrated by Paul. No one had ever seen him manhandle Catherine or any other woman—at least not until Margaret Rickter took the stand.

Margaret Rickter, a retired nurse, had never personally met Paul or Catherine but she claimed she'd seen them together and it had not been pretty. She was a witness with testimony akin to that of Jacques Szwarcbart, the neighbor who claimed he saw Paul dumping a bag of garbage at four in the morning. The facts of their stories were a bit loose, but they gave the jury something else to think about.

Rickter claimed she'd been in the vicinity of East Eighty-sixth Street sometime during Thanksgiving week 2005 when she saw a young couple arguing on the street. She was not sure what day she'd seen them that week but felt it was probably Friday, sometime around noon.

"Well, I was walking slowly because I had had a hip injury, so I it took me at least two minutes to kind of inch my way up that side," said Rickter. "Then I paused because I had had a spasm in my hip joint and I rested for about a minute, and I was a little closer up then, when I stopped."

"When you walked past them, how close did you get to them?" Casolaro asked.

"I think it was close enough that if I wanted to reach my hand out, I could have touched them."

"Could you describe for us what was going on between them?"

"I was looking at them because they appeared to be arguing about something, and the gentleman was holding the woman in a way that left me uncomfortable, which is why—"

Dawn Florio objected at this point.

"Just describe for us what you saw," Casolaro said.

"Okay," Rickter said. "I saw the man holding the woman and I saw them and could hear in some way that they were arguing about something." She said the man was holding the woman above her left elbow and "I could hear the woman saying, 'Let me go,' and I could tell by the volume and the way they were—you could tell it was an argument."

Rickter described the woman as "approximately twenty, twenty-one, or twenty-two years old, extremely beautiful, slender. She appeared tall to me, but anybody over five feet, five inches is tall to me, so I would say she was about five-seven, five-eight, maybe a little bit taller, porcelain complexion, big dark eyes, dark hair, and very well dressed."

She described the man as a bit taller than the woman with "dark hair, shiny wavy hair and it looked like it had some kind of treatment, like a satiny treatment, which makes your hair shine, very wavy. It looked like it was a little bit longer than shoulder length. He had a chiseled chin, very—a masculine type of a face—slender, casually dressed with a very elegant soft black leather jacket.

"White, they were both wearing very beautiful white shirts. And he was wearing—I remember boots. I remember black boots on him."

The clear implication was that Rickter had seen Paul manhandling Catherine and wearing boots just a day or two before the murder. Rickter said she was later shown a photograph of Catherine Woods and she identified it as the woman she'd seen that day.

Casolaro did not ask Rickter to identify Paul, for good reason. While Rickter had picked him out of a photo array when she first came forward, she'd been unable to identify Paul at a preliminary hearing, when he was sitting at the defense table between his two female lawyers. That was certainly a major problem with her story.

Florio, in her cross-examination, got the four-feet, eleven-inch Rickter to admit that she'd thought the man was about six feet and much taller than the woman. Paul is only five feet, seven inches and was about the same height as Catherine.

But that wasn't the worst part of Rickter's testimony for the prosecution. She seemed to lose most people in the courtroom when she began talking about a "premonition" she'd had months later, one that compelled her to walk by the building where she'd seen the couple arguing. "And when I walked by that building, there was a private sanitation department picking up the trash from the apartment of Catherine Woods.

"There was a bookcase and on the bookcase clearly I saw a large Bible, a blue Bible that was engraved 'Catherine Elizabeth Woods.' I took that Bible. There were a few miscellaneous items. I immediately took them home, called the police, and asked them to immediately come over. I did not want to do anything with that but give it to the police. And I called the police, and they came and took those items."

"And how did you know that it was Catherine Woods's garbage?" Florio asked.

"There was a Bible that said, 'Catherine Elizabeth Woods,' and there was a porter there and I asked him—when I saw it, I was very upset when I saw this Bible and I saw these things, and some of them were bloodstained. And I asked the man that was bringing these things out from the 355 apartment building, 'By any chance, are these items belonging to the apartment of Catherine Woods?' And he said, 'Yes.'"

Florio did not ask Rickter about her testimony at

the preliminary hearing at which she could not identify Paul as the person she'd seen on the street. Rickter stepped down without either side asking if she could identify Paul. Neither side knew what answer she would give, and it was just too risky.

43

The Twelve Hairs

One of the most intriguing pieces of evidence found in Catherine's bedroom were the twelve hairs lodged between the fingers of her left hand. Even to the casual observer, it would seem at least possible that Catherine had pulled out the hair of her murderer. There was nothing under her fingernails except her own blood, but there were those twelve hairs, which might point directly to the murderer.

But did they?

The hair and fiber examiner who inspected the hairs for the NYPD was Valerie Wade-Allison, a nine-year veteran who had analyzed hair in nearly seven hundred cases. She gave the jury a brief education on the types of hair in the human head, but the most important questions came down to those twelve hairs in Catherine's hand.

Wade-Allison testified that she'd been given only two hair samples for comparison—hair belonging to Catherine and Paul. David's hair was never checked against any of the hairs in Catherine's bedroom, despite the fact that he had discovered her body and, at least initially, was a strong suspect in the case.

When Wade-Allison compared the hairs in Catherine's hand and elsewhere in the apartment with Paul's hair, there was not a single match. It seemed hard to believe that Paul, with his long flowing hair—even if it had been tied back—could have engaged in a violent life-and-death struggle and not have shed a single hair.

If the hairs had been analyzed for DNA, it would have made things more definitive, but for whatever reason, no DNA test was performed on them, even though Wade-Allison stated in her own report that "all of the recovered hairs may be suitable for mitochondrial DNA testing."

Why wasn't the DNA testing done? The authorities have never provided an answer.

This irked Paul's mother. "I can understand that maybe they felt strongly it wasn't David," Ivette said. "But don't you think that maybe a hair sample or two should have been tested as well? Why only Paul's? It's a good thing, because it's not Paul's, but then how can you have this poor woman with hair in her hand and no attempt is made to identify it? That makes no sense to me."

Paul's defense team felt the same way.

Lead investigator Steven Goetz had been at the trial every day even though, because he was a witness, he was not allowed to sit in the courtroom prior to his testimony. He was working nights, but he showed up every day at the Criminal Courthouse, on his own time, to be there for Jon and Donna Woods. He was afraid they'd be lonely and emotionally overcome by all the testimony. Goetz is particularly close to his father, and as a father himself, he felt a kinship with Jon Woods. During the trial, Goetz and his father even took Jon out to dinner on a couple of occasions, doing what the detective could to make this horrible ordeal a bit less horrible. Later, when talking to friends about their experience in New York or talking to the National Organization of Parents of Murdered Children, the Woodses would always make a point to let everyone know how well they'd been treated by Goetz and his brethren in the NYPD. To the Woodses, New York cops truly were "New York's Finest," the nickname they go by in the city.

Now, in the second week of the trial, Goetz was finally in the courtroom, having been called as a witness. After describing for the jury the murder scene and how David and Paul had appeared during questioning, Goetz was asked about Paul's now-infamous diaries. Observers knew what was coming because of all the stories in the press, but this was the first time the jury would actually hear Paul's own words and get a glimpse into his heart and mind. Goetz told Casolaro the diaries had been seized in a search of Paul's apartment. The prosecutor asked Goetz to identify the diaries, and then Casolaro was off and running, reading excerpt after excerpt, even ones written back when Paul was in college and dating a girl whose nickname was Boo.

One entry began: *Boo is helping me transform into the person that I want to be!*

Paul had written that he told Boo he loved her even though he knew she had a boyfriend and he was nothing more than a friend to her. Clearly he was troubled by the situation, as related in these words, which Casolaro read to the jury: *I feel so crushed. I am trying to let her go but I'm too captivated by her.*

Paul went on and on about his unrequited love for Boo and instructed himself: *Stop thinking about Boo. Stop thinking about Boo. She is poisonous, dangerous, unstable. You are not ready to handle her love.*

Casolaro was using the diaries to get the point across to the jury that when a woman rejected him, Paul could be unstable and obsessed, with the implication being that he'd acted the same way when Catherine had rejected him.

In the next entry, Paul commanded himself to be a victim of Boo's no longer, writing:

> *This crowded world is empty*
> *Compared to the crowds in my head*
> *Deciding on the knife*
> *Skin versus metal*
> *Vein versus blade.*

After Boo, Paul dated a student named Amanda, yet another woman who didn't reciprocate his love. As he wrote:

> *I wonder if she is just fucking random guys that she thinks are hot or if she's getting to know another more intimately. I still remember how she was my baby and how it makes me sad to know she was just using me. . . . It's not worth giving my love away to someone who can just forget me in a week and start fucking around with their—with other guys. She is a sly whore playing the innocent card because it gets her far. I wish I had listened to my soul.*

For a guy who affects a peaceful exterior, it was apparent that Paul was a tormented soul. Casolaro wanted the jury to hear about Paul's "rage":

> *All this hate—for what? I still feel she's fucking S.M. And so what if she is? She's not yours. You don't own her. You can't save her. You can only save yourself. And yet I feel as if my soul is dying at times—Am this pent up rage—unable to kill— unable to find retribution. I just want peace. I don't want them to affect me anymore. They're seeing into everything. I just want them to die or to leave or to be as miserable as I am.*

In an entry dated "12-01-04," about a year before Catherine's murder, Paul wrote these much-discussed lines:

> *She wipes clean the shaft*
> *that cuts her throat*

and returns back to her day
her shoes
her home
away from her home somewhere
out in the Midwest
where boys are dirty
and girls are princesses.

And then, in spring 2005, there is a clear reference to Catherine:

I saved her from rape, but she still wanted to take the risk of stripping for money though she might be drugged and molested again . . . I wake with sadness in my heart every day for the loss of Catherine Woods.

Let her go
She said she hates you
She wants you out of her life
So let her go
Her journey is different than yours
She must burn more than you wanted her to
You can't save her
She doesn't want to be saved
She doesn't understand your love
She said she despises you
Let her go
You hurt her more than you loved her.

But Paul finds he cannot let her go:

> *I look at other girls and it's not the same. . . . Beautiful Catherine, love of my life. How can I make you understand this erotic subjugation to lusty men hurts you more than you know. I see that you would rather choose them over me. Maybe if I had money it would be different . . . Catherine, you are so much more than this, and what's crazy is that you don't see that you can quit being treated like a whore and still be independent. I will wait for you forever if possible because I believe you are my soulmate. Love always, Paul.*

But in the very next sentence, after Paul found out that Catherine was still living with David, his anguish was palpable:

> *Catherine turned out to be lying too. She was sleeping with David and the others the entire time she told me how she was true and in love with me. How easy it has been to compartmentalize our hearts from our actions, from our minds. As if I didn't really mean anything to her.*

Reading aloud entry after entry, Casolaro was making Paul look worse and worse. He next read a song Paul had written on October 12, 2005, called "The Killin Machine." It is filled with violent and misogynistic lyrics:

Girl
The way you move your hips
Is so wicked divine
Tryna hold us down
But ya can't crown the mastermind
Hellhounds wanna pounce
And rip you apart with a scream
Betcha get violated
Gripping on The Killin Machine

After reading these lyrics, Casolaro said, "I have no further questions of Detective Goetz, Your Honor." He hadn't asked one for more than half an hour.

Laura Miranda began the cross-examination of Goetz by bringing the jury back to the evidence, noting that no murder weapon had ever been recovered.

"In fact, it wasn't recovered from Paul's apartment?"

"That's correct," Goetz said.

"In fact, there were no traces of blood recovered on any items recovered from Paul Cortez's apartment, correct?"

"That's correct."

Miranda also got Goetz to admit that despite what had been reported in the newspapers, no security video camera had ever captured an image of Paul from the night of the murder.

As for Paul's journals, Miranda noted that the excerpts read by Casolaro were chosen from thousands of entries. And she pointed out that the journals were exceptional for what was *not* in them.

"In all the journals that were recovered from Paul Cortez's apartment, there is no mention by Paul that he hurt Catherine or that he killed Catherine, correct?"

"That's correct."

44

Spence

When Erin Moriarty and Patti Aronofsky heard that Spence Lebowitz was going to be the prosecution's last witness, they looked at each other. What on earth could he add? They'd interviewed Spence four months after the murder, at The Back Page sports bar where Spence had met Paul after Catherine's murder, and Spence seemed not to remember much at all. Moriarty was actually upset that they'd even bothered to interview him and felt that Spence was such a waste of time that he was not included in the hour-long CBS broadcast about Catherine's murder. Now he was being put on the stand as the crucial last witness.

It promised to be an interesting afternoon.

Lebowitz, a twenty-six-year-old hairstylist and friend of Paul's, was friends with another trainer at the Equinox fitness club, which is how he met Paul. The two became friendly, and at exactly 7:57 on the night of Catherine's murder, Paul called up Spence and asked him if he wanted to hang out. Spence was already at an Upper East Side bar called The Back Page, and he suggested Paul meet him there to watch the New York Giants football game, which was being broadcast that evening. The game went into overtime, and the Giants lost after the team's kicker missed three field goals.

Like everyone else in Paul's life, Spence knew that Paul had broken up with a girlfriend, but he did not know Catherine by name. "He was in love with her and didn't know how to get her off his mind," Spence said.

Spence, who said he was drinking Miller Lite beer, said Paul came in, sat down at the bar, and ordered a glass of water.

"Do you remember how Mr. Cortez was dressed and what he looked like that night?" Casolaro asked.

"His hair looked like it was gelled back and he was wearing a black leather coat, jeans, and black boots," Spence said.

Moriarty and Aronofsky couldn't believe it. Could this be the same Spence they had interviewed the year before? Back then Spence had said on-camera that he was drinking Corona beer and remembered very little about the way Paul was dressed. What's more, this hairstylist had also said on-camera that Paul had been wearing his hair in a ponytail.

In the on-camera interview, Moriarty had asked Spence: "Did you get a close look at Paul?"

"Nah. I wouldn't say a close look at him at that point. You know, I was so caught up in the game that I didn't pay attention."

She tried again. "How was he dressed? Do you remember?"

"Yeah, he was wearing a jacket. It was cold out. It was cold out. So he was wearing jeans and a jacket."

Now, on the stand, Spence was much more forthcoming, telling the prosecutor not only that Paul was wearing boots but "they were a buckled boot." He then identified a Sketchers boot as the same ones that Paul had been wearing that evening. Spence picked out the boot from an array of line drawings that featured *only* Sketchers boots. It was a little like shooting fish in a barrel, and it was a devastating blow to Paul's defense. Spence became the first and only person who said that Paul—on the night of the murder—was wearing the exact style of boot that could be matched to the boot-prints on Catherine's shirt and bedsheet.

Laura Miranda realized what had just happened and was beside herself. She asked Spence, "Isn't it a fact that nowhere in any of the statements that you made on that date, November 28, 2005, did you indicate what shoes Paul Cortez was wearing?"

Casolaro objected, and Judge Berkman sustained the objection.

"We've never heard that this witness ever identified our client wearing a pair of shoes," Miranda implored the judge.

"Yes," Berkman said, "but a prior omission is not, in itself, inconsistent. So until you make such a showing, I'm not permitting you to elicit this."

Spence went on to say that the first time he told anyone about the boots Paul was wearing was in October 2006, nearly a year after the murders, when Casolaro questioned him.

Miranda pressed on in an attempt to discredit the witness. "Well, isn't it a fact that you were high from marijuana on November 27, 2005, when you met with Paul Cortez?"

"After we met up, when we had hung out that night, before I went home, we smoked."

"Toward the end of last year, is it fair to say that's the first you discussed with Mr. Casolaro that Paul Cortez, what shoes he may have been wearing that night?"

"It was the first time I had discussed with anybody . . . the entire situation about that night," Spence said.

But that was not true. He had given an interview to *48 Hours Mystery* well before he spoke to Casolaro in October 2006.

"I was asked if I could point out the shoes, and I pointed out the shoes," he said. "I went through all the pictures on my own and I pointed out the shoes that I pointed out just before and I never spoke about it again."

"And when you saw Paul Cortez that night, you didn't see any blood on his jacket, did you?"

"No, ma'am."

"You didn't see any bruises on his hands, did you?"

"No, ma'am."

"You didn't see any bruises on his face, did you?"

"No, ma'am. I wasn't paying attention to that."

Miranda attacked Spence's testimony on the boots one more time. "When you were questioned by the detectives, at any point were you informed that there were bootprints at the scene of the death of Catherine Woods?"

"No, ma'am."

"And when you met with Casolaro, were you informed of that?"

"No, ma'am. I was asked to identify what he was wearing, if I could identify. And that was when I'd say he was wearing a black leather coat, blue jeans, and black boots. And then I was asked to identify, if I could identify the boots."

"Well, isn't it a fact that Paul Cortez was wearing loafers that night, black loafers?"

"I remember boots."

"And didn't Mr. Paul Cortez have long jeans on that night?"

"He had jeans that went down to his boots. . . . They weren't capris," Spence said sarcastically.

After Spence stepped down, Casolaro stood up: "That's the people's case, Your Honor."

It was now the defense's turn.

45

The Defense Case

The defense began Tuesday afternoon, and the first in a parade of character witnesses was school chum Wilfredo Acosta, a friend of Paul's who had met him when they both attended the Poly Prep Country Day School in Brooklyn. Acosta was now a no-nonsense marine determined to make the jury see Paul as he knew him.

The two had played football together, acted in school plays, and often, Acosta would invite Paul to spend the nights at his house to avoid the long commute back to the Bronx. Acosta's stories about Paul were sweet reminiscences of a busy youth, but they didn't seem to amount to much. It was certainly not evidence, and Acosta did little more than serve up platitudes about Paul being a good guy incapable of any type of violence.

But one had to wonder if it had any effect on the jury. After all, nearly every outrageously violent crime seems to be almost immediately followed by television interviews with bewildered neighbors and relatives describing the murderer as a "nice guy." Still, Casolaro couldn't let Acosta leave the stand without having a bit of fun for himself.

"You said Paul was a very good actor, is that right?" Casolaro asked.

"I would say he's very talented, yes."

"And he appeared in productions and was very, very convincing in the roles he played, correct?"

"Yes, sir."

"And he played many, many different kinds of roles, didn't he?"

"That is correct, sir. But one thing is certain, I always knew it was Paul. When he was onstage, he always brought himself to the role."

"And to be a good actor he studied, didn't he, to become a good actor?"

"Yes, sir."

"And as you pointed out before, you would have to prepare a role to be a good actor, is that right?"

"That's correct, sir."

"And among the preparation you do is, you learn what the true feelings and the true reactions of the character you're playing is, don't you?"

"That would be one method, sir."

"And you try to get into the role and be that person rather than yourself, is that correct?"

"I'm not an expert on acting, but perhaps, sir."

"Well, Paul's very, very good at submersing his real personality and getting into character, isn't he?"

"Objection," Florio said at last. It was clear that Casolaro was priming the jury, trying to get them to consider that when Paul did take the stand, he would be "in character."

"I wouldn't say that, sir," Acosta said.

The next witness was a woman who was allowed to testify without giving her name. The jury was told she wanted to remain anonymous "for business purposes." This woman and her fiancé had lived with Paul for five months, when they were doing a summer play in college.

"Paul to me," she said, "is one of the most peaceful people I have ever met and has introduced me to many, many spiritual things in the way of meditation and yoga."

She said she knew about Paul's relationship with Catherine and that she had seen him a month before the murder when he seemed "sad about it" but never angry.

Paul's friend and co-worker Jaki Levy took the stand next. He was one of the few members of Paul's inner circle who had seen Paul and Catherine together, and he testified that when he met them at a café in July 2005 "they were very affectionate toward each other. . . . They were kissing each other very passionately," he said. "They were almost horizontal. If any of you were there, you would have probably told them to get a room. They were very, very tender with each other and very affectionate."

Jaki's testimony was intended to counter the prosecution's underlying belief that Paul's relationship with Catherine was very much a fantasy created in his own mind, that while they'd initially been lovers, she later soured on him and considered him just a friend. In fact, Casolaro only half-jokingly told some acquaintances in private that he believed Paul and Catherine had never even had sex.

But that's not the way Jaki saw things. He said that he was in Paul's apartment in early November 2005 when Catherine phoned Paul late at night. "She called him around eleven or midnight, pretty much as we were going to bed, and had asked to see Paul again," he said.

At that point, Jaki said, the relationship was on the rocks and Paul was seeing another woman, an actress.

On the day of the murder, Paul had called Jaki several times, once in the afternoon and twice in the hours immediately after the murder, at 7:12 and 8:06 p.m.

"Did you actually speak to Paul Cortez at 7:12 p.m.?" Florio asked.

"Yes, I spoke to him both times."

He said each call was about three minutes long. Florio wanted to know what Paul's demeanor was during the call at 7:12 p.m., which was maybe thirty minutes or so after Catherine had been stabbed twenty times and had had her throat cut twice. Jaki answered that

Paul "was pretty calm, pretty positive, and I would say just generally positive. He was looking to make a lot of positive moves."

It *was* hard to believe someone could butcher another human being and be so cavalier so soon after.

Another male friend of Paul's came next, and he, too, asked that his name not be used. He was sworn in as a John Doe. He talked about Paul's reputation for peacefulness and how Paul had introduced him to various Buddhist writings.

It would seem that there wasn't much to attack in his testimony, but Casolaro found an opening.

"Did I hear you correctly, that you said that one of the reasons you thought Mr. Cortez was peaceful is because he studies Buddhist texts?"

"That is correct."

"Do you know what the Taiping Rebellion is?"

"The Taiping rebellion, I believe, was in China. It was in the eighties," John Doe answered incorrectly. "That was when the students rebelled against the government."

"Are you aware that the bloodiest war in the history of this planet where anyone got killed was in the nineteenth century, between two Buddhist sects in China? Are you aware of that?"

"Not as much as you are, sir."

Miranda called for an objection, but Casolaro said, "No further questions."

John Doe could not believe Casolaro's chutzpah. "Jesus Christ," he said.

46

Paul Takes the Stand

The next day, after a few more defense witnesses had come and gone, to little effect, Laura Miranda said the words that everyone had been waiting anxiously for: "Your Honor, at this time we call Paul Cortez to the stand." Here, at last, was the main attraction.

The highlight of any murder trial is when the accused takes the stand. Everyone wants it, but it happens very infrequently, and when it does, it's because the accused is confident or innocent or both. And no matter how much the jury is instructed that the accused need not take the stand, any defendant who does so scores at least a few points for having the courage to get up there. It is no doubt high stakes for everyone. In a murder trial, the defendant is putting the rest of his life—sometimes his very life—on the line.

For the defense, it is a risk that the jury will take something the defendant says the wrong way or even hate him completely. For the prosecutor, it's a lot of stress because of societal expectations. We've all seen the television programs where the prosecutor breaks the defendant down and he admits his crime. That virtually never happens in real life. And on TV, it is the prosecutor who asks the defendant, "Did you kill your wife/lover/husband?" In real life that is rarely the case. The prosecutor knows the defendant will say no, so why give him a chance to deny the crime?

That day, Paul was wearing a blue sweater and had his hair tied back in a ponytail. He was confident and looked at the jury frequently, almost as if they were a group of his friends. Paul was a very unlikely murder defendant in that he was intelligent, articulate, and attractive. It was easy to imagine that he should have been the one asking the questions. He made sure to be very respectful of the judge and the process as he described his family history and his education and the sacrifices he'd had to make.

Defense attorney Laura Miranda made sure to elicit Paul's whole life.

"My mom would help me wake up at 4:30 in the morning to eat breakfast and take a train ride," he said. "Well, a bus to the train. Trains. The 6 to 125th; the 4 to Atlantic; the R to the last stop in Bay Ridge."

It's a foreign language to anyone but a committed New Yorker, who understands what a long ride Paul is describing. Paul talked about how he loved to sing and dance from an early age and how he'd taken up writing down his thoughts in a journal back in grammar school. He said comic books gave him a love of drawing, and he often doodled and drew figures of warriors in his books.

Paul made sure the jury knew that he was hip to the world, sophisticated and educated, well beyond the experiences of a poor Latino boy from the Bronx. He mentioned traveling to Argentina, London, New Mexico, and Minnesota. On occasion, he even took a shot at Casolaro, such as when Miranda asked him if he'd had a chance to review his college journal entries about his old girlfriend Amanda.

"Yeah, yeah," Paul said, "I remember the wonderful reading Mr. Casolaro did yesterday."

It was almost like he was being inclusive by sprinkling the district attorney's name throughout his testimony. Talking about acting, Paul said, "What you do is delve into that emotion and kind of embellish it. Mr. Casolaro used a good word. It's kind of developing a fantasy of the experience. You try to feel every emotion connected with that so you can actually translate it onto the stage."

Miranda gave Paul a chance to talk about how he'd been jilted by women in the past and had gone on with his life. Why should this time be any different? He wasn't some crazy stalker who lashed out at women after they'd rejected him. He was a sophisticated, good-looking guy who knew that relationships had their ups and downs, and he took the breakups in stride. Miranda mentioned the episode when, according to Paul, his girlfriend Amanda slept with his best friend.

"Did you continue to be friends with Amanda after the breakup?"

"Yeah, we did."

"What about after she slept with S.M. [Paul's best friend]? Did you continue to be friends after that?"

"Yeah, both times," Paul said slyly.

In fact, he said, he was still in touch with Amanda and reeled off her home phone number from memory.

Miranda introduced the text messages Catherine had sent Paul during the turbulent Thanksgiving week. "Did you also on November 23rd receive a text message from Catherine Woods on that date?"

"Yes."

"What was the substance of that message, November 23rd, 2005?"

"It says, 'I know. I love you.'"

Miranda had Paul read other entries from his journal, the less offensive ones that had been skipped over by Casolaro. One mentioned "the Gardens of Kamala," a reference to the Herman Hesse classic *Siddhartha*. Paul said the poem was about the rape Catherine had suffered in Brooklyn when she first came to New York. Again, the point was that he was a trusted confidant of Catherine's. Why else would she have shared such intimate details of her past? He claimed to have visited Catherine's apartment "fifty-something times," and said she wasn't the first woman who'd confided in him about past sexual abuse.

"And when you say you've been with other girls who've had similar experiences, what do you mean you've 'been with them'?" Miranda asked. "Have you been intimate with them?"

"Yeah, there's usually a time where sometimes you're having sex with them, making love, and they kind of like shut their eyes, or a couple of times I've had girls break down on me and just cry for no apparent reason and then stop. What's going on? And then telling me the whole history of them being in that situation, and then kind of, you know, comforting them through that."

This was Paul the understanding guy, Mr. Touchy-Feely. It certainly wasn't the sexually aggressive guy Monica encountered on New Year's Eve 2004, but she was not called to testify. Paul's testimony seemed to be going over fairly well with the jury. He often made eye contact with them. He was surely very different from most murder defendants they'd read about in the newspapers.

Miranda turned the conversation to David Haughn. Again, Paul was Mr. Understanding, "[Catherine] didn't want to just send him home because she still cared about him, still loved him, and she wanted to make sure that they maintained a friendship," he told the jury.

Miranda asked Paul to recall what Catherine had told him about an incident with David that occurred the summer before the murder.

"Basically, they had an argument and he got really mad and he basically threw all these dishes on the floor and just kind of destroyed the dishes," Paul said. "And I called her and I was like 'What are you doing?' She was like, 'I'm picking up broken dishes.' I was like, 'From what?' and she's like, 'Well, you know David just got mad and stormed out.'"

Paul told the jury how, shortly after that, David called him and told him, "Where's my girl? You better not be with her."

Paul told Catherine this, and he said she told him she would take care of David. "So I guess she told him never to call me again, and he never did after that," Paul said.

As the afternoon wore on, Paul revisited others' testimony about Catherine's topless dancing, the April incident where she called him after being drugged and assaulted, and his phone call to her father. The stories were similar to what others had said, but basically Paul gave the jury his side of the story. He denied, for instance, that he had told Jon Woods that Catherine had been using drugs and was a prostitute.

"I guess something got lost in translation, but I did tell him Catherine had at one point been using drugs and drinking and things of that nature when she had first come to New York, but as far as I knew her, she had never done any of that. We drank maybe a couple of times at a bar, and about three times we smoked pot together. And that was the extent of it. To my knowledge, she was completely clean. She was always very busy with work and her dance schedule, but anyways, I told him that.

"I told him the situation with David, how David wasn't really contributing and how she basically wanted him out and . . . she was still trying to salvage him as a friend . . . and all of that. I told him all about our relationship, that we had been together, and he thanked me.

"We hung up and we basically—before we hung up, he asked me to see her and just try to get her not to go to—it was actually that night—to the strip club that night because he was going to fly in the next day and, you know, talk to her about the situation and I, I was like, 'Well, okay, I'll try.' He hangs up."

Paul agreed that Catherine was angry that he'd called her father and told him she didn't want to see him again. Miranda asked him to read the passage from his diary where he referred to that springtime breakup.

"Sure," Paul said, as he picked up the diary. "It says, 'I saved her from rape, but she still wanted to take the risk of stripping for money though she might be drugged and molested again. I tried all I could to make her heal and vanquish the demons that kept herself abusing. She thought I betrayed her when I told her father of her nighttime secret life. I wanted her to stop so that she would heal and love me without boundary or pain, but she would never stop.

"'It's like trying to stop the river's downward path in the summertime with your bare hands. No, you must wait till the winter, when nature's freeze grips the sultry flow to stillness.

"'I loved her more than the others, but I still could not keep her close. I myself had too much separation anxiety, fear of dishonesty, and unfinished healing to do myself, but I still wanted her all. How well deceived we lovers allow ourselves to be. I wake with sadness in my heart every day for the loss of Catherine Woods.' "

"And when you wrote that entry, at any time did you intend any harm to occur to Catherine Woods?" Miranda asked.

"Not at all, not at all."

Casolaro broke in: "I'm sorry, I couldn't hear you?"

"Not at all," Paul said again, looking directly at Casolaro.

Miranda took this as an opportunity to ask *the* question: "Did you kill Catherine Woods on November 27th, 2005, Paul?"

"No, I did not."

"Did you want any harm to come to her?"

"No, I did not."

"Now, why did you write that entry and what did you mean when you wrote that entry?"

"I was sad about the whole situation. I felt like I was trying to do a good thing and I understood that I did betray her trust by calling her father, but in that moment, I didn't—I was trying to help. I didn't know what was the best thing to do to help and I figured if she wouldn't listen to me, she might listen to a voice of authority, you know, someone she cared about, and I knew she cared about her family a lot, so that's when I called Mr. Woods.

"And then I say I make an analogy of like how you can't really stop someone from doing what is in their nature to do and I kind of liken it to a river, and it says, 'It's like trying to stop the river's downward path in the summertime with your bare hands.' It's impossible because it goes through your hands and it just rushes past you."

Paul said that Catherine called him about three weeks after the incident to make up with him. Miranda then introduced itemized phone records that showed a phone call made from Catherine's to Paul's cell phone. The call took place on April 23, 2005, and lasted seventy-seven minutes.

Casolaro interjected to point out that there was a phone call the day before from Paul to Catherine that lasted eleven minutes—the point being that it was Paul who initiated contact with Catherine after the fight and not the other way around.

Miranda had not yet addressed the most damaging evidence against Paul—the cell phone calls made from her neighborhood just before the murder and his apparent "bloody fingerprint" on her bedroom wall. But that's exactly where she was headed with her next series of questions.

"Approximately how many times do you believe you were intimate with her from August 2005 to November 2005, at her apartment, specifically?" Miranda asked.

"At her apartment? Um, from August until November, you're saying?"

"Yes, 2005. If you know."

"I don't know. Maybe like ten times. Mainly, we were at my place. I liked to have her at my place. It was just more convenient. I had my own music. It was my first apartment, too, and it was on the top floor. So it was just—whenever she wanted to smoke, she could go onto the roof, and we would hang out there, as well. It was just a better situation."

"When you say 'Whenever she wanted to smoke'— did she smoke cigarettes?"

"Cigarettes. Yeah."

"At any time when you were intimate with Catherine at her apartment from August 2005 to November of 2005, did she have her period at any time?"

"Yes."

"When you were making love with her at any time while she had her period, would there be—would there be messes or accidents?"

"Um, yeah. Like, you mean—I know what you mean. Yeah."

"I mean, would you get your hands dirty at any time?"

"Yes."

"Did you ever get your hands on the wall when you were intimate with her when she was . . ."

"I might have. Yes."

So there it was: a possible way for Paul to have left a bloody fingerprint on Catherine's wall. The defense was floating the theory that if that was Paul's fingerprint on the wall, it was possible that he'd left it there on a previous occasion when Catherine had her period.

The theory was that, during sex, Paul had gotten Catherine's menstrual blood on his fingers and wiped it on her wall.

The theory was a bit far-fetched, but the defense was desperate. They had not lined up any fingerprint experts who were able to challenge the way the police had found the print, but they had to find a way to explain away the print, and the menstrual blood theory is what they came up with.

The press was incredulous. So was Casolaro.

The day was winding down, but Miranda wanted to address the lyrics to the song "The Killin Machine," which had been introduced by Casolaro. She wanted Paul to explain why he'd written it and what it meant.

"Now," Miranda said, "could you—could you sing that song for us, 'The Killin Machine'?"

Judge Berkman quickly interjected: "No, he cannot. He may not sing a song."

"It's entirely different from the way it sounds, the way it's read from the way you read it or the way you sing it. Judge, I would request that you make an exception in this case."

"No."

"Judge, the people are basically using this to prove that my client had the intent to kill Catherine Woods. I would request that you make an exception and allow my client to sing this song."

Berkman would not be moved. "No."

At that point, Paul said, "It's actually a nice song."

That was probably the wrong thing to say about this particular song, as the jury would soon find out.

Exasperated by the judge, Miranda gave up. "And can you read the song for us, since you can't sing it?"

"Okay," Paul said. He began reading it in a sing-song or hip-hop kind of way:

> I feel the surge
> Her electric rush is pushing me up to the verge
> Breakdown bitches
> Never gonna shatter my urge
> Cut the shy lean
> Girl
> Better change your scene
> With a gang of lunatics
> Grippin on The Killin Machine
> Get ya steel need
> Bleedin' on The Killin' Machine
> Eyes dialate
> Shakin on The Killin Machine
> You got violated
> Fixin for The Killin Machine
> Meet me on the way out
> You looking real fine
> Girl
> The way you move your hips
> Is so wicked divine
> Tryna hold us down
> But ya can't crown the mastermind

Hellhounds wanna pounce
And rip you apart with a scream
Betcha get violated
Grippin on The Killin Machine"
Kind of goes back.

"What was the purpose of writing this song?" Miranda asked.

"Well, my drummer and I were talking one day. He was telling me about this girl that he was dating. And—it's kind of a funny, sort of embarrassing story. But, whatever. He was saying that no matter how big a guy's penis is, after you've been with her for a while, she's always gonna want the next size bigger. So we had a good laugh at that. Then we invented this machine that is like basically—this is a really raunchy, bawdy story. I'm sorry. This was our humor. We made this machine that was like a dildo attached to these winged things."

"Did you actually make it?"

"No. We actually envisioned it. We were cracking up at the idea. You would crank it like this [gesturing] and go ZZZZZZZ."

"In-and-out motion?"

"Yeah. So, we were cracking up creating this machine. He was like, yeah, you know, that will pulverize—pulverize her and beat that pussy and all that stuff. And then I started realizing, I was like, you know, isn't it funny how in our society today, guys are always like, 'Yeah, I want to fuck the shit out of that girl,' whatever. And guys are so—they equate violence with sex. So I made this song sort of, like a combination of those two themes of, like, violence and sex and how, like, you know, a lot of the—a lot of the words are kind of double entendres between violence and sex. And it's just kind of to hold up the mirror, as it were, to how most guys in today's society view, you know, sex."

A female juror in the back row winced at Paul's graphic description of today's sexual mores, or at least the way he'd interpreted them. She wasn't the only one. Moriarty remembers thinking right then that there was something seriously wrong with Paul. And it wasn't just his words but how he said them. He seemed extraordinarily animated as he grew more and more vulgar.

"Was it your intention at all to, you know, create violence and sex? Was that your intention?" Miranda asked.

"No. Not at all."

"Was it your intention to harm Catherine Woods?"

"Not at all."

"When you say, for example, 'Her electric rush is pushing me up to the verge, breakdown bitches,' what did you mean by that, 'They never gonna shatter my urge'?"

"Well, when I was writing it, I remember the way Alex looked on the guitar while he was playing it. And like electric guitar, but also like electric rush, pushing me up to the verge of . . . of . . . of ejaculating, coming, you know. 'Breakdown bitches never gonna shatter my urge.' All the girls who are all about drama, whatever, is not gonna shatter my urge to go out and, you know, my—copulate. I guess my manhood. Whatever. And then it talks about a girl, saying, 'Cut the shy lean, girl. You better change your scene.' So, like, I'm picturing, like, a bar. You know, sometimes girls are just leaning off to the side, looking shy. And he's like, you know, let's change the scene. Let's go back to my place so we can go and have sex. 'With a gang of lunatics grippin on the killin machine.' The gang of lunatics, when I sang it, was the guys in Monolith."

"Did you intend any harm to happen to Catherine Woods when you wrote the song?"

"No, I did not."

When Paul was finished, more than a few people in the courtroom were shocked by his gutter language and how he'd seemingly gone out of his way to graphically explain more than he had to. Some of the sheen was wearing off his supposedly sophisticated exterior.

He remained on the stand the rest of the afternoon. The Johnston and Murphy loafers that he said he was wearing the day of Catherine's murder were introduced. The shoes were cut a bit high and, with the pants leg down, looked very much like boots.

Miranda asked about the nature of the couple's relationship and why he'd phoned Catherine as much as he had. Was he obsessed? Paul denied he was. "Basically she would play the princess role on me, like 'I'm the princess and you have to come and woo me back.' And I would do it, and it was what it was. That's how it kind of operated."

It had been a long day. Paul had not disappointed, but had he done himself any good?

And what would tomorrow bring?

47

Paul—Day Two

It was now Friday in Paul's murder trial and, as the day began, his lawyer asked questions about Paul's whereabouts on the day of Catherine's murder. Paul said the last time he'd seen her was on Saturday; she was on the elliptical machine at the Equinox fitness club and he said she had suggested they get together "soon."

The next day—soon enough for Paul—he was working at the Bikram Yoga studio in the morning but sent Catherine a text message "reminding her, you know, we should go hang out, get some coffee, some tea later on in the day." He mentioned three-thirty as a good time. They later exchanged phone messages but kept missing each other. Meanwhile, Catherine spent the day with her friend Christina Dupont, and met Christina's boyfriend. When Paul had not heard from her by the afternoon, he called Stephanie Bucci and ran those errands with her.

He admitted he'd upset Bucci when he made those remarks about licking strawberries off her body, but he insisted he was only joking. By 5:00 p.m., he was back in his apartment at East 106th Street when Catherine reached him on his cell phone. It was, he said, the first time they'd spoken that day. He said they were in the middle of a conversation when they got disconnected.

"And how did she sound when she was speaking to you?" Miranda asked.

"She sounded a little bit edgy, you know, a little bit preoccupied, like either she was doing something or she had just been doing something. I don't know, a little bit rushed, so I called back several times and I didn't get her, which is when it went straight to voice mail. And then she called me back and then she told me that she really had to go, that she was getting ready to go to the club to work. She was like, 'I really don't want to go tonight, but, you know, I have to.'"

"Did she tell you why she didn't want to really go that night?"

"No, she didn't explain why. But, you know, I was trying to keep her on the phone, so I kept asking her, you know, 'well, tell me about your day.' Like, what was going on?"

Miranda asked, "Why were you trying to keep her on the phone?"

"Well, I just wanted to see how she was. She sounded a little bit disturbed, and I hadn't really spoken to her. We said we were going to meet, so I just wanted to speak."

Paul said he tried calling again and got disconnected again. He said he was worried and then recalled that, at least once before, he'd been able to talk Catherine out of going to work by just showing up at her apartment and taking her out to eat. "I decided, you know, I would go into her neighborhood and, and see if she wanted to do something. So I took the bus to 86th Street and I called her as soon as I got off the bus. Then I went to the Starbucks that we usually hang out [at], on 84th and Second, and I had the book with me that I just got from Steph, so I was just waiting at Starbucks, calling her, reading the book, and just waiting for her reply."

Paul's story was that he relaxed at Starbucks, making a few calls to his gym clients to lock in their workout schedules for the coming week. He admitted that he decided not to attend band practice because feelings among his bandmates were bruised of late and he didn't feel like having a confrontation with them. When he was unable to connect by phone with Catherine again—despite trying seven times in a row—he said he walked home to East 106th Street, stopping to eat chicken at a Popeye's restaurant on the way. Later, he said, he met up with his friend Spence at a bar, smoked marijuana, went to another friend's house to watch the Jets play football, and then went home.

The following morning, Paul testified that he went to work early to train a client and then returned a message from his mother, met her, and found out that Catherine had been killed.

He told the jury how he'd been questioned by police for about five hours and had done everything they'd asked of him—without a lawyer being present. Paul said he'd had no food, that the cops had promised him pizza but never came through. Detective Goetz—sitting in the courtroom next to the Woodses—was astounded that Paul was whining about not getting his pizza just hours after his girlfriend had been killed. Paul then dissected yet another of his poems, and Laura Miranda asked him for at least the third time if he'd killed Catherine. Again, he answered no.

"Do you think she still loved you?" Miranda asked.

"I knew she still loved me. Just the other day, she wrote in a text message, 'I know. I love you.' "

"Did you love her?"

"Of course."

"I have no further questions for this witness, Your Honor."

Now, it was the prosecution's turn.

48

Cross

Peter Casolaro stood up and immediately began using Paul's own words against him.

"So, you don't harbor any resentment against women for their hurting you in love, right?" Casolaro asked.

"In the beginning when things happen and arguments happen and things happen, natural reaction is to be upset and to be hurt," Paul said. "I may have expressed that several times. But overall, at the end or a later time, there's always reconciliation."

"Do you recall writing in your diary that 'love hurts,' that 'you have to choose between loneliness or love,' and that 'love is pain'? Do you remember writing that?"

"I've written a lot of poems," Paul said.

"So you don't remember writing it?"

"If you have something to refresh my memory, I will take a look at it."

"Do you remember ever writing that because of the pain you've experienced from love, you've 'become a misogynist'?"

"I might have said that, yes."

"Do you remember ever writing that 'You want to fuck all these girls and to rip their hearts with your hard cock and to turn them to stone'?"

Miranda called for an objection, but Judge Berkman overruled her.

"You don't remember writing that?" Casolaro said.

"It may have been in a poem. Maybe."

"May have been," Casolaro said sarcastically. "You remember other things in great detail, but this you're having trouble with. That's not memorable to you?"

"Objection," Miranda cried again, and this time her objection was sustained.

"Do you remember writing that since your mother and other women hurt you, you want to 'bury every girl in the ground'? Do you remember writing that?"

"I may have written that for *Hamlet*. We [classmates] were working on [that] our first year [in college]. I remember drawing those—those experiences, trying to work on that. So I may have written that, yes."

"Do you remember writing that you wanted 'to tear their cunts apart and kill that which hurts'?"

"Objection," Miranda said.

"Overruled," Berkman answered.

"Do you remember saying that 'love hurts more than life itself,' and that 'love is just pain'?"

"Maybe."

"And do you remember writing that you wanted 'to kill that which causes pain'?"

"Maybe. I—I don't remember actually."

Casolaro returned to his original question: "But you don't harbor any resentment against women—is that right?"

"No, I don't."

"Now, Mr. Cortez, this is your fingerprint, your hand here on the wall in [exhibit number] 32, isn't it?" Casolaro said, showing Paul the exhibit with a handprint on it.

"Objection," Miranda said. "My client is not a scientist."

"You may answer the question," Berkman told Paul.

Casolaro asked again: "Is that your handprint on the wall of Catherine's bedroom?"

Paul would not take the bait. "No, it is not."

"Well, what was all that testimony we heard yesterday about menstrual blood on your hand and touching the wall?"

"Um, I didn't hear anything about menstrual blood that touched the wall," Paul said. It was a curious answer, and Casolaro called him on it. "Didn't you tell the jury that you were having sex with Ms. Woods, you got menstrual blood on your hand, and you touched the wall?"

"No. I never said that to the jury. No."

What Paul *had* said was that he had had sex with

Catherine at a time when she had her period and that it had been messy. It was left to the jury to conclude that perhaps he'd gotten blood on his finger and wiped it on the wall.

"So, then you have no explanation why your fingerprints and her blood would be on the wall of her bedroom?"

But Paul is no dummy, and he turned the question to his advantage. "Well, I believe Alex Chacko [the fingerprint expert] made it very clear that the fingerprint was a latent fingerprint that was not visible to his eye. After he put that amido black stuff on, that reacts with protein, then the fingerprint was lifted. Then, after, I heard the testimony that the blood above the fingerprint was Catherine's blood. The fingerprint itself they never tested."

"I guess that means that you didn't touch the wall with your hand then, ever?"

"I'm sure I touched almost every wall in that apartment, and my fingerprints should be all over that apartment."

"But when you had Ms. Woods's menstrual blood on it, did you ever touch the wall?"

"Like I said, I don't recall. It may have been a possibility."

"Did you see a bloodstain on the wall ever in the times you were in the apartment?"

"I don't recall that."

"You don't recall seeing blood on the wall of the

bedroom while you were in the apartment?" Casolaro asked incredulously.

"Objection. Asked and answered."

"Overruled."

"No. I don't recall seeing any blood on the wall. . . . I don't ever recall seeing blood on the wall."

"So why did you then testify that you had menstrual blood on your hands when you were in the apartment?"

"Objection, Your Honor. Form."

"Sustained."

Miranda seemed more upset by the questions than Paul, who kept his composure despite the assault from Casolaro.

Casolaro continued: "So it's your testimony, then, that you don't know how the police identified your fingerprint in blood on the wall?"

"Objection," Miranda said for the umpteenth time. "My client does not have a burden [of proof]."

"That is correct. He doesn't. And the objection is sustained, although not for that reason."

"So, Mr. Cortez, is it your testimony, then, that your fingerprint was on the wall in her blood?"

"Objection, Your Honor."

"You may answer the question."

"Like I said, from the testimony of the experts, there's a difference between a latent print and a patent print. And the latent print is a print that's not visible, that a substance needs to be used in order to bring it out. The experts have testified that the print was latent. Patent print is when something is in blood or any substance and is put on a wall."

"Didn't you hear Mr. Entenmann testify that he cut out that section of the wall because he saw a bloody fingerprint there?"

Casolaro's statement was untrue. It was *not* what Entenmann had said. Miranda called Casolaro on it: "Objection."

"Sustained."

Casolaro moved off the bloody fingerprint at last and onto Paul's conflicting statements about where he was when he made the seven rapid-fire phone calls to Catherine's cell phone just before her murder.

"Mr. Cortez, you—you said that you were in Catherine's neighborhood that day, is that right?"

"Yes, I was."

"And that you had gone to a coffee shop—I'm sorry. Was it a coffee shop? I don't remember."

"Yes. It was Starbucks."

"And you were there for a period of time, and you called her a number of times from that coffee shop?"

"Her and a lot of my clients, yes."

"So, the cell site chart that we put into evidence was correct, is that right?"

"Objection," Miranda said.

"The objection is sustained."

"And you said now that you—you were questioned by the police the next day, and you told them about this, right?"

"I didn't tell them specifically that I was at Star-bucks. I said that I went to get something to eat at her neighborhood, and I told them the place."

"Well, the detectives had just accused you of com-mitting a crime, is that right?"

"They didn't accuse me of committing a crime. They said I was a suspect to the crime."

"They had asked you had you committed it, hadn't they?"

"Oh yes. They asked me if I—yeah."

"Then after they asked you if you committed it, you told them, 'Well, I'd been in the neighborhood that afternoon,' is that right?"

"No. I said, 'No. I did not commit this crime.' And then maybe about two and a half hours later that—me being in her neighborhood came out." Paul was insist-ing he had told detectives he was near Catherine's apartment that day but claimed they had not written this down.

"And the detectives didn't say, 'Oh, you were in the neighborhood,' and follow up on it at all with you?"

"They did a little bit. I said I was in the neighbor-hood. Well, first I said I went out to eat. They asked me where. And I said, 'In her neighborhood.' Then they asked me where. And I said, 'At Popeye's.' Actu-ally, I said, 'At a chicken spot.' I couldn't remember if it was Popeye's or Pudgy's at the time. And I said that. And they were like, 'Okay.' Then they asked me, 'When was the last time you had spoken to Catherine?' I said I was at home."

It was a fine distinction because Paul had testified that the last time he actually spoke to Catherine was when he was at home. He didn't reach her when he made the calls from her neighborhood.

Casolaro wasn't buying it. "And the detectives never concentrated with you on your movements, even though you told them you were in the neighborhood that day?"

"Yeah. I just related that to you."

"You mean they didn't say, Where were you at this time, where were you at that time, where were you at this time?"

"No. No."

"The detectives never said those things to you?"

"I remember them asking me if I knew where I was around this time. I was really unclear. I had not been able to even check my cell phone at this point. That's when they asked me for the cell phone, actually, and I gave it to them, and they were checking it themselves."

Paul was not shaken by Casolaro, and was even able to slip in little asides like this one, which let the jury know how much he had cooperated with police—he'd even given them his cell phone voluntarily.

"Didn't the detectives ask you where you were between five and eight p.m., and didn't you tell them you were at home?"

Paul repeated himself: "I said I was at home and then I said I went out to eat, and at that point I went and called clients and called Catherine and said I came back home."

"When you wrote out your statement, which was three pages long, you didn't put in that you had left your home at any place, did you?"

"No. And I didn't put in I went to see Stephanie, either. I didn't put in a lot of things in that statement."

"Well, but the detectives were asking you about your whereabouts at the time of the murder, Mr. Cortez, when you wrote that, weren't they?"

"Yeah."

"What you left out, according to you today, is your whereabouts at the time of the murder?"

"Like I said before, it was a very stressful situation, and I did not want to be part of this in any way. I didn't volunteer any information that they didn't ask for."

"So you mean you're not going to tell them your whereabouts at the time of the murder when they ask you your whereabouts at the time of the murder?"

"Objection. Asked and answered," Miranda said.

"Overruled."

Paul blamed the detectives for having bad work habits: "No. I did tell them where I was. But the fact that they didn't go into a minute-by-minute detail is something on them. Just like they didn't ask to see my hands until four and a half, five hours later, until Goetz came in."

Casolaro wanted the jury to see that he felt Paul's answers were absurd. "So the love of your life, as you've written in your diaries, is dead, the police are asking you for information in their investigation, and your decision is to withhold information about where you are at the time of the murder?"

"Well, I know I didn't do it. I was trying to give them information that might lead to information to someone that did do it."

"Oh, and the way you'd lead them to someone else is by not telling them where you were, is that correct?"

"Like I said, I definitely told them where I was."

"When you were asked to write it down, you withheld it?"

"I did. I omitted that."

"And as you said, you omitted other things as well, right?"

"It wasn't a conscious effort on my part to omit things. I was just trying to get it over with and done."

"That's what you wanted. You wanted to get out of there, right?"

"Yeah."

"So the love of your life is murdered, and you're not saying, 'God, how can I help? What can I do?' You're saying, 'Gee, what time can I go home?' "

"Objection."

"Correct?" Casolaro pressed.

"No."

Miranda was still trying to get her objection heard. "Misleading. It's misstating the evidence," she said.

"You may answer the question," Judge Berkman told Paul.

"Okay. After I provided the information that I thought was helpful for them, for that case, I wanted to go home. They asked me the same questions over and over again over a period of six hours."

"And by the way, you never told them in that six hours that David had been violent with Catherine, did you?"

"Yes, I did."

"Oh. They left that out, too? They never mentioned that in the statement? You certainly didn't put that in your written statement, did you?"

"Right. Just like I never put in my meeting with David."

"You wanted them to find the real killer, right? And you wanted, as you said a minute ago, to lead them to the person, is that correct?"

"Well, I was hoping that they would find the person, yes."

"So you were leaving it up to them, and you weren't going to give them this important clue that David was a violent guy with Catherine, right?"

Paul claimed he had told the police about David and about the fight in which Catherine said David had broken some dishes.

"When you were memorializing your statement, which was going to be your contribution to this investigation, you left all that out, correct?" Casolaro asked.

"Like I said, if I would have written everything that I knew about Catherine Woods and our relationship, it would have filled a novel. And I was basically exhausted, emotionally and physically and everything, and I—I left out a lot of information. Yes. I did. But I told the police—"

"That was the choice you made, to leave that out, correct?"

"That's true. I told the police everything I'm telling all the people here now. It wasn't a conscious choice to leave those things out."

"When you decided to write your statement out, you said that you didn't want to be involved. So that was another reason you left things out, correct?"

"Yeah. I was definitely scared."

Casolaro tried again to trap Paul with his own words: "So you made a decision not to tell the police the whole truth in your statement?"

"Well, I said I didn't volunteer any information like 'Oh, yeah, well, I was waiting at Starbucks four or five blocks, you know, from her house.' "

"And you did that because you didn't want to get yourself implicated in the case, correct?"

"That was one of the reasons, yeah."

"And so," Casolaro summed up, "when you decide it's in your best interest not to tell the truth, you don't tell the truth?"

"Well, it's two completely different situations. At the time that I'm talking about, I'm surrounded by cops, and I just found out my girl died. And now I'm trying, and I've sworn and everything to tell the truth and the whole truth."

Casolaro would not let it go. "So truth-telling for you is a situational event?"

"No. Not at all."

"Correct?"

"Not at all."

"Did I just misunderstand your last answer, then?"

"Well, you're implying that I would lie just for anything, and that's not true."

"Well, you lied to Alex Casella that day, didn't you?"

Casolaro was referring to Paul's telling the guitar player from Monolith that he'd slept through band rehearsal on the night of Catherine's murder.

"Yeah, I did."

"You lied to him just because it was inconvenient for you to go to practice, correct?"

"He and I both knew the truth of what was going on."

"So then it's okay to tell a lie if the other person knows you're lying?"

"Well, it was—that was our relationship at that time. It was growing very distant. And I told him, 'Listen,' you know, 'we'll talk about this later,' and he agreed."

Casolaro switched topics. "So you've looked at the telephone records a lot, as you said, over this period of time before the trial, is that correct?"

"I looked at it, yes," Paul said.

"So you're aware that in January of 2005, you called Ms. Woods 175 times, is that correct?"

"I'm not aware of that. But it could be."

"In February, you called her 119 times, is that correct?"

"I'm sure she called me just as much on both occasions."

"In March, you called her 145 times, is that correct?"

"She called me just as much as I called her."

"She called you, say, in October, 292 times, the same as you called her?" Casolaro asked.

"Possibly. I don't have the phone records in front of me."

"You said that the reason you called her so much on October 19th, the day where you made calls to her, was because she was angry at you because she had caught you checking her phone for other men, is that right?"

"Uh-huh."

"She told you, 'I'm really angry at you, leave me alone,' or words to that effect, correct?"

"Well, she was angry at me, and she didn't want to speak to me at that moment, yeah."

"But you kept calling?"

"Yeah. I kept trying to apologize."

"And you called and called and called and called and

called, even though it was pretty clear she didn't want to pick up the phone, right?"

"It was pretty clear that she had turned off her phone, and I was trying to catch her when she picked it back up."

"What you were interested in was you wanted to get in touch with her. You didn't pretty much care that she didn't want to talk to you, is that right?"

"I'm sorry. I don't understand."

"You didn't care that she didn't want to talk to you. You wanted to talk to her, right?"

"I wanted to reconcile the situation."

"So you had no intention of respecting her wishes to be left alone, correct?"

"Well, there were a lot of times that she would say things like that, and then we would just call each other and make up."

"So in this particular instance, though, she wasn't calling you to make up. You were calling her minute after minute after minute after minute. Correct?"

Miranda jumped up at last. "Objection. Asked and answered."

The judge would not sustain it: "Overruled."

"And so what mattered on October 19th, in that situation, was what you wanted, not what she wanted, correct?"

"What mattered is that we reconciled the situation and that we weren't being mad at each other."

"And she didn't want to hear from you, and you kept calling until you finally wore her down, right?"

"No. I wouldn't say that."

After more testimony about Paul's many phone calls to Catherine, Casolaro turned the questioning back to Paul's writings. "Now, you wrote this song 'The Killin Machine.' You say that's about sex, is that right?"

"It's about how men, especially in our society, they—they use sex as violence or they equate sex with violence. Like I was saying, there's certain slang—maybe not in your generation, but in our generation—terminology that's like, you know, 'I want to fuck the shit out of this girl,' or, you know, 'I'm gonna beat that pussy good.' There's all this violent—like the way they talk about sex now. It's no longer like, you know, fifties, how it's all like love and romance, stuff like that. So I'm writing a song that is a hard rock song. I'm getting this point across and [it's] entertaining at the same time and—"

Casolaro had heard enough and so had many in the courtroom. For all his savior faire, Paul seemed unaware that spouting vulgarity on the stand was not going to endear him to some of the women in the jury box.

"So I take it your answer is a yes?" Casolaro asked.

"Yeah."

"And so you equate killing with sex in your song title?"

"I definitely do not."

"Well, you wrote it?"

"Yeah. I've written a lot of things."

"The girl in that song, she's a very attractive young woman, isn't she?"

"Well, if you're implying Catherine, no, it's not about her," Paul said. "It's definitely about attractive girls, how you meet them in the club and you're kind of gaming them a bit, you know. And then, eventually, you meet up outside, go to the place, have a great night of raw sex, hot sex, whatever you want to call it, and that's the rock 'n' roll part of it."

"Once again, the answer is yes, it's about an attractive young woman?"

"It's about attractive young women and the men that want to have sex with them."

"And your sex machine that you write about is not made of plastic or rubber or things that sex toys are made of. We even have those in my generation. It's made of steel. Is that right?"

"Well, steel is a hard element. So the idea of steel is an erection being rock hard or steel hard."

"Knives are made of steel, too, aren't they, Mr. Cortez?"

"So are guns," he answered.

"And so are swords, is that right?"

"Yeah. So are cars and a lot of other things."

"And the way that—the result that this sex machine has on the people in your song is it tears the woman apart with a scream, is that right?"

"Right. That's a common use of guys nowadays. They say, 'I want to tear that pussy apart.' "

"Really?" Casolaro asked. He was egging Paul on, but Paul seemed not to realize it.

"Yeah."

"Then, boy, I'm out of it, you're right. Of course, when women have sex, their eyes dilate, too, right? Just like dead people's eyes?"

"Objection."

Finally, the judge sustained one for the defense.

"Well, [were] your woman's eyes dilated when she's on the killing machine, Mr. Cortez?"

"Did you ever see *your* girlfriend's eyes when she's coming?"

It was an outrageous and provocative question for someone on trial for murder, and the judge was not about to let Paul go there. "I think Mr. Casolaro is asking the questions," she said.

The district attorney moved on to another of Paul's poems, "The Gardens of Kamala," which Paul said was "written for a lot of girls who have gone from the pain of being raped."

"That's why the girl is from the Midwest, living away from home, and has a dog, just like Catherine Woods, right?" Casolaro asked.

For once Paul agreed with him. "Yeah. That's definitely referring to her."

"And so it's a complete and utter coincidence that you write a poem about [her] getting her throat cut, and your girlfriend just happens to be murdered by having her throat cut in exactly the same way?"

Miranda was on her feet. "Objection."

Berkman agreed: "Sustained."

"Total coincidence, right, Mr. Cortez?"

"Objection."

"Sustained."

The whole afternoon, Casolaro and Paul were locked in a war of words over what the symbolism in Paul's poetry did and did not mean. It went on and on, probably too long for the jury. Casolaro seems to have made his point—that Paul enjoyed using violent images and in fact drew knives on a page of his journal. Paul said these images were inspired by all the comic books he'd read as a child and meant nothing.

Finally, Casolaro returned to the day of the murder. "Now, when you were in her neighborhood on the day she was murdered, you testified that you were worried about her and that's why you called so much, correct?"

"Well, something had seemed wrong, and that's why I had called so much."

"And so you called a number of times, and in the last number of times you never reached her, correct?"

"Right."

"And then you just stopped calling, correct?"

"Well, I left several messages on her phone and, you know, that's basically the way our relationship was for that month of November. We pretty much tried to give each other a little bit more space, and I figured I called, I tried to see her, I left a message. I left actually three messages, two or three, and in it I said, you know, 'Please call me when you get out of work.'"

"And even though you were worried, you gave up and stopped calling, correct?"

"Well, there was nothing I could do."

"You were in the neighborhood, right?"

"Yes."

"You could have stopped by, right?"

"After that time with David, she told me never to do that again. I respected that."

"Now, that day when you were down by her apartment, you left to go home directly from the Starbucks, is that right?"

"No. After Starbucks, I went to eat at the Popeye's. And then from there I went back to Second Avenue, crossed over to check what time that store was going to be open, the paint store, the paint and home repair, and from there I went home."

"And you didn't ride a bus or a train to go home, right?"

"No, no, I didn't."

After hours of cross-examination, Casolaro was finally winding down with a series of questions that seemed to flatter Paul but in fact were going straight to motive.

"You're very well educated, correct?"

"I would, I would say I have had the privilege to go to very good schools, yes."

"And you're very smart? You did well in school, correct?"

"Not by virtue of grades, but by virtue of talent and just hard work."

"Okay. You're very talented? You're a talented writer, correct?"

"I can't stipulate to that," Paul said, picking up the lingo of the courtroom.

"Well, you have succeeded to some degree with your talent, correct, as a writer, a dancer, a singer, correct?"

"Depending on who you ask. It's not my position to say how good I am."

"And you certainly keep yourself very fit?"

"I was a personal trainer, yes, I kept fit."

"And you're very articulate as we see here in court, correct?"

"Thank you," Paul answered.

"And so your competition is this uneducated, really slow, not-so-much-to-look-at rube from Ohio for Catherine, is that correct?"

"Beauty isn't just an external thing. There is obviously something that she loved about him, and I respected that."

"And she wouldn't give him up for you, would she?"

"I never asked her to give him up. I wanted her to respect her own wishes to want to give him up, because he was constantly, at least from what she told me, you know, mooching off the relationship and everything, and she really couldn't get him out. And he always used manipulative tactics, like, you know, 'I'm gonna hurt myself if I don't get back with you,' and things of that nature in order for her to keep him."

"And she never chose you finally over him? Correct?"

"She loved him and she loved me. To my knowledge, he had moved out . . . in August and she—I know she was still seeing him, but to my knowledge, they were friends."

"She never moved in with you, did she?"

"No, I didn't, I didn't. That wasn't it."

"No more questions, Your Honor."

49

He Was Very Affectionate with Her

Ivette Cortez followed her son to the stand. As the mother of the accused, she had been allowed to attend the trial even though she would be called as a witness, and she'd been there every day for her son. She wanted to stand by him but almost couldn't bear the way he was being described. "They're describing, quite frankly, a monster," she said. "And it's just something that has hurt us all so deeply because you see things in the paper, and the average person just takes it at face value and they will believe it."

At her core, Ivette wished her son had never met Catherine. "I just feel that my son is in the situation because he fell in love with the wrong person, plain and simple," she said. "His life would have been completely different if Catherine Woods was never part of his life."

As she took the stand, Ivette wanted to portray the Paul she had known her whole life. She told the jury a little bit about raising Paul in the Bronx. She spoke of the time she'd gone to the Bronx Zoo with him and Catherine.

"He was very affectionate with her," she said. "You know, a lot of hand-holding and giggling, and we had a very nice time together. And I think even at one point my son realized that I must have felt like a third wheel because he made it a point of being between both of us so he could hold both of our hands as we walked through the zoo, and we had lunch."

Again, Paul's lawyers attempted to show the relationship went both ways—that Catherine enjoyed being with Paul as much as he enjoyed her company.

"And when you went to Paul Cortez's apartment, did you see any of Catherine Woods's belongings in his apartment?" Dawn Florio asked her.

"Well, it was obvious to me that I felt my son made a home for her at his place. I noticed there was a lot of junk food around the house and Paul doesn't eat junk food, as far as potato chips and those kinds of things, so I was joking with him. 'Finally you're now out of the house and you're eating junk food.' He was like, 'No, no, I keep those for Catherine.' "

Ivette recounted the last time she'd seen Catherine, which was only two weeks before her murder. "My son makes it a habit of visiting me at my job from time to time and we will go out and have lunch and he'll tell me his news as far as what's happening with the band or the job or whatever, and this one particular time he did come with Catherine.

"I treated them to lunch because I always feel like they're starving artists and they never have any money in their pocket anyway, so we went out to lunch. And

I just noticed in the way they held on to each other and you just noticed people—they were turning heads. They were an attractive couple. I don't know if it's a mommy thing or I guess just that they were so beautiful to see people that they are in love or they have the chemistry or whatever, just you notice these things.

"If you take the time you notice, so we had lunch. And I will always remember Catherine's baked potato smothered in catsup."

The rest of Ivette's testimony concerned how she'd told Paul about Catherine's murder and how he seemed to be carrying on just fine at Thanksgiving, even though Catherine and his friend Jaki did not attend.

After Ivette's testimony, the defense rested its case. The defense was noteworthy for what it did *not* present. There was no scientific evidence or experts to rebut the prosecution's account of how the left index fingerprint had been processed, no one to blow any holes in it. Also no expert had been called to cast doubt on the technology of telephone cell sites. The prosecution made the cell phone technology sound completely foolproof, but—in a city as crowded as New York, where the buildings are literally on top of one another—was it possible that a call could bounce from one cell site to another?

Defense attorneys Laura Miranda and Dawn Florio had always maintained that they were not given enough time to put together a proper defense, and the weakness of their presentation was showing. Money plays a huge role in criminal cases. The prosecution has nearly unlimited resources, but the amount of money Paul's family had to spend on his defense was limited. While his friends and family managed to raise seventy-five thousand dollars, the money went to pay lawyer fees. Paul's attorneys successfully petitioned the court for money to hire expert witnesses, and Paul's lawyers, according to a source, did have an expert look at a photo of the fingerprint *after* it had been enhanced by prosecution experts. That expert reportedly confirmed the fingerprint matched Paul's. Obviously, that expert was not called to the stand.

The evidentiary phase of the trial had lasted more than two weeks. Closings were scheduled for Monday morning.

50

Miranda for the Defense

The courtroom was packed on Monday morning, and there was a new addition thanks to Judge Berkman. She had approved a request by *48 Hours Mystery* to have a videocamera present for closing arguments. Cameras in the courtroom are relatively rare in New York, but the argument was that once the evidence was in, the appearance of a camera could not possibly affect the outcome of the case. As usual, jurors were told they would not be videotaped.

Expectations were high as Laura Miranda stood to give the defense's closing argument. Miranda loved to box as a hobby, and there was no doubt that as she stood she was entering the ring for the main event—she was fighting for the underdog. Miranda reminded the jury once again that Paul was innocent until proven guilty. She began with a prop—empty paper cups—telling jurors that the state's case was built on illusions as empty as those cups, and it was doomed to fail. Miranda pointed out that Paul had never been arrested for *anything*. He was, she said, simply not a violent person.

Miranda wanted the jury to see evidence of Catherine's love for Paul. She put up a display. "I want to show you Paul's telephone in-box. And I want you to remember that. Because on November 23rd, you will see that Catherine Woods sent him a text message with an asterisk on it. It says, 'I love you.' It says, 'I know. I love you.'

"He has no motive to kill this woman whom he loves. He has absolutely no motive. Look at his behavior throughout. Because the prosecutor is going to get up and say, you know what, he's acting; you know, he's following a script. Right? That's what he's gonna say to you. But that's not consistent with any evidence in this case. All of his character witnesses tell you they've known Paul Cortez, they've known him since he was in high school. His very close friend, Will Acosta, who's serving our country as a marine, tells you he's a gentle, caring, peaceful soul, that he's always been like that. Right? He tells you that he gave up contact sports to sing and dance.

"Look at his conduct when he meets David Haughn. He's going to his girlfriend's house. Right? He runs into another guy at his girlfriend's house that he knows is her ex, but he's there. Paul says, 'Let's talk,' in the quiet, submissive way that he is.

"And he's able to have a conversation with David Haughn, and he tells him what's going on, and they walk. There's no physical violence against David or Catherine at that time or any other time. Right? So, what motive would he have at this time to do something that he's never done in his life? And Paul, his parting words with David isn't like when David calls him, like, 'You better stay away from my woman.' It's 'You know what, let me know if you need anything. Call me.'

"That's why the person that you saw, Paul Cortez on the stand, is the same person. He's exactly the way everybody else has described him."

After leaning heavily on Paul's good character, Miranda switched tactics and went on the attack—against David Haughn. If anything was going to save Paul, it was selling the jury on the concept that Paul was the wrong man and that the real killer was David.

Miranda said David implicated himself in Catherine's murder by statements he gave to police that night. "David Haughn doesn't say, 'Oh, I left at six o'clock.' No. David Haughn doesn't say that. David Haughn says he left twenty minutes before he made that 911 call. Right?

"He made the 911 call at 6:59. Twenty minutes before is 6:39. But this prosecutor, they have their case, and their witnesses are for the purposes of establishing their case. They don't want David Haughn in the apartment at the time that [neighbor] Andrew Gold says that he hears those noises."

Miranda turned to the case's physical evidence—specifically the hair found in Catherine's hand. "Catherine had hair in her hand and she had hair on her body. Right? They were hairs that were never tested for DNA. We do know that from their testimony, their own witnesses say that every single one of those hairs, the forty hairs in her hand, the hairs all over her body that were retrieved, were dissimilar, they were not Paul Cortez's hair."

She turned to Paul, who was sitting listening with his hair tied back. "And look at his hair," Miranda said and then she ordered Paul, "Take down your hair."

He did, and it fell down to his shoulders.

"There was a struggle in that apartment, and it took time. The medical examiner told you there were twenty bruises. Catherine was struggling. No human being deserves to die that way. She was struggling. If you can see, she was on the floor. She was bleeding. She was cut. She was slashed. Whoever is struggling, especially someone with long hair, whoever was struggling, there would be evidence of that.

"But David Haughn doesn't give any hair samples, and no DNA tests are done of his hair. Right? And there are hair samples there that weren't tested not only for DNA but for characteristics. There was a gray hair, a nonpigment hair. We don't know whose hair it could have been. But it was in her clasp when she was struggling for her life. And if they're stepping on her, you know, they're holding her down, it's not taking five minutes. It could be taking ten, fifteen minutes.

"And then you have to clean up. Right? And this prosecutor wants you to believe that Spence—I would say he's a pothead. When I asked him if he still, if he did pot frequently, he said, 'No, ma'am. Not anymore.' Right? But he comes here, and he testifies after not being asked at the time on the date, November 28th and 29th, when he was interviewed, he's never asked about the shoes the person is wearing. I mean, isn't this an investigation? They know they have shoeprints or bootprints. He's never asked about that? And he doesn't talk about it. He's not asked to focus on it. But meanwhile, he said four months ago, which is October, almost a year after the events, that he actually remembers the shoes that Paul Cortez had on that night. As if—I would think the person who killed Catherine Woods would get rid of those shoes pretty quickly because there was a lot of blood in that apartment. In the bedroom, particularly.

"But Spence Lebowitz says he doesn't remember whether Paul Cortez had blood on his jacket. He doesn't remember whether Paul Cortez had cuts and bruises. He kind of says . . . no . . . because I wasn't paying attention to that. Well, what would give you reason to believe that he was paying attention to his shoes?

"And you know what shoes Paul Cortez was wearing on November 27, 2005. And I'll show you the DVD at P.C. Richard, and you'll see these are the shoes that he was wearing."

Miranda wanted to be sure the jury could see the security camera video of Paul and Stephanie Bucci at P.C. Richard because, she said, it showed that Paul was wearing shoes, not boots. The judge said she would allow the jury to have the tape when they considered their verdict.

"Did the cops ever take any boots out of his apartment? No. You think they would have, for purposes of the investigation. You know, they took his leather jacket. It wasn't introduced into evidence. And that's because there's nothing that incriminated Paul Cortez. In fact, Detective Goetz said that, you know what, when he did the search of Paul's apartment, that there were absolutely no traces whatsoever, whatsoever, of Catherine Woods's blood, of any hair, of any fibers.

"And you know what, what even confirms that he's not guilty of this crime, that there's reasonable doubt? There's absolutely no fiber, no hair, no DNA. There's nothing in Catherine Woods's apartment that proves beyond a reasonable doubt that Paul Cortez committed this crime. There's nothing there.

"The prosecutor is going to focus on the print, and I will get to that. Because, you know, Entenmann says it's a patent print, which means it's visible. Chacko says when he gets that piece of Sheetrock, right, it's a latent print; it's not visible. He said that two, three—I don't know how many times he said it. And he wasn't the only one who said it. Anna Branigan also said it. Anna Branigan is the witness who comes here and takes the stand and says she acknowledges that, you know what, I know there is human error, and that's why we have supervisors, right. But I'm perfect. I never make mistakes. And I tell you, that arrogance, in and of itself, is dangerous.

"They said they have—in addition to the boot— they have twenty-six different shoes, Sketchers, that matches that sole that was on that print on that bed. Right? It's not proof beyond a reasonable doubt that Paul Cortez committed this murder. He doesn't even have Sketchers boots in his closets. Believe me, if he did have Sketchers boots or Sketchers shoes, they were there the next day."

Again, Miranda contrasted her client with David. "I ask that when you deliberate, you consider David Haughn's behavior. David didn't have a life. Catherine was his life. And if she asked him to leave there again, he couldn't stay in New York City.

"Paul Cortez, on the other hand, he had a life. He had his career. He was writing lyrics. He was writing poetry. He was dating other women. He was intimate with other women. And the prosecutor is going to say, well, he came here and he's not telling the truth. And the judge will tell you that he's an interested witness. But you have a choice. First of all, you have to focus on their case to determine the proof beyond a reasonable doubt. But you have a choice when you listen to Paul Cortez, you know, whether you believe he's telling the truth or not. He didn't come here and say: 'Oh, yeah, yeah, you know what? I remember. I put my hand up against the wall that time when she had her period. Yeah, I definitely remember that.' He didn't say that to you. He said, 'It's possible.' And the prosecutor was horrified because he hadn't noticed that. Well, you know what? In the dark, you may not notice it. And you know what? That print was not visible. Their own witnesses, several of their own witnesses said that. And the proof—what was tested was the blood above the print. That's what was tested. There's no proof beyond a reasonable doubt either that that was the blood from menstruation or that was the blood from that day—if you believe that there was blood on that print. But wouldn't it make sense if the bed was in this corner, and they're making love, that that would be where he would put his hand? That's a reasonable doubt."

Miranda was hot now and marching all over the courtroom in defense of her client, practically screaming at times. She brought up the fact that there was a record of Paul calling Catherine at 6:33 p.m., during or immediately following the time the state said he had allegedly killed her.

"His last phone call is at 6:33. And the prosecutor may say to you, 'Oh, he just made that call to cover it up so you believe he didn't call her.' If you believe there was reasonable proof beyond a reasonable doubt that he was in there at that time and that David Haughn wasn't right. But you know what? There's no proof beyond a reasonable doubt of that. And don't you think if somebody was trying to cover up, he would have called her five more times or ten more times? And he didn't. He called her one more time. He told you: I was trying to get hold of her. I called and left her a message and told her to call me when she gets out of work.

"But then, if you see the next phone call that he makes at 6:50, he starts making calls to his clients because he's prepping for the next week. He has to schedule his clients' appointments. I mean, who's going to do that afterward? And did any of them come in to say he was bizarre when he called me? Of course not. He was being normal. He was doing what he usually did Sunday nights to get his schedule together."

Miranda moved on to the number of phone calls that made it appear that Paul was always calling Catherine but she was almost never calling him. That impression, Miranda said, was absolutely false.

"In November, she called him 76 times. They spoke 311 minutes. It was less than October, yeah, because they were still, you know, getting over things. But in October, she called him 150 times, and they spoke 745 minutes. In September, it was 34 times. There were periods there that they didn't speak to each other and, you know, he wasn't calling her. There were ten days at a time that neither one of them were calling each other. But even those 34 calls, they spoke 135 minutes. In August, 138 calls. They spoke 712 minutes in August. They spent a lot of time on the phone."

She pointed again to Paul's good character and the way he reacted after he met David and found out that he was still living with Catherine. It was not, Miranda said, the reaction of someone who is violent and insanely jealous. "He writes about that incident and it's a single page and he just says, you know, he's hurt. 'Catherine was lying to me.' He doesn't say, 'I want to kill her. I want to hurt her' or 'I'm going to kill her. I'm going to hurt her.' After he finds out that she and David Haughn are still sleeping together, all he does is, he says, you know, he expresses his feelings and then he goes, 'I'm going to start dating other women because, you know what, I have to accept her for who she is. She is gonna keep on stripping and either I deal with it and I accept it or, you know what, I don't spend any more time with her.'

"Paul Cortez is charged with a very serious murder in the second degree and you cannot unfortunately give Catherine Woods her life back, but you can give Paul Cortez his life back. And when you focus on all of the evidence and the lack of evidence in this case—how it's inaccurate, how it contradicts itself, how their own witnesses and their conclusions are not supported by evidence—then you'll understand that this case demands that you come back with a verdict of not guilty. And I thank you very much for your time and your patience and your attention."

Soon after she finished, Miranda realized she had failed to show the jury the DVD of the security videotape from the P.C. Richard electronics store. She requested she be allowed to do so, but Judge Berkman refused. "If the jury wants to see it, they will see it," the judge said.

51

"If You Believe That's His Fingerprint . . ."

Many of those in the courtroom thought Laura Miranda did a fine job in her closing, leaning heavily on her best asset—Paul himself. Outside the courtroom, she was feeling very good about her presentation, shadowboxing in the courtroom hallway. She had one very good point—it was difficult to believe that such an educated, articulate, and sophisticated young man who had dedicated his life to peace and meditation was capable of murdering the love of his life so viciously.

But Assistant District Attorney Peter Casolaro was intent on explaining to the jury why this was not only possible but was exactly what had happened. He addressed Paul's character immediately. Casolaro talked about the nature of love and how it could turn to hate and how, in that respect, Paul was no different from a lot of people—he reached his breaking point on November 27, 2005.

"For all the defendant's attempts to convince you in court while he was on the witness stand that he was in control of himself and think of how many times he said to you when Catherine didn't do something he wanted or when she wouldn't drop David or stop stripping, how many times did he say to you, 'Well, that was cool with me. That was all right.' For all of his attempts, you know, you could see the signs that he was, he was losing his grip, he was cracking up.

"What I want to talk about is the most important part of this case . . . and that is the evidence that actually puts him in the apartment participating in the murder. Because the People's case is designed not to prove that Paul Cortez is the *kind* of person who would have done this, but that, in fact, he *was* the person who did this.

"Let's concentrate on what shows that he actually committed the crime. . . . Let's start with the most important piece of evidence in the case, which is the bloody fingerprint. We heard a little bit about it in defense summation, but let's talk about it in more detail here."

Casolaro held up a photograph of the fingerprint found on Catherine's wall, the one taken by John Entenmann. "Here it is. Here's the print. In this photo here, you can see there's the print right there in the middle of the wall, okay? Right there in the middle you can see."

Casolaro's contention was the handprint had to have been made at the time of the murder, and he spent a fair amount of time explaining to the jury why that had to be so. Casolaro went on and on, using terms like "ridge characteristics." His explanation was complicated, and it's questionable whether the jury understood what he was talking about, but he got very worked up about it.

He challenged the defense's explanation that the fingerprint may have been left on the wall earlier, possibly in Catherine's own menstrual blood. "I can't imagine any woman that would leave a bloody menstrual handprint on her wall. He says, 'I put it on in the dark,' but it had to be there, to be there for some time, so it's obviously going to be noticed in the day.

"And then they kind of backed off that a little and sort of, then just sort of argued on the second day of his testimony that, well, we really don't know how it got there, but it could have been some other type of protein that was there other than blood that reacted with the amido black and that meant that, you know, that you could, you could now see the print. Well, what are they talking about? What other type of protein? I mean, is somebody putting eggs or peanut butter, steak, on the wall? I mean, what are they talking about?" Casolaro was indignant.

"It's the protein in blood that reacts. . . . I mean, I mean, are they trying to suggest there are some protein in menstrual blood that isn't regular blood? Well, there is no expert testimony about that. Blood is blood. In fact, the only expert testimony you heard in this case is that that fingerprint had to be put on the wall at the same time that the blood was sprayed on the wall. And you can see for yourself. Remember what I told you in opening, you don't have to take my word for it. Take the evidence into the jury room. Look at it yourself and you will be able to see that.

"You know in her summation, the defendant's attorney concentrates on the fact that Mr. Chacko said you couldn't see the print, but what Mr. Chacko is talking about was in very, very technical terms. Of course . . . he could see the print because that's what he tested. That's where he put the amido black. What he means when he says, 'I can't see the print,' is that 'I can't see the prints sufficient for comparison purposes,' which is what his job is—to bring out the print in such detail that can be compared."

But that was *not* what Alex Chacko had said on the stand. He plainly said he could not see the print before applying the chemicals.

"You know, it's like eyeglasses," Casolaro continued. "You wear eyeglasses not to see. You wear eyeglasses to see *better*. And that's precisely what Mr. Chacko's job is, to enhance the prints so it can be seen better. So all you have to do is look at the first photo he took and you can see that the print is absolutely visible, and that's why Detective Entenmann cut it out. That's why Mr. Chacko tested that particular area, and that's why we have the beautiful print for comparison.

"Now, you may ask, 'Well, how come if he touched the wall we only got one print?' And the answer is, we were incredibly lucky, just incredibly lucky. His hand was in motion and somehow that hand, that finger came off the wall when his hand moved. And it was just dumb luck.

"If you believe that's his fingerprint put there in her blood—and you should believe it—then that's it. The defendant is the killer.

"All the other evidence is nice. All the other evidence helps, but that [fingerprint] proves he's the killer. No matter what you think about his character witnesses, no matter what you think about the rest of our case, his fingerprint is in her blood, put there at the time of the murder, and there is no other, no innocent explanation for that."

Having explained the fingerprint endlessly and to great effect, Casolaro mercifully moved to the other main piece of evidence against Paul—the cell site records and Paul's incessant calling.

"It's the defendant's persistent use of his cell phone that again puts him in hot water here. Clearly he does not realize what we now know about cell towers and how a phone can be tracked.

"Now, it's true Miss Woods calls him . . . and they talk. Now, we know one thing about this phone call, and that's what he told the police in his statement the next day. We know that something in his phone call disturbed him, that he was upset by the phone call, because Catherine was short with him, and on the stand he even admitted, he had said there was something wrong, so he then calls her back twice. Now, he made it seem like, 'Oh, I called, I called,' but look at the number. Look at the time difference, how short a time it is before he starts calling back. He calls back in a very short time.

"All we know for sure is that he told the police he was upset about something and he called her constantly. Now, she does call him back. She is clearly getting these messages, and she calls him back at 5:11 and they have this one-minute, twenty-three-second call. Another really short call. We have no idea what the substance of that call is, but we know something about it disturbed him, because he calls her back twenty-two seconds after that call ends. Twenty-two seconds from the end of that call to when he calls her back again.

"So something disturbed him because he wanted to call her back so quickly, and then in the next twenty-eight seconds, he calls her three more times. So there is something . . . as casually as he tells you on the stand that everything was okay and 'we could talk,' as calm as he described it, he was not calm on that day. He's urgently calling her in [a] matter of seconds after she last spoke to him."

Casolaro pulled out the cell-site records to show that the next thing that happened is that there was a thirteen-minute gap, and Casolaro explained that by saying that Paul was on the subway on his way to Catherine's apartment. There is no cell phone service on New York City subways. When Paul began calling again, he was near Catherine's apartment, according to the cell site records, which put him only a block or two away.

Casolaro painted a picture of Paul getting closer and

closer to Catherine's apartment and dialing her cell phone continually. But then, the calls stop. The question is, why?

"For the first time since he started calling her—and that's this gap from three and a half minutes to 6:00 to 6:33—a thirty-seven-minute gap. And we know, if he's not right on her corner, he's very, very close during that thirty-seven-minute period. And the other thing we know is that he's not making any phone calls to anybody during that period of time. Now, it just so happens that that's the time of the murder."

Casolaro said that based on the testimony by neighbor Andrew Gold, the district attorney puts the time of the fatal encounter between Catherine and her killer at 6:20 p.m., certainly no later than 6:35 p.m.

"So that's the range of the murder, and all of that time we know from the records that Mr. Cortez is right in the neighborhood and that he's not calling anybody. Now, the records don't put him in the apartment. That's exactly correct, but the fingerprint puts him in the apartment. So now we know not only is his print found on the fresh blood, but his own cell phone records tell us that he has the opportunity to put that print there, because he's there at the critical time."

What about the phone call from Paul to Catherine at 6:33 p.m.? Why would he call her if he'd just killed her? Casolaro said that because the phone call was only one second long, he believes that Paul accidentally hit the Redial button on his phone, realized his mistake, and cut it off quickly.

Casolaro was making a very strong case for Paul's guilt, but he had yet another point to make and this point would get picked up in all the newspapers the next day, probably because it had the ring of truth and smacked of common sense.

"Paul never, ever, ever calls Catherine Woods again after the murder. The guy who called her 51 times a day, 47 times another day, who calls her 292 times a month, never calls her after she is dead. And he says he didn't find out about it until 10:30 the next morning. So that means for sixteen and one-half hours, from six o'clock to ten-thirty in the morning, he doesn't call her. Not at all.

"Now, remember, this is prime time to call her because David is at work between eleven and seven in the morning. And that's why, on his phone records—I want you to look at the phone records in the jury room—you are going to see him calling all hours of the morning, because that's when David isn't there. Yet on this day, the day she is murdered, there are no calls during prime time. And also you got to look at that time in terms of the persistent way he is calling her. After that one-minute-and-thirty-eight-second call where he says to the police she was clearly upset, he's calling, calling, calling, calling. Time of the murder, he stops. Never calls again.

"Is that a coincidence? Is that why he stops calling her? Or is it because he already knows she is dead and there is nobody to answer the phone?"

Casolaro went on and on, but that one sentence made the biggest impression of the day. In the rest of the summation, he described Paul as a continual loser in romance, a loser whose rage against women was building by the time he met and fell in love with Catherine.

"In his secret diaries there's a lot of rage against women. And that's the important thing. Because by the time he meets Catherine Woods, he's zero for four or zero for five in trying to get successful relationships with women. So when he enters his relationship with Catherine in 2004, it again becomes the all-consuming relationship. . . . He's calling her well in excess of 150 times a month. He's calling her dozens of times each day.

"He says, 'Well, she called me just as much.' Look. If you look at the phone records, you're going to see that, on average, he calls her ten times to every four times she calls him. Yes. She calls him a lot. Especially in the beginning. But it's certainly not as much. It's easy to say now, 'She's calling me because she loves me,' because, of course, she's dead and she can't answer. You're going to look at the records, and you'll see a pattern from June up to September, that ten-to-four ratio, and all hours of the day and night. In September, something happens, because in September you're going to see the calls fall off radically. She's like hardly ever calling him, and he's not calling her at all. It's clear. And we don't know what happened . . . the relationship changed dramatically. She's not as eager to call him anymore. You'll see that when you look at the records.

"In September he makes a big push to get her back. He calls her 299 times in October. He does this for a while. Then it wears off pretty quickly. If you look at the first two weeks in November, she doesn't call him at all, hardly at all. Just a handful of calls, at most. It's clear something happens—whatever happened in September, there was some kind of holdover.

"By November—first two weeks in November—she's not calling anymore. Very, very little. He makes one last attempt—you'll see it in the records—and he bombards her with calls in the middle of November. . . . But then something else happens. Because on November 25th, the day Mrs. Rickter sees what she sees, Catherine Woods stops calling the defendant and, essentially, doesn't call him anymore, except for what you saw on the chart on November 27th, where she has those two very brief phone calls. . . . So something has happened that she's now pushing him out, and she's cutting off contact, and she's slipping away from him.

"She pushes him away. She does the stripping. She hangs out with David. It's not working the way he wants it to work. . . . So on November 25th, for whatever reason, which is lost now—as I told you, it was in [my] opening, we don't know—she cuts him off for some reason. And for the next two days, three days, through the 25th, 26th, and 27th, she's basically ignoring him. And then, on the day of the murder, he calls her, and she blows it off.

"How do we know that? He wrote it in his statement to the police. He said, 'She was very, very short with me. Something was wrong. I wanted to call her again.'

"So he calls and calls and calls . . . she's not calling him back, so he runs down to her neighborhood. He calls and calls again when he gets in her neighborhood. She's still not picking up. She still won't answer. And then he sees David come out, and he goes in.

"And what happens then? He reached the breaking point. That's exactly what happened. He reached his breaking point. His incredible narcissistic vanity must have been so bruised, along with the fact that he couldn't have what he wanted.

"Look at him. He's: 'I'm a college grad. I'm the guy with the great dramatics background. I'm the star of all those shows. I'm the lead singer of a rock band. We're really serious.' He's vain to the nth degree. 'This beautiful woman who I'm madly in love with, done all these things for, saved from herself, she's hanging on to this unsophisticated guy from Ohio who's nothing but a leech, just sucking her blood, a part-time doorman, very slow, who can't compare to me at all.' What's happened to him? Friend. Once in a while [they'll] have sex. Instead of becoming the love of his life, which is what he wants.

"Couple that with all his previous rejections, you

just have to say to yourself it's like a volcano, where the person you are is building up, building up, and building up. And the volcano seems passive, dormant. And then, all of a sudden, boom! There's a huge explosion. That explosion in this case was murderous rage. And Catherine Woods just happened to be in the wrong place at the wrong time."

Casolaro had more to say, but it didn't really matter. It was a terrific closing argument, and Paul Cortez was in a lot of trouble. His only hope was for one juror to believe he was not the kind of person who could commit such a murder. True, it would mean a hung jury, not an acquittal, but it seemed like Paul's last best hope.

52

Inside the Jury Room

By the time the closing arguments ended and the judge delivered her instructions, the jurors were more than ready to deliberate the evidence. They adjourned behind closed doors, on the eleventh floor of the Criminal Court building in Lower Manhattan, each eager to know what the others were thinking.

"On one hand, you have this bloody murder, a horrific crime," said one female juror. "On the other hand, you have this seemingly harmless, peace-loving individual with no history of violence. How do you put these two things together? It's very difficult."

It was clear immediately that Paul's personality and charisma would loom large. "I honestly didn't have any opinion when I went into the jury room, but I wanted him to be innocent," the same female juror said. "He's this creative person. He's worked very hard with his life. He had no history of violence, and he had a loving family. His mother was in court, and his very supportive friends only had nice things to say about him. They never got one person to say anything nasty about him the whole trial."

Others liked the way Paul faced the jurors while testifying. "I felt like we weren't really in court," she said. "I felt like we were at somebody's apartment just talking to him, like we were having a cup of coffee. It was really strange."

But not every juror was a fan. One described some of Paul's behavior on the stand as "inappropriate" and pointed to the moment he was asked to identify the shoes he said he was wearing that weekend. Paul did so, but then joked that when he'd worn them, they had shoelaces. "It seemed to me like he doesn't want to believe that this is court and he is on the stand. And it's his life, you know? I thought, 'What is he thinking? Where does this come from?' This is not a funny situation."

And oddly enough, it wasn't *only* Paul's character that offended this female juror, who had emigrated from Europe to this country as an adult. She didn't much like Assistant District Attorney Peter Casolaro, either. "The prosecutor was displaying a lot of hate, and when anybody does that, it's very difficult [for me] to listen to what he has to say," she said. "I was almost biased against the prosecutor because his opening statement was so hateful. He made it hard for me."

But most others disagreed and thought Casolaro had made a lot of sense, especially in his argument that Paul had never called Catherine again after that Sunday night because he knew she was dead. It seemed inconceivable that Paul, a veritable cell phone junkie, would simply stop calling—unless he had a reason. "He didn't call her after the murder and he was always calling her before that," the juror said. "And then he just stopped?"

That juror thought Paul was clearly lying to police in his written statement. "He remembered every little incident of . . . meeting Catherine, but then towards the end, he couldn't remember anything. He remembered speaking to Mr. Woods—everything—but he couldn't remember the last day he saw her?"

Most thought Paul was indeed obsessed with Catherine, and it was the phone calls that proved it. "Three hundred phone calls in a month?" one woman said. "That's ridiculous."

But while the fingerprint and the phone calls were considered very important, Paul's diaries were not. The jurors more or less dismissed them, despite all the time spent poring over Paul's words. "We really didn't look at the journals or the diaries that much," said one woman who voted guilty from the beginning. "There was other evidence we looked at, and it was actually bigger than the journals, so we didn't take that into account."

When the jurors polled themselves, the first vote was seven guilty, five not guilty. Clearly, there was a lot of work to be done.

As always, the jurors brought their own history and

experience into the deliberations, and even though it had nothing to do with the evidence, sometimes that history swayed them one way or another.

One of the women on the "not guilty" side was a recent widow. Her deceased husband had been an artist, and for that reason she admitted being biased in favor of Paul's innocence. "My husband died three years ago, and I had just got over grieving for him, and he himself was an artist," she said. "Although I didn't relate personally to the defendant, I saw him in the abstract. What they said about him, the little details, reminded me of people I know who are artists, musicians, or whatever. My husband was always scared of the police so, in a way, I felt it upon me to sort of fight for him [Paul]. Maybe I was fighting for my husband's life or something, and I realized that I have this bias. And that's why, in my head, I tried very hard to get rid of the forensic evidence."

But the forensic evidence was not going to be dismissed so casually. In fact, one young woman on the jury said that the fingerprint told her all she needed to know. "I just went with my gut, and I just felt he was guilty and that was his fingerprint on the wall," she said. "I made it an important piece of evidence because you didn't have a murder weapon. That was the closest thing that made me say, 'Oh yeah, Paul was in that apartment at the time of her death.' "

But the European immigrant argued against the fingerprint. She said she'd once had her own fingerprints taken and had had to do it over and over because the inked impression was not good. Because of that, she said, she felt fingerprints were not an exact science. She ruled it out completely and could not be swayed on that point.

Eventually, the widow became Paul's biggest defender in the jury room. No matter what the evidence, it seemed she could turn it around to Paul's favor. When the jurors deliberated about Jacques, the neighbor who said he'd seen Paul throwing out garbage at four in the morning, this woman told them it was a perfectly reasonable thing to do. "I throw my garbage out at quarter to one in the morning because I knew the garbage gets picked up around that time," she said. "So maybe his garbage pickup was four-thirty so he's throwing it out at four o'clock. I don't think there's anything particularly suspicious about that, which some people thought was terribly peculiar. How that relates to the fact that he did the crime or not, I don't know."

One thing just about all the jurors discounted was the testimony of Margaret Rickter, the elderly woman who claimed to have seen a couple resembling Paul and Catherine fighting on East Eighty-sixth Street during Thanksgiving week.

"I just felt that was ridiculous."

"She was just a busybody."

"That was just silly."

As usual, the European woman went one step further and said that Rickter's testimony proved that Casolaro would do anything to convict Paul.

And then, of course, there was David Haughn, who as expected created problems for the prosecution. "I actually thought he could have done it," said one juror. "I thought he was more likely the type of personality to do it rather than the defendant. I think he had actually assaulted her at one time."

In fact, there was no evidence that David had ever assaulted Catherine, except for Paul's account claiming that Catherine told him David broke those dishes. But to say the least, the source of that information was a bit biased.

As the first day of deliberations wound down, there was a lot of confusion in the room. The arguments were all over the place. Some jurors pointed to Catherine's topless dancing. Had the police really checked whether or not someone might have been stalking her? No one from Flash Dancers or Privilege testified, and the jurors wondered about why not.

Jurors also argued that the defense could have done more. Why hadn't the defense brought in an expert witness to counter the prosecution about the fingerprint? It was further proof, the jurors said, that Dawn Florio and Laura Miranda were "sloppy" and "unorganized."

Because the defense had not introduced any experts, said one juror, "we're stuck with what we have."

At least one juror said she was willing to consider the possibility that the fingerprint might have been left in Catherine's menstrual blood, but "we would've needed another expert to tell us that that was possible, and we didn't have it. So her theory without any backup was difficult to accept."

The jurors made a list of the evidence they would ask for: the testimony of various police officers, the recording of David Haughn's 911 call, David's statements to the police, various crime scene photos, Paul's Johnston and Murphy shoes, the line drawings of those Sketchers boots that Spence had looked at, part of the testimony of the medical examiner and of fingerprint expert Annabelle Branigan, and finally, the DVD recording of the security videotape from P.C. Richard that the defense was so anxious for them to see.

Judge Berkman said she would grant their requests but told them they'd have to wait until tomorrow to get the proper equipment to hear the 911 recording and to see the DVD. When Miranda heard that the jury wanted to see the DVD, she thought it was a very positive sign.

The next day was the only time the jury deliberated for an entire day. Much of the day was devoted to the reading back of the testimony they had asked for. It seemed to onlookers that the jury was interested in establishing a clear time line for when the murder took place and, at the same time, trying to get a read on where Paul and David were during that time.

They sat politely in the courtroom and listened, but behind the scenes, positions began to harden. Different items took prominence. Some jurors began questioning Annabelle Branigan's testimony on the fingerprint match simply because she'd been so adamant that she'd never make a mistake. That didn't sit well with the jurors. "A lot of people had a problem with that," one said.

The fact that Paul admitted lying to Alex Rude about sleeping through band practice also became a problem. If he lied once when it suited him, why wouldn't he lie again? Jurors were further troubled by Paul's written statement that never mentioned he was in Catherine's neighborhood around the time of the murder. One woman wondered about Paul: "I thought, does he know the truth? Is something wired differently in his brain?"

But the widow who was Paul's defender was willing to believe that he'd been too afraid to tell the cops he was in Catherine's neighborhood. "He doesn't trust the police," she said. "I think that's quite credible."

The deliberations continued into the afternoon, and gradually the vote became ten-to-two to convict Paul. But the two holdouts could not be swayed. It seemed nothing could convince them that Paul was guilty, and there was talk of a hung jury. Weariness was setting in, along with exasperation and anger.

The jurors decided they would take a break and come back the next morning.

The next day, someone suggested they all settle down and take another look at the DVD submitted by the defense, the security videotape showing Paul Cortez and Stephanie Bucci walking into the electronics store to buy the humidifier. "We didn't know why it was important, but the defense wanted us to see it," said one juror.

Miranda had gone out of her way to tell them to look at it, and so they looked very carefully. What was it she had wanted them to see? They gathered around to watch the tape on a large television screen. They played it a couple of times, until one juror said, "Stop it right there. Freeze it right there."

They looked carefully at Paul walking into the store. What was he wearing—shoes or boots? Everyone was tired, but they were desperate to latch on to anything that would prove once and for all whether or not Paul was guilty. "There it was," said one juror, "the evidence was staring me in the face."

The jurors agreed they all were seeing the same thing. The DVD—which had never been played in court—became the key piece of evidence, more important than the forty-five witnesses who had testified, more important than the so-called bloody fingerprint, more important than the cell phone calls or Paul's or David's demeanor on the stand.

One juror burst into tears. "It's the first time in my life I've ever cried in public."

A male juror wrapped his arms around her. The jury alerted the bailiff.

They had reached a verdict.

53

"Monsters Don't Always Look Like Monsters"

It surprised a lot of people, but Jon and Donna Woods did not stay in New York to hear the jury's verdict. They had listened to all the testimony and the closing arguments, but then they decided to get back to their lives. Whichever way the trial ended, Catherine was gone forever. "There's no happy ending to this," Donna said. "It isn't like anybody really wins."

Jon agreed: "We've lost a daughter, and the Cortez family will have lost a son, more or less. It's a no-win proposition for everybody when something like this happens."

What *was* important, Jon said, was for them to hear the testimony. "We wanted to hear firsthand everything that was going to be said there," he said. "I tried to approach this with an open mind. We didn't want to hear things secondhand or read them in the papers."

The trial was stressful and exhausting, and it took a lot out of them. Aside from the details of the crime, they were living in New York, the city that they will forever associate with their daughter's death. No one could blame them for feeling out of step with the city's glamour and fast pace. What's worse is that court did not convene on Wednesdays, a day when the Woodses were left to themselves, a day when they could not help but feel adrift. Detective Steven Goetz would set aside part of those days to be with the Woodses, but it was difficult for them to "enjoy" New York under those circumstances. In the end, they'd just had enough.

"I just want to take my brain and put it somewhere so I don't have to think for a while," Donna said.

They said the hardest part of the trial was not the medical examiner's testimony about the way Catherine died but, rather, hearing the defense presentation. "I felt like I didn't have a voice," Donna said. "It was frustrating, and I wanted to say, 'Wait a minute, that's not how it was exactly, that's not how Catherine was.' That part has been very, very hard for me."

Donna loathed watching Paul on the stand. "He has this nonchalant attitude," she said. "He's been smiling; that was rough for me to watch. When he finished testifying, I didn't know whether I should leave or whether I should stand up for the performance that he gave. I felt that he was performing."

She said she had never thought of one thing until the trial—the fact that Paul had never contacted them after Catherine's death, before he was arrested. Supposedly the love of his life had been butchered mercilessly and "he didn't call. He didn't send flowers. He didn't send a card. We never heard from him."

Catherine had told them that Paul was a friend, nothing more, and none of the testimony had convinced them otherwise. "She just wanted her space," Donna said of Catherine. "She didn't want to be involved in the drama of a boyfriend/girlfriend-type relationship. She wanted to do her thing. She had also shared with me that she thought Paul might be gay, and she was happy about him being gay because that would mean she could keep him as a friend and she never had to worry about the relationship going in that other direction."

It wasn't the first time someone had suspected Paul was gay. Both Danielle and Monica, the women Paul had been sexually aggressive with, had sensed the same thing. In fact, in Danielle's police report, she said that Paul told her that at one time he had been a male stripper and an escort, but there is no proof of that beyond that one reference. Danielle said she thought Paul's abhorrence of stripping was some type of transference and that he actually hated himself for having once tried it.

The Woodses considered him, at his core, a liar and a murderer. They were horrified by the lyrics in his songs and even more so by the way he explained those lyrics on the stand, going out of his way to disrespect women, Jon said. He and Donna came away from the trial thinking two things: Catherine had not given up on her dream and had not turned to drugs and prostitution the way they say Paul told them. Second, they were leaving New York convinced that it was Paul who had murdered their daughter.

"Monsters don't always look like monsters," Donna said. "He stabbed Catherine twenty times. He slit her throat from side to side and then stabbed her larynx. There is no doubt in my mind that he's a monster. I think he's extremely dangerous."

Sitting through the trial had been rough, they said, and they'd had enough. It was time to return to Columbus. Whatever the verdict, they would handle it in the privacy of their own home.

Ivette Cortez, meanwhile, had everything to lose. Her baby boy was fighting for his life, and she was going to be there for him. Her large family wrapped her in its embrace, and overall they were upbeat. They believed in Paul, believed he had not killed Catherine, and were optimistic the jury would find him not guilty.

"In my heart," Ivette said, "I think, 'not guilty,' but it is up to the jurors."

Paul's uncle Louie, Louis Rosario, felt he'd soon see his nephew a free man. "I really feel a not-guilty verdict is gonna come up," he said, "and I'm just gonna scream for joy in the court. They'll probably throw me out, but what the hell. I can't wait for our boy to come home. I feel that confident."

Laura Miranda and Dawn Florio were on edge. Florio thought Miranda had done an "amazing" job in her closing and felt the jurors were with them, whereas she thought the jurors seemed rather subdued while listening to the prosecutor. Waiting for the verdict is the worst time for a lawyer, but both were hopeful.

Marguerite Shinouda, Paul's biggest supporter outside his family—the woman who'd put her life on hold to raise money for his defense and to sit through nearly every day of testimony—believed the jurors would do the right thing and come back with a not-guilty verdict. She felt the prosecution's case was confusing, given that one fingerprint expert had said the print was patent or visible and the other had said it was latent or invisible. She'd believed in Paul when she met him at a retreat in her house, and she believed in him still.

Nothing could shake her faith.

54
Verdict

Later that morning, the jurors walked back into Judge Berkman's courtroom. Everything was happening very fast. After two and a half days of deliberation, the jury was coming back with a verdict.

It's always shocking how quickly a trial ends after all the weeks of testimony and evidence. People you've spent weeks with suddenly disperse, and you likely will never see them again. It takes only a matter of minutes for a trial to end, and then the court personnel move on to the next case.

In a murder case, there is tension in a courtroom that exists nowhere else. This is not a reality show—this is real life, and a man's future is at stake. The court clerk asked the jury foreperson, "Has the jury reached a verdict?"

"Yes, the jury did."

"Madame Foreperson, how say you to the one count of the indictment numbered 6433 of 2005, charging the defendant with the crime of murder in the second degree? Do you find the defendant guilty or not guilty?"

In a strong voice, the foreperson said, "We find him guilty."

There was no reaction from Paul. Those close to him said he was simply too stunned to react. But his mother, Ivette, collapsed in a heap of loud sobs and later fled the courthouse.

Detective Steven Goetz was pleased that all his hard work had paid off in a conviction, but he did feel badly for Ivette. "Just because I arrested their son doesn't mean I don't have feelings for them and that I don't realize what they're going through right now," he said.

Before all parties were dismissed, the jurors were polled one by one as to their verdict. It didn't change anything. Paul was still guilty. Judge Berkman set March 23 as the sentencing date.

The Woodses had just arrived in Columbus that morning, because a snowstorm had forced them to remain in New York a day longer than they'd wanted. They were still in the airport and had stopped in a cell phone store when they got the news of a verdict.

Jon Woods, in his usual low-key way, simply said, "I was very relieved it came through that way. I think justice was served, but there are no winners in this."

In an interview, jurors who agreed to talk to *48 Hours Mystery* said "the tipping point" that convinced the two holdouts to vote guilty was the DVD of the store security camera that the defense had urged them to watch. The more they watched, the more they became convinced that Paul was wearing boots—not shoes—in the video. It became the determining factor in their decision, the one piece of evidence that persuaded the two holdouts to switch their votes to guilty. It was ironic—of all the pieces of evidence, one introduced by the *defense* was the one that got Paul convicted.

Not long after, *48 Hours Mystery* hired a forensic scientist to take a look at the videotape in an attempt to determine if the jurors had made a correct assessment, that Paul is seen wearing boots, not shoes. Erin Moriarty and the producers working on the show found it impossible to say—no matter how often they froze the frame and looked at it on the best possible monitors—what kind of footwear Paul was wearing.

Gerald Richards, who does forensic examinations for a living, agreed to take a look. After examining the video, freezing the frame and enlarging it, he finally said, "It suggests that it's more likely the boot than it is the shoe."

But Erin Moriarty wanted more than that. She pressed him: "What is your opinion, after looking at this videotape? Is Paul Cortez wearing either the Johnston and Murphy shoes or is he wearing boots?"

"I can't be definitive about it," Richards said. "I can't tell for sure, based on the information we have. It's probably more likely than not that these are boots as opposed to shoes. And that's based on reflections, based on the shade area and based on comparison with other shoes and boots in that picture.

"But again, more likely than not is just what it means. It isn't positive by any stretch of the imagination."

"You mean it's not one hundred percent?" Moriarty asked.

"It's not absolute. There are some cases we can absolutely say this is true or absolutely this is not true. This is not one of them."

"But would you say it's more likely than not that these are in fact boots and not shoes?" Moriarty asked again.

Richards said the quality of the image was too poor to be definitive. "From a legal standpoint, that's about fifty-one percent. I might go to fifty-two percent."

The bottom line, Richards said, is that people will see what they want to see. When the jurors watched the tape, they zeroed in on his footwear—they said Paul was wearing boots.

And they were so sure of it they were willing to bet his life.

PART IV

AFTER THE VERDICT

You know, I have a tendency, even after almost three decades, to try to see how a homicide makes sense, and it's almost silly, because a homicide doesn't make sense.

Judge Carol Berkman

55

"The Mistake of Our Lives"

Ever the defense lawyers, Laura Miranda and Dawn Florio—even a week after the verdict—were still ticking off reasons why they felt it was impossible that Paul could have killed Catherine. But nothing they could say now was going to change the outcome—Paul Cortez, a hero to his family, a Renaissance man who had grown up with such promise, was suddenly, and sadly, a convicted murderer.

"You can't take it personally, because it's a job," Florio said. "You feel bad, but we know we've done everything and our whole team has done everything, but of course you're disappointed, especially when you have an innocent man. You just have to keep going to help your client."

But the verdict definitely stung, Miranda said. "It's just devastating because you get to know Paul and you see the kind of person that he is. That he's kind, that he's peaceful, and just interacting with him since last April, he's not somebody who loses his temper. He's not somebody that's vindictive. He's not somebody who carries revenge."

"He's not somebody who could have done this," Florio said succinctly.

They both thought that Paul had helped himself on the stand. "We thought he did great," Miranda said. "He was himself, he was polite and sincere, and no matter how much the prosecutor tried to rattle him, he wasn't."

The defense lawyers had not yet heard what the jurors had said about the videotape. Moriarty asked them about Spence Lebowitz.

"I take it that neither one of you believes that Spence really remembers the shoes."

"No way," each of them said.

Moriarty asked them why they had wanted the jury to watch the DVD from P.C. Richard. "We introduced it into evidence to show the clothing that Paul was wearing," Florio said, "and his demeanor. That he was happy and communicating with Stephanie."

"We also wanted to show his hair," Miranda said.

She said the prosecutor, who provided them with a copy of the DVD, had not entered it into evidence because "he wasn't wearing the boots that he hoped Paul was wearing. So he didn't use it."

Miranda said before they gave the DVD to the jury, they studied it over and over again—"like ten times"—to be sure that Paul was not wearing boots. Moriarty finally told them the news. "What if I told you that the jurors, all twelve jurors, looked at that videotape and believed he was wearing boots?"

"That would amaze me," Miranda said, "because they don't look like boots at all. They looked like the Johnston and Murphy shoes that come up to the ankle."

"What if I told you," Moriarty asked, "that two individuals who were on the fence, who might have hung the jury, came to their decision based on that videotape? And convicted him?"

"You know what?" Miranda said. "It would be the mistake of our lives. And I'm sure the prosecutor would be grateful to hear that. Because he didn't even think it resembled the boots. That's why he chose not to introduce it. So that amazes me. It's terrible. And you know I'd feel responsible for him being convicted.

"But I can't imagine that they would have believed that those were actually boots. Because it didn't look like boots. It had the height that his Johnston and Murphys had."

"Did you by any chance have an expert look at it before you submitted it?" Moriarty asked.

"No. No," Miranda said.

"There was no time to have an expert look at it," Florio said. "We were in the middle of the trial. And we didn't have anything to hide. We weren't scared of the video. That's what he was wearing."

"They [the jurors] decided based on looking at that videotape that Paul must have lied on the stand when he said he was wearing shoes that day," Moriarty told them. "Are you surprised?"

"I'm absolutely shocked!" Miranda said. "I'm amazed, because to me, it looked like the Johnston and Murphy shoes. That's why I put it in."

But Florio said she was not surprised and that she felt the two holdout jurors had taken the easy way out. "A lot of times jurors, when they want to convict and they want to hold someone responsible for such a gruesome crime, they're just looking for an excuse," she said. "There's so much, in my opinion, reasonable doubt in this case. And I think that was just a way out for them."

56

Sentencing

On March 23, 2007, the murder trial of Paul Cortez reached its conclusion—the sentencing. There was still one important decision to be made, and it was up to Judge Berkman. She would decide whether Paul received a sentence of fifteen years to life or the maximum sentence of twenty-five years to life.

Jon and Donna Woods attended the proceedings with their teenage daughter, Tori. Paul's mother and relatives were there for him. It was Jon who delivered the impact statement for the family. "Your Honor, the brutal and horrific murder of Catherine Elizabeth Woods was devastating to our family. Catherine not only lost her life, but was robbed of her dignity as a result of the vicious thrashing associated with publicity in the trial.

"Our family is only consoled by the fact that we knew the real Catherine for the past twenty-one years. One very memorable card that was sent to us said it all: 'It's not how long a flower blooms, but how beautiful.'

"This thought will forever define our memories and

feelings about Catherine. Our hearts will never be quite the same.

"Paul Cortez savagely ended the life of a young twenty-one-year-old woman who was responsibly pursuing her lifelong dream of a being a professional dancer. Our family has forever lost a beautiful part of our lives.

"Your Honor, we request that Paul Cortez be given the maximum sentence. We hope he will be kept off the streets forever. He is a murderer deserving nothing less than a life in prison."

Peter Casolaro spoke next for the state: "There are times, Your Honor, when a defendant who has no criminal record, as this defendant, and who has a strong educational background and strong family ties [is] deserving of far less than the maximum sentence. However, Your Honor, I don't believe that this is one of those times."

Casolaro went on to describe Paul as a danger to all women. "We have a person of remarkably violent nature, with a malevolence toward women, who has a deceitful personality and who is indifferent to the suffering of others. I think that, Your Honor, plus the absolutely brutal nature of the crime really takes away any reason to give any mercy or leniency to the defendant. And for all those reasons, Your Honor, the People would recommend the maximum sentence."

Dawn Florio rose to speak for Paul. He chose not to speak on his own behalf. Instead, Florio yet again told the court about all of Paul's childhood achievements. "He would like the family to know that he did not kill Catherine Woods and he's very sorry for their loss and he's grieving for Catherine Woods and he hopes that the real killer is found," she said.

She went on to rail against Casolaro, whom she accused of being "very inflammatory" in his closing remarks and said, "I am imploring the court to impose a minimum sentence of fifteen to life. Mr. Cortez loved Catherine Woods very deeply. He grieves for her every day. He suffers because she is gone."

Now it was Judge Berkman's turn. Berkman had already received the presentencing report on Paul, put together by a Queens consulting service. Paul was despondent after the verdict but nonetheless had put on a good face for Cynthia Santiago, the forensic social worker who'd written the report. Plenty of Paul's friends and family had written letters on his behalf, but it wasn't so much their testimonials that are touching but the record of Paul's young life. Because in his younger days he was such a special person and student, the presentencing report is about as sad and heartbreaking a document as one is likely to find.

Her whole life, Ivette was the chronicler of Paul's success, and thanks to her, the presentencing report contains Paul's report cards from grades two through six, his certificate of scholarship from St. Aloysius, letters from teachers written more than a decade earlier attesting to Paul's creativity. One begins, "I have been teaching students for over sixteen years and every now and then I come across a truly gifted youngster. Paul is one such student."

The proof of Paul's prowess is all there: a special award as a member of the P.S. 85 glee club, the letter recommending Paul to The Buckley School, his acceptance letter from Poly Prep Country Day School, his Bachelor of Fine Arts degree from Boston University, and lots of programs of theatrical performances he took part in.

Cynthia Santiago ended her report this way: "While not excusing Paul's conviction, the details of his history suggest not a hardened criminal to whom a maximum penalty should be sought, but rather a young man that is worthy of leniency. I respectfully submit that nothing in Paul's background should compel the court to seek the maximum sentence but rather have the court consider that this is a young man that is worthy of leniency, and should be sentenced to the mandatory minimum."

Judge Berkman briefly addressed the parties before giving her decision and began on a philosophical note:

"I think when we lose a loved one that loss creates a hole in our lives, and the hole doesn't get fixed, doesn't get healed. I guess what we do is learn to walk around it to live with it in various ways. And the family of Catherine Woods has to learn that still, as does the family of Paul Cortez.

"As for Paul Cortez, the evidence here establishes, notwithstanding his denials, which he's entitled to, that he is the author of his own tragedy. But one has to feel bad for his loving family, particularly his mother, who has faithfully attended I think every appearance of this case.

"I thought long and hard about this because Mr. Cortez is a person of great apparent talent. There are a lot of people who come forward and support him and want to believe in his innocence and, therefore, do believe in his innocence. And no doubt continue to believe in his innocence; notwithstanding the jury's verdict and anything else that could be said to them, and that's their prerogative.

"The extraordinary brutality of this homicide against a woman whom the defendant says he had a close and intimate relationship with—I don't know what to make of all that. Much of the evidence as to the relationship comes from Mr. Cortez.

"I think it does merit what the family of Catherine Woods is asking for and what the people are asking for here. Notwithstanding that Mr. Cortez, who still has the gift of life, has other gifts as well, and I recognize that, he is sentenced to a term of twenty-five years to life."

It was another day for Paul's mother to cry her eyes out.

57

48 Hours Talks to Paul

CBS News producer Patti Aronofsky had been meeting with Paul Cortez in jail for more than a year. The two had met probably a dozen times, but Paul had always resisted Patti's request for him to sit down and tell his story on-camera—at least before the trial. He did promise Patti that someday he would do an on-camera interview. In the meantime, the two talked about life and the murder, and Paul told Patti that he desperately wanted to find Catherine's real killer. He seemed to trust Patti but would not grant an interview. And besides, his lawyers had advised him to say nothing before his trial.

During the trial, Paul was on a high after he testified, and it seemed like he'd finally do the interview. But then came the verdict, and Patti heard nothing from Paul for days. Not surprisingly, Patti had heard from Paul's friends and family that he was depressed.

And then, finally, Paul called. Patti told him that this would be a chance for him to tell his story and take back his life from the tabloids, at least a little bit. He consulted with family and friends and finally agreed to talk to Erin Moriarty with the cameras rolling.

On March 27—not even a week after his sentencing—Moriarty, Patti, and two television news crews set up in a room on Rikers Island, New York's notorious jail just across from LaGuardia Airport. You can see it nearly every time you take off from the airport, but most flyers have no idea it's so close. The jail is actually a series of low-rise buildings where New York holds two types of prisoners: those who've not yet been tried and those who have been convicted and are awaiting transfer to a state prison. It's not a happy place.

Paul was very nervous for the interview, the first and only time he's spoken to anyone on the record about the case outside the courtroom. He didn't look especially confident, and had lost the swagger he'd displayed in court. He was pale, and had finally cut his long hair. Now Paul was sporting a crew cut.

He did not have the same relationship with Moriarty that he had with Patti, but Paul had told relatives that he thought the first hour done by *48 Hours Mystery* back in May 2006 was fair because the broadcast had portrayed Catherine as more than just a stripper. Paul's lawyers were in the room for the interview.

Almost as soon as the cameras began rolling, without being asked, Paul said, "I didn't do it."

"That was my next question," Moriarty said. "Did you, in fact, kill Catherine Woods?"

"No, I didn't."

"You've had so much time to think about this. If you didn't kill her, then who do you think did?"

"I don't know. I have no idea."

Paul talked about the shock of finding out Catherine had been murdered and hearing that David Haughn was a suspect, but he didn't take the easy way out and accuse David of the murder. He just talked about how he talked to the police voluntarily and told them everything he knew.

"Did you ever think you'd be in this situation, Paul?"

"Oh, gosh, no. It's probably the worst thing that has ever, ever happened. And I wouldn't wish it on anyone."

"What's the worst part about it?"

"There's so many bad parts. Losing someone I love is one of the worst parts. I've lost so many people that I love, though, out of this. Out of this whole thing. A lot of friends I've lost. Family."

"You're twenty-seven years of age. Just turned twenty-seven, right? . . . If none of this had happened, what were your dreams? What did you think you would be doing right now?"

"I thought I'd be in a rock band, onstage singing. Possibly signed. My band and I were working hard. I wasn't sure if that was going to be the band, but I've been making music my whole life, so I thought I'd be something artistic. I thought it'd be something that dealt with the arts or singing, dancing, Broadway, something. That's kind of what I've always done."

He talked about his dream of being on Broadway as a dancer, pretty much the same dream Catherine had had. Paul told the story of how they'd met at the health club and how, afterward, it was Catherine who called him.

"How would you describe Catherine?"

"Gosh, so many words," he said. "She's, like I said, open and compassionate. Very beautiful. Very sensitive. Very giving. Very big heart. Her heart was so big, with animals and with people on the street. Homeless people, she would always give to them. And cabdrivers. She would always give them extra tips, you know? She was just such a beautiful person. And I think that's why I fell in love with her."

"How close were the two of you?"

"We were incredibly close. We called each other every day at all hours, whenever. I made it clear to her that she could always come by my place or call me whenever. It was never a problem. And we talked about everything. She told me a lot of things about her and her life that I know are private things that one wouldn't just tell anyone."

Paul said he knew that she was living with David when they first met, and he had tolerated it because he knew how much she loved David. She'd told Paul that David was on his way out, and he'd believed her.

Nothing was off-limits in the interview. Paul spoke candidly about Catherine's topless dancing and his disdain for it. He admitted he'd tried to get her to stop, even going so far as to call her father, but nothing worked. Sometimes, whenever he mentioned her name, he smiled and called her "my best friend."

"I took her out on her birthday. I didn't have much money. Being a trainer, you're kind of always living from check to check. But I had scrounged up enough money to buy her this silver necklace that had a single pearl on it. I thought it was beautiful and she liked it, too. I got that for her for her birthday, and we did the whole thing. We went out for dinner dressed up and everything, and turned heads everywhere, you know. She was stunning, especially when she dressed up. She loved that gift and . . . funny thing, she was like, 'Oh, a pearl, that's my birthstone.' And, I was like, 'Oh, yeah, I knew that.' "

Paul laughed, remembering the good times that now seemed so far away. In the next breath, he talked about David, and it was clear he was hurt that Catherine had continued living with him.

"Wasn't that hard, if you're in love with someone and she's living with another guy?" Moriarty asked.

"Yeah, yeah. It was . . . she tried to kick him out several times, but he always came back and she would always feel bad for him, and that was that. Eventually she told me he did move out in August 2005. She told me he moved upstate, and to my knowledge, from then up until the end in November, he was living upstate."

"You didn't know," Moriarty asked, "that he had actually moved back in with her?"

"No," said Paul, "I didn't."

It was an interesting point because the prosecutor's theory of the crime was that Paul, on the night of the murder, had waited until David left before rushing into the apartment and ambushing Catherine.

"So, January, February, March, and April, did you think you loved Catherine? Would you say you loved her?"

"Yes."

"Do you think Catherine loved you?"

"Very much so. She told me every day on the phone, in person, making love. She always expressed it to me."

Moriarty pressed him. "But at the same time, she's living with another guy."

"Yes. To my knowledge, their relationship was strictly platonic. They were friends and they were roommates, and that's how she made it seem, and I respected that. I didn't think she really had any need to lie to me. I trusted that. I wasn't comfortable with it, but it was nothing that I ever blew up about or anything like that."

"If the two of you were in love with each other, why didn't she tell any of her friends that she was dating you?"

Paul looked surprised. "I don't know. I thought she did."

"Catherine's friends say they heard your name but they say that Catherine never told them that she was dating you. Why not?"

"I don't know."

"Do you think David could have killed Catherine? Honestly, what do you think?"

Sitting in jail, it would have been easy for Paul to lash out at his rival, but he held back. "I have gone through so much because people have prematurely and falsely accused me of doing this, of killing Catherine, that I don't want to do that to David. He might have or he might have not. I don't know, and it's not my job to find that out."

"But who else could have killed Catherine?"

"It could have been a stalker from where she works," Paul said. "She was very beautiful. I know that profession isn't safe. I don't know, it could have been any number of people."

"Did Catherine ever talk about any particular individual who was either stalking her or showing an inappropriate interest in her?"

"Not to my knowledge. I know she met people there at the club, but she never really talked about the details of it, and I didn't really want to know about the details of it."

"Catherine was all David had. Could you imagine that he would ever kill the one person that he loved? She was like a parent to him."

"Anyone can imagine that," Paul said. "What if the person that is everything you have tells you, 'All right, it's really over now. Get out.' What do you do? You can imagine a ton of scenarios, but I don't know what happened that night."

Paul said again that he was disappointed but not

upset that Catherine had chosen to spend Thanksgiving with David and not him. He said she'd told him that she felt close to David and that he had no one else. Paul said he understood.

As he went through the day of the murder one more time, he reiterated that he had never had a pair of Sketchers boots. "What was your reaction," Moriarty asked, "when your friend took the stand at trial and said, 'He was wearing boots that night,' and then pointed out the Sketchers boots?"

"That was a huge surprise to me. When the DA asked him to come in, the media had already accused, tried, and convicted me, and possibly, he believed I was the guy and wanted to do them a favor and pointed out the boots."

"Why would Spence do that?"

"I don't know. We weren't really sober that night," Paul said, mentioning that they'd smoked pot.

Moving on to the phone calls, Paul said that he'd told the police the truth—the last time he spoke to Catherine, he was at home. It was not the last time he called Catherine. In his mind, it was an important distinction.

"You never mention that you were right down in her neighborhood just blocks from her home. Why not?"

"I just remember being in a haze at that point," he said. "I was still in shock. I had just found out that someone that I loved dearly was killed and that I was a suspect for it as well. I wanted to put in things that I thought might be helpful for their investigation."

"Didn't you think it would look worse if they found out that you were right down there?"

"No. Everything they asked me, I answered truthfully and I gave them everything they asked me for."

"Why wouldn't the police put that down in their report?"

"I don't know," Paul said.

"Did you forget to tell the police in the statement that you were right in her neighborhood?"

"Honestly, I can't remember. I just remember being bombarded, and I just wanted to go home."

Moriarty, who is a lawyer, kept the questions coming. At times, Paul's lawyers stepped in and told her she was being "too prosecutorial."

"Here's another thing that bothered the jurors," Moriarty said. "Before six o' clock, you're calling Catherine more than a dozen times because you're concerned about her. But then, after six, the next thirty minutes, there are no phone calls at all. Nothing. And it just happens to be the time that Catherine was murdered. I mean, how do you explain that? No one sees you. You're not making any phone calls. There's just this gap."

"I made many phone calls to many different people."

"From 6:00 to 6:50 there's one one-second phone call to Catherine, at 6:33. Otherwise, you're not seen by anybody. No one talks to you. How do you explain that?"

"There's nothing to explain. I called her many times and I left messages . . ."

"That was before six."

"Yeah. And I figured after I left the last message of, 'Hey, call me when you get out of work,' I figured that was it. I went, after that, to get something to eat. And then I finished calling clients and stuff like that after eating. And that was it."

"But do you understand why it might look bad that, before six, you're calling clients, you're calling Catherine. You're on the phone constantly. And then there's this gap where no one sees you, you're not making any phone calls. And then, at 6:50, you start calling people again. You meet with people. That's a big gap."

"Like I said, I was eating at the time. I understand why, in retrospect, why the police did arrest me and put me in here. And they used that as being one of their circumstantial pieces of evidence. But . . ."

Moriarty cut Paul off. "Paul, you loved this woman. She lied to you over those months. Did you, in fact, that night just snap and kill her?"

"No. I would never do that. I loved her so much, I could never do that. There was no reason for me to snap. That's not in my nature to even do that sort of thing. We had our relationship, it was the way it was, and it was more distant over that time. We weren't boyfriend and girlfriend at that point. I didn't want to incessantly call her to bother her or anything like that. The night before that . . . I never called her, you know, numerous times. It's just the way our relationship was."

"Here's another thing that bothered the jurors. Whenever you had unresolved problems with Catherine, you called her and tried to resolve them. After that evening, after you didn't hear back from Catherine, after you called her just about thirteen times that evening, you never called her again. Sixteen and half hours and you never call her again. The prosecutor says that's because you knew she was dead."

"No," Paul said. "That last phone call that I made, I left a message, and I told her, I said, 'Please call me when you get out of work.' I just figured that would be that, and I'd speak to her either in the morning or the next day."

"But if you were worried about her, why didn't you call her in the morning when she got home from work and before you went to work?"

"There's nothing I could do. I got home really late and I was actually late, maybe five, ten minutes, getting into work. And so it was just one of those mornings that, you know, I figured I would just call her after work. But it didn't happen that way."

"Did you ever think you'd actually go on trial for this?"

"Never. Never. No."

"Tell me about the trial," Moriarty said.

"I don't really know much about the law or anything like that. You know, procedures of court or anything like that. But it just didn't seem fair. It seemed so slanted for them to convict me. Everything just was so slanted to get this conviction."

"At one point, in the trial, the prosecution brings in your writings. According to the prosecution your writings reflect a violent nature."

Paul sighed. "They took 13 different excerpts from 25 diaries, each of which are at least 250 pages each. Some of the writings they took out were from five years ago. And then they tried to turn it around and say, 'Oh, well, you know, because of this specific line on this date, it means he hates women.' It's not it. If you looked in all my writings, you would see I've written about everything I could have experienced at the time or felt at the time."

"But you'd admit that some—if you just looked at some of these lines, I mean they sound pretty damaging."

"You can take anything out of context and make it sound the way you want it to fit. And tailor it to your needs."

Moriarty pulled out some of Paul's writings: "Let me just go through a few, just so that you can explain . . . We don't have time to go through a lot. The ones that I thought that were probably the most important. At one point, Paul, you wrote, 'She wipes clean the shaft that cuts her throat.'

"And then Catherine's throat is cut. That's how she dies. The prosecutor says that's just too much of a coincidence."

"That's a poem that was written in January or February of 2005 [about eleven months before Catherine was murdered]."

"But you knew Catherine then."

"Yeah, I knew her then."

"You're talking about Catherine in that line."

"Not necessarily. It's almost like an everywoman that has been damaged by rape or some sort of molestation. It's a poem. Poetry is just filled with symbolism and all kinds of things. To say that I had been plotting this thing since even before I met Catherine, or since February . . ."

"Well, you knew Catherine then. I mean, when you wrote this you knew Catherine," Moriarty said.

"Yeah, but I mean to say I was plotting this thing eight months before I knew her is ridiculous."

"Are you saying that it's just a coincidence that that's how she dies?"

"Yeah. I'm saying that. I didn't know what was gonna happen to her that night. And, I mean, let's say if she had gotten shot, I had written songs about people shooting. And so they would have just used that against me. Or if she had gotten, I don't know, hit by a car or something like that. I've written things about that, and they would have just used that against me."

Paul also pointed out that that poem was about the rape that happened to Catherine when she briefly lived in Brooklyn.

"The prosecution says that you were a volcano ready to erupt. And Catherine was the last straw, that you'd been hurt by so many women. And her betrayal was the last straw."

"That's not true," Paul said. "I have so many outlets. I do yoga, I meditate, I'm in a rock band, I sing, I draw, I write poetry. You know, I do all those things to sublimate everything that I'm feeling, or just to express myself. Whereas other people bottle it in and they hit a wall, or throw things around. I don't do that. I make it into art."

"You decided to take the stand. Was that a tough decision?"

"I wanted my voice to be heard by the jury because it hadn't been heard before. And anything that anyone knew about me was just through the tabloid press, saying, like, how crazy I was and what a monster and everything, complete fabrications of the kind of person that I am or what I'm about. So in a sense it wasn't really that hard. The only reason I felt that I might not want to take the stand is just because I didn't want my words to be twisted against me. But in the end, I just figured if I just armed myself with the truth and just say everything that happened, and how I really felt about things, that they couldn't twist that around."

"What did you think was gonna happen? Tell me about the two and a half days before the verdict. What was that like for you?"

"I didn't really eat. I didn't really sleep. It's such a weird feeling."

"What did you think the jury was going to do?"

"I thought at least they would not be able to decide."

"A hung jury."

"Yeah, a hung jury. I did not expect, whatsoever, that they were gonna say guilty. I didn't think it would be possible in our system for that to happen."

"Did you really even hear it when the verdict was announced?"

"I remember hearing it and then I just heard all these sobs. Just people crying, and I don't really know what happened after that. I kind of just felt like my heart was . . . it was a very similar feeling when I first found out about Catherine's death. It's just kind of like your heart drops to your stomach and then it just kind of obliterates you."

"Why do you think the jury found you guilty?"

"The DA was good at spinning his lies. And good at making me into a monster that I wasn't. I don't know what's in their head, but I tried my best to just tell them who I was, and what happened, and I guess it just wasn't enough."

"What do you do at this point? What now?" Moriarty asked.

"Well, now comes the appeal. You know, try to survive every day and try to comfort my family every day and friends. And just try to be strong until justice can be served."

The interview was winding down, but Moriarty was troubled by Paul's demeanor during the interview. There was no passion behind his answers and he was speaking very quietly. She was also troubled by his body language. "You don't look at me a lot when we're talking. Is there a reason? Are you uncomfortable with that?" she asked.

"No. This whole scenario is a little bit weird, with the lights and all these people around watching me say these things. So forgive me if I'm not looking at you the whole time."

The interview ended, the bright lights were turned off, and as he was led away, Paul motioned for Patti to come over. He didn't think he had done very well. "You did fine," Patti said. "You answered a lot of tough questions. Maybe you'll change some minds."

Paul was clearly depressed. "Well," he said, "it doesn't really matter. I told the truth to the people who mattered, the jury, and they didn't believe me. What does it matter? I did this because I promised you I would."

And with that, corrections officers led Paul back to his cell.

58

The Appeal

Not long after the verdict, Paul moved ahead with his appeal. He got a new lawyer with a famous last name— Nathan Dershowitz, brother of Alan Dershowitz, the well-known criminal appellate lawyer who, among others, had defended Claus von Bülow, who was accused of putting his wife, Sunny, into a coma. Paul had heard Dershowitz's name bandied about the inmate pipeline on Rikers Island and asked supporter Marguerite Shinouda to reach out to him. It turned out Dershowitz was already familiar with the case. He agreed to represent Paul for the appeal because he believes Paul simply did not receive a fair trial.

Dershowitz said he was "startled" by Paul's conviction, given that he saw any number of reasons for which the jury could have found reasonable doubt. "I mean, you have hairs found in Catherine's hand, interwoven in her fingers, and no DNA was done on those hairs," he said. "You have blood on David's pants and no blood-spatter expert looked at it. You look at the evidence with respect to a knife that was found in the kitchen—there's an indication that it has blood on it—and you don't find any checking as to whether or not there were fingerprints on it."

Above all, Dershowitz said, those hairs in Catherine's hand should have been sent out for DNA testing. "Catherine was obviously fighting off her killer," he said. "She has hairs in her hand and those hairs should be examined. And if you look at the testimony at the trial, it's startling as to what was said. You have an expert who says the hairs were not similar to Paul's hairs. They were 'somewhat similar' to Catherine's. What does that mean? Nobody ever asked the question, what do you mean 'somewhat similar'? Human? Blond? Dyed? Straight? I have no idea.

"And those questions were never asked. You can do DNA testing on hairs even without roots. You can do DNA testing. If you have the roots, you can do DNA testing, nuclear DNA testing. Which will tell you to a certainty who it was."

And because the hair was tested against Paul's hair, it is a known fact that the hairs did not belong to him. It was a no-lose proposition for the defense and yet no further testing was done.

A big part of the problem at trial, Dershowitz says, is that Paul's lawyers were outmaneuvered by prosecutor Peter Casolaro, who did "a good job of pulling out little pieces of evidence and presenting a picture which made some sense."

Dershowitz says that Casolaro, while "a very persuasive advocate," often "went over the line" in his summation, and that it would make a good appeal issue. "I think he frequently testified and made statements [in his closing] that I just think were grossly inappropriate, particularly with regard to the so-called 'bloody fingerprint.'

"He's supposed to take evidence from the trial, summarize the evidence, and make presentation to the jury," Dershowitz said. "He's not supposed to be the expert. . . . Here's a prosecutor who has no scientific knowledge . . . and [during the closing] he's making all of these presentations in terms of smudges, in terms of pixels. That's not his job!"

Dershowitz said that no expert during the trial argued one way or another about whether Paul's fingerprint could have been on the wall before the blood went over it but that Casolaro put on a lengthy presentation to the jury telling them why that could not have happened.

Casolaro was contacted for a response to these and other matters concerning the trial but did not return phone calls.

But it wasn't just what was left out of the case that troubles Dershowitz—it was also the admission of certain prejudicial items, such as Paul's journals. "I have six or seven problems with the admission of the diaries," he said. "Let's take the first problem I have: Had Paul been abusive to other girlfriends, which he was not, but had he been, that evidence could not have been admitted. It's inadmissible evidence.

"To then take writings, where he's free-associating, and selectively choose a few things from 250 pages of 25 volumes . . . and suggesting that that's representative is grossly inappropriate. More than that—so he writes things. He writes some things on violence. He writes some things on love. There was never an expert psychiatrist who testified that people who write things like this then go off and commit crimes.

"We are incapable of predicting behavior on the basis of writings of that type. So it would never be admitted. But to then proceed the other way around, and say, 'Oh, he wrote something. Therefore he must have done this,' is just a grossly inappropriate use of the writings.

"It conveyed an image of Paul that was an inaccurate image. And the prosecutor made a lot of use of that inappropriate image, conveyed Paul as a misogynist. There's no evidence that Paul ever behaved in a manner which would suggest that he's a misogynist."

And what about the jurors' contention that Paul must have been guilty because he was seen wearing boots in the DVD from the electronics store made on the day of the murder, a DVD that was provided to them by the defense? Dershowitz did not come right out and say Florio and Miranda had made a huge mistake, but it was obvious what he was thinking: "The first thing you're taught in law school is that you never ask the witness a question unless you know the answer," he said. "Why? Because the worst thing a lawyer can do is to provide the evidence for the other side. It's very disturbing to me that the jury would convict on the basis of such speculative evidence.

"A trial has to be fair, a proper presentation of the evidence."

According to Nathan Dershowitz, Paul's trial was anything but fair. Dershowitz said he expected to file an appeal in late January 2008 just as this book was going to press. He said the basis of the appeal would be ineffective assistance of counsel. The appeal, he said, would focus on what he claims was Dawn Florio's failure to properly interview experts who could bolster a forsenic case for the defense. In addition, Dershowitz claimed, Florio failed to properly cross-examine the expert witnesses put forth by the prosecution.

Additionally, the appeal will state, according to Dershowitz, that Florio had a conflict of interest with Paul because, at the time of Paul's trial, she was under indictment by the Manhattan District Attorney's office for passing contraband to an inmate. Dershowitz will charge that the court did not adequately advise Paul that, if he wished, he could ask for new counsel.

59

What We Know and What We Don't Know

After all is said and done, is there any way to know what really happened to Catherine Woods on the night of November 27, 2005?

Examining the trial testimony, the evidence, and the interviews done for *48 Hours Mystery,* we are left with some very compelling questions: There were no bloody footprints leaving Catherine's room. Why not?

And how did Paul manage to leave the crime scene without being covered in blood? Police sources say Paul's jacket, which he was seen wearing both before and after the murder, contained a speck of blood that they say was female but too minuscule to type. If that is true, why wasn't that evidence used against him at trial?

Why did David Haughn say he could clearly see Catherine's body when he first came upon the murder scene even though her body was not visible to the first responders?

How could Paul have viciously stabbed Catherine more than twenty times and not have left a single strand of his long hair anywhere in the apartment?

Yet, with all the questions that remain, there is considerable evidence that ties Paul Cortez to this unspeakably brutal act. What we do know is that in early November 2005, Catherine was distancing herself from Paul, because she caught him checking her cell phone to see whom she was calling. She told him she wanted to take a break, according to Paul. On the night of the murder, Paul was frustrated by his inability to reach Catherine by phone and he traveled to her neighborhood. We know he did not tell police in his written statement that he was near her building when he made those phone calls. We know that Paul's fingerprint—however you care to characterize it—was found on Catherine's blood-spattered wall. We know he never called her again after 6:33 that Sunday night. We know—because Paul admitted it to us—that he had no idea David was still living with her.

On that evening, Catherine was refusing to take his calls or to call him back, but he did know that she had to go to work.

The evidence—contradictory as it sometimes is— suggests that this is what might have happened:

Paul went to Catherine's apartment—as he had in the past—to talk her into dinner instead of going to work. He stood on the sidewalk across the street from her building, hoping to intercept her when she came out to go to Flash Dancers, but then he spotted David, who came out first. Once again, Paul realized that Catherine was lying to him and he was enraged. The moment David walked down the block, Paul charged into the building. The lock on the exterior doors was faulty, and Catherine may even have buzzed Paul in.

Once he was in the apartment, there was an argument about David living there, about Catherine's job, about Paul's obsessive behavior. Catherine may have told Paul to get out of her life, and Paul just lost it. In a manic state, he grabbed a knife from the kitchen and stabbed Catherine repeatedly, cut her throat, and ran out of the apartment, managing to avoid passersby on a cold and dark November evening.

Moments later, he even subconsciously dialed Catherine's number by rote, just as he had done hundreds of times before. But then he realized that she was dead, and he cut off the phone quickly. That was the one-second phone call at 6:33 p.m. As he walked home, Paul knew he needed an alibi and began to provide one for himself, calling clients to schedule appointments for the next day and then phoning Spence to meet for a drink.

Sometimes the facts can be so stark and unrelenting that we want to turn away. So it is with Paul Cortez. It's painful to a lot of people to picture him as a killer. He's intelligent, well educated, charismatic, and talented. It's a thought that struck Patti Aronofsky from the very moment she went to visit him in the city jail. "He was someone I'd be happy to have dinner with," she said.

That's the mystery of Paul Cortez. You don't want to believe that someone like him could be guilty of such a brutal, unforgivable crime because he is, after all, someone so much like all of us.

But there is one person who has no trouble calling Paul a murderer—Detective Steven Goetz, the chief investigating officer. "There is no doubt in my mind that Paul Cortez killed Catherine Woods," he said.

"But why?" Moriarty asked.

"I can't answer that," Goetz said. "Only one person can answer that . . . you can't get into somebody else's head . . . but I go to bed every night knowing that Paul Cortez is in jail and he's the killer of Catherine Woods."

Epilogue

When thinking about her daughter Catherine, Donna Woods finds comfort in the words of legendary writer E. B. White. It was White who wrote one of the most cogent essays on what New York City represents to those who come here seeking fame and fortune. According to White, there are three New Yorks: the New York of those born here, the New York of those who commute into the city every day for work, and finally, the greatest New York, the one of those who come here "in quest of something." Catherine, of course, falls into the third category, and when Donna thinks of her, she thinks of these words from E. B. White:

> And whether it is a farmer arriving from Italy to set up a small grocery store in a slum, or a young girl arriving from a small town in Mississippi to escape the indignity of being observed by her neighbors, or a

boy arriving from the Corn Belt with a manuscript in his suitcase and a pain in his heart, it makes no difference: each embraces New York with the intense excitement of first love, each absorbs New York with the fresh eyes of an adventurer, each generates heat and light to dwarf the Consolidated Edison Company.

That is the New York of Catherine Woods.

Jon Woods has found his own place in New York—at the front of Macy's Thanksgiving Day Parade. His daughter was murdered over the Thanksgiving Day weekend of 2005, but that did not stop Jon from accepting an offer in 2006, and again in 2007, to lead the Macy's Great American Marching Band. Musicians from different states comprise the band, but it doesn't matter where they come from. Whenever Jon Woods leads the band, he is in his element, in the city that his beloved daughter so loved.

Paul's Letter from Prison

Paul never again spoke publicly about his conviction after being interviewed by Erin Moriarty, but his supporters did post a long letter from Paul in prison on his new website (www.freepaulcortez.org). The letter is in Paul's own hand and dated 12/24/07.

In it, Paul states—with more conviction than he has in the past—that he did not kill Catherine. It's also clear that the reality of prison life is taking its toll as Paul writes, "even my faith in God is waivering [sic]." He lashes out against his former lawyers, the criminal justice system, and even some of his supporters. The letter is clearly a plea to the world for help.

"There is such extreme indifference, cold-heartedness that I wonder if there are any truly good people in this world," he writes. Paul paints a harrowing picture of his life as it is today and he is convinced of one thing: "A killer is out there who has literally gotten away with murder."

Not sure what to read next?

Visit Pocket Books online at
www.simonsays.com

Reading suggestions for
you and your reading group
New release news
Author appearances
Online chats with your favorite writers
Special offers
Order books online
And much, much more!